D0734338

# Rosie

## The Ultimate Guide for Rosie O'Donnell Fans

## PATRICK SPRENG

A Birch Lane Press Book
PUBLISHED BY CAROL PUBLISHING GROUP

A Birch Lane Press Book
Published by Carol Publishing Group
Birch Lane Press is a registered trademark of Carol Communications, Inc.

Editorial, sales and distribution, rights and permissions inquiries should be
addressed to Carol Publishing Group, 120 Enterprise Avenue, Secaucus, N.J.
07094

In Canada: Canadian Manda Group, One Atlantic Avenue, Suite 105, Toronto,
Ontario M6K 3E7

Carol Publishing books may be purchased in bulk at special discounts for sales
promotion, fund-raising, or educational purposes. Special editions can be created
to specifications. For details, contact Special Sales Department, 120 Enterprise
Avenue, Secaucus, N.J. 07094.

Photos courtesy of Photofest.
Book design by Cindy LaBreacht.

Manufactured in the United States of America
10 9 8 7 6 5 4 3 2 1

Library of Congress Cataloging-in-Publication Data
Spreng, Patrick.
    Everything Rosie : the ultimate guide for Rosie O'Donnell fans /
Patrick Spreng.
        p.    cm.
    "A Birch Lane Press book."
    Includes bibliographical references and index.
    ISBN 1-55972-452-8
    1. O'Donnell, Rosie.    2. Comedians—United States—Biography.
3. Motion picture actors and actresses—United States—Biography.
4. Television personalities—United States—Bibliography.    I. Title.
PN2287.027S67    1998
792.7'028'092—dc21
    [B]                                                                98–6651
                                                                         CIP

## TO ROSIE,

the nicest thing
to happen to TV,
and all her fans

# Acknowledgments

First and foremost, I must thank my family—my wife, Jean, and my son, Evan. Without their support and faith in me, I never would have taken on a project of this magnitude.

I must also thank my friends Erin Noll, Jim Parish, and Joe Bob Briggs, all of whom encouraged me to find my inspiration and write something—anything. And, of course, my editor, Mike Lewis, for asking me out of the blue to write a Rosie book in the first place and for guiding me through the maze euphemistically called the publishing business.

I would also like to thank the following people for their help in writing this book: Desiree Devereaux, Ruth Dworin, Linda Jones, Jean Kalich, Lou Kersten, Kasia Kowalewski, Kamal Larsuel, Molly Wohlgemuth, and the entire Rosie mailing list.

# Contents

# Introduction

**HOW I GOT**

**TO JUNE 10, 1996**

**WITH ROSIE**

I first became aware of Rosie O'Donnell from her early films. I remember going to *A League of Their Own* to see Tom Hanks and Geena Davis. It was a wonderful movie, and the stars did a terrific job, but I came away with a real admiration for the brash, gutsy third baseman who could juggle bats and throw two baseballs with one hand.

Then came *Sleepless in Seattle*, which I wanted to see because it starred Tom Hanks and Meg Ryan. Again, I was impressed by the woman with the tender heart and the New York City attitude who played Ryan's friend. She was a buddy, a pal, a friend, an Everywoman to whom you felt close before you even met her. She was an equal, someone you could talk to and know that you would be treated with respect.

Next, for me, came *The Flintstones*. I was not all that interested in seeing this picture, but my preadolescent son was, and when I found out that Rosie was playing Betty Rubble, I agreed to take him. And I'm certainly glad I did. I enjoyed every minute Rosie was on-screen, from her tittering giggle to the cloth tied around her ankle to hide her string-of-roses tattoo. Unfortunately, that wasn't very often, and the rest of the picture was much less interesting, as its relatively poor box office seemed to indicate.

It was not long after seeing *The Flintstones* that I read somewhere that Rosie was active on America Online (AOL), the dial-up service that was quickly becoming the most popular commercial online service in America. I logged on to my AOL account and did a member search on "rosie o'donnell." To my surprise, up popped her screen name, "ROSIE OH O." It was common knowledge that many well-known celebrities had accounts on AOL and other services, but they usually made a point to hide their existence by either using a pseudonym or having their name removed from the system's member lists. Rosie didn't do that. She welcomed mail from her fans.

So sometime in the fall of 1995, I sent her electronic mail (E-mail), first simply asking if she were the same Rosie O'Donnell of film and TV fame. She responded, in her usual terse form, that indeed she was the one-and-only Rosie. Knowing how easy it is to impersonate someone else in the online world, I continued to exchange E-mail with her off and on over the next few months while I became more and more convinced that she was no impostor.

Rosie told me about her most recent film called *Beautiful Girls*, where she got to play opposite Timothy Hutton and Matt Dillon. They had filmed in the Minneapolis, Minnesota, area in early spring, and she complained about the cold weather. She also complained about the difficulties of mothering her newly adopted son, with all the travel necessary to make movies. I shared the fact that I also had an adopted son and that we were often separated for weeks at a time because of my travels as a consultant.

The last time I heard from Rosie was during the holidays at the end of that year. Apparently she was putting all her time into creating *The Rosie O'Donnell Show*, because she no longer responded to my E-mails. In the meantime, I spent most of the first five months of 1996 working in Baltimore and returned home to a world of leisure (and unemployment) in early June. I made a point to be in front of my television set on June tenth for the first live showing of *The Rosie O'Donnell Show*.

I was pleasantly surprised by what I saw. Rosie was bringing back the kind of talk show that the viewing public could really be excited about. For the first time in years, those of us who are not insomniacs could watch our favorite celebrities being adeptly interviewed by an enthusiastic, self-professed fan.

My immediate reaction was to log on to the Internet and see what I could find out about Rosie on the World Wide Web. And what I found was nothing. Knowing an opportunity when I saw one, I began creating the ACME Rosie page. I had already created a couple of celebrity-fan pages on the web—one for actress Karen Allen *(Raiders of the Lost Ark, Starman, National Lampoon's Animal House)* and another for the Los Angeles Dodgers (the ACME Dodger page)—so I knew what I was doing and quickly had the site ready for prime time.

Meanwhile, I was watching Rosie's show every day and even taking notes. In September I was contacted by Mike Lewis at Carol Publishing Group, who logged on to my web page and asked me to submit a proposal to write a biography of Rosie. Fortunately, my proposal was rejected, and George Mair and Anna Green produced the fine book *Rosie O'Donnell: Her True Story* for Carol. Then, in August 1997, Mr. Lewis contacted me again to do a proposal for a follow-up book, and that's what you are holding in your hands.

While this book has a great deal of biographical information, it is not a biography. I don't pretend to be a psychologist. I present a great deal of biographical information, mostly in Rosie's own words, and let you, the reader, put it all together into the person we call Rosie O'Donnell. For a more in-depth biographical analysis, read *Rosie O'Donnell: Her True Story* and the many other Rosie biographies now available.

*Author's note:* Any typos you see within transcripts of Rosie's online chats are exactly as they appeared on the screen and are the result of the typists' excitement and/or poor secretarial skills.

# Everything Rosie

# Everything Rosie

**NAME** Rosie's real name is Roseann O'Donnell (no middle name). She was named after her mother, Roseann Murtha O'Donnell. "When I was a kid, my family called me Dolly. That's because my older brothers couldn't pronounce my name when they were little, and they also thought that I looked like a dolly. So they called me Dolly until I was eight.

"Patty Cossick, from across the street, gave me the nickname 'Dolly Bloomer Bottoms.' I always wore bloomers instead of shorts, so Patty called me Dolly Bloomer Bottoms." Early in her stand-up career she was confused with Gilda Radner, whose character Roseann Rosannadana sounds much like Roseann O'Donnell. So one comedy club owner christened her "Rosie," and she's been called that ever since.

**BIRTHDAY** Rosie was born on March 21, 1962, the first full day of spring. At publishing time, she had just turned thirty-six.

**CHILDHOOD HOME** Rosie was born in Flushing (Queens), New York, but she grew up at 17 Rhonda Lane, Commack, New York. "It's suburban hell. Tract row houses one after another, exactly the same. Different-colored shutters were the only way you could tell them apart." Her childhood house is still there, on Long Island. Rhonda Lane is just northeast of where the Northern State Parkway and the Sunken Meadows State Parkway intersect, about two miles north of Exit 53 on the Long Island Parkway.

**ANCESTRY** Rosie's parents were Irish Catholic. After the death of her mother in 1973, her father moved the family back to Ireland for nearly two years before returning to Commack.

**FATHER** Edward O'Donnell is an electrical engineer who designed cameras for spy satellites either for Fairchild or Grumman, depending on whom you ask. He has remarried and lives in North Carolina. He and Rosie are still estranged; she feels he wasn't "really available for his kids. I've never told my father I love him, and he's never really told me. Those words were never said in my house.

"I was raised in an aura of neglect. My father was grief-stricken and quite incapable of dealing with five small children and no wife. The father I have in the [stand-up] show is a lot nicer and a lot more approachable than the father I had in reality. My father in reality is not the affable Irish leprechaun."

**MOTHER** Roseann Murtha O'Donnell was a wife, mother, and president of the local Parent-Teacher Organization (PTO). She died on March 17, 1973 (St. Patrick's Day), four days before Rosie's eleventh birthday. She was thirty-nine. Rosie was first told her mother had died of hepatitis, then, later, cancer of the liver and pancreas. But she recently learned that her mother actually died of breast cancer. "My whole life revolves around my mother's death. It changed who I was as a person. I don't know who I would be if my mother had lived, but I would trade it all in to see. Psychologists say that a trauma like the death of a parent at an early age can stop further emotional growth. I guess that's why I'm still ten in so many ways."

Rosie and her siblings were not allowed at the funeral, which took place on Rosie's eleventh birthday. Rosie remembers getting birthday gifts from weeping friends and family, who also brought casseroles.

"There is also a lot of denial. The family has been brought up to ignore the elephant standing on the kitchen table. For instance, when my mother died, I didn't even know what she died of until I was sixteen.

They told us she died of hepatitis. Figuring we were little and wouldn't know what that meant. I looked it up. I was in fifth grade, and it said a disease you got through dirty needles. I remember thinking, in a ten-year-old's rationalization and justification, that it was from sewing."

Because her mother had been president of the PTO, a memorial plaque was mounted on the wall in the main hallway of her school. Whenever she would walk by, Rosie thought her mother's body was buried in the wall behind the plaque.

**TELEVISION** "Well, I tell ya, I watched TV because I didn't have parents that were [there]. My mom died, my dad was really absent from the house, so that was the nurturing. And in some ways the parenting that I got, believe it or not, was through the TV. I would see families—in the seventies there were a lot of families with no mom: *Courtship of*

*Eddie's Father, Eight Is Enough,* and the Bradys. They were broken families, but they met each other and came together. So I had all these fantasies, from watching those shows, that my dad would meet Abby from *Eight Is Enough* or Nanny from *Nanny and the Professor* or Mrs. Livingston would come and live with us. And I was really nurtured by TV because there was such a void of parenting and nurturing in our family. So, hopefully my son will not seek that through the TV. Hopefully I'll be able to give that to him so he'll be able to watch it for entertainment only."

"I faked [mononucleosis] in seventh grade for the Mary Ryan–Jack Pinelli wedding on *Ryan's Hope.* It was hard faking [mono] for a week so I could watch it all."

**ELEMENTARY SCHOOL** Rosie attended Rolling Hills Elementary School in Commack. In the first grade she was already practicing signing her autograph. "When I was a kid, I always fantasized my success would be to this degree. I fear people will think I'm stuck up and say, 'Yeah, right, like she knew she'd be this famous,' but you have to dream it to live it." In the second grade Rosie made her stage debut as Glinda the Good Witch in *The Wizard of Oz.* In another grade-school play, she was Piglet. "I was pretty much in a play every year from then on."

Her third-grade teacher was Miss Boy, and a great one at that. "She read to us every day, encouraged us to be creative, to write, to draw, to paint. I was kinda shy back then, sitting quietly in the last row, wishing I could be a little more like [my classmate] Billy Sheerin."

"Billy was fearless. I think he knew every joke there was and wasn't afraid to tell them. When he ran out, he made some up. Silly, nonsensical jokes. . . . 'Why is the rug green? 'Cause my sneakers are blue.' Then he would roar with laughter. Contagious, side-splitting, milk-coming-out-of-your-nose-type laughter. Before long, the whole class was laughing with him. I can still see his shaggy blond hair, sparkly blue eyes, and loopy grin. To me, Billy Sheerin was the king."

Another classmate of Rosie's, Amy Golditch Bernard, tells how Rosie helped keep other kids from being bullied. "It seemed then, when I was just eight years old, like the most horrible time in my life. But as long as Roseann was around, everything was all right. She was my hero."

**HIGH SCHOOL** Rosie graduated from Commack South High School (their team was the Spartans) with the class of 1980. She maintained a B average while participating in nearly every activity imaginable. She was elected homecoming queen, prom queen, senior class president, student council executive board, class clown, and personality plus. She was on the yearbook staff, in the Drama Society, Senior Follies, and Leader Corps, and—not surprisingly—she was a candy-sale committee member. Rosie played varsity tennis, junior-varsity volleyball, baseball, basketball, field hockey, and other sports, as well as playing drums in a rock band. She tried stand-up comedy after doing killer impressions of Gilda Radner for her friends and in a school follies production. "Being popular was easy for me, because of my humor and desire to please. I was more interested in making my teachers laugh than the students. I was always trying to get the teachers, who were around the age of my mother, to like me and validate me."

**SUMMER JOBS** "I was a day-camp counselor for little kids when I was fourteen or fifteen. I also painted T-shirts and sold them to a kids' store. I later learned that the paints I used came off after two washes."

**DATING** Rosie's first kiss, with Craig Blitz while playing basketball, occurred about this time. "The ball bounced into the garage. He kissed me, and it bounced out again."

"Most teenagers go through sexual discovery and angst [during high school]. I didn't. I went through working at comedy clubs and being very asexual. I started doing stand-up comedy when I was sixteen. I'm thirty-one years old and have yet to really date seriously."

**COLLEGE** At her father's insistence, Rosie enrolled on scholarship at Dickinson College in Carlisle, Pennsylvania, where she majored in prelaw. She worked part-time in the school post office. She eked out a grade-point average of 1.62 (on a 4.0 scale) her freshman year. She left Dickinson, transferring to the Drama Department at Boston University. While in Boston, she worked at a nearby video store. After about six months, she was told by one of her drama professors that she "would never make it as an actress." Still, she might have stuck it out had she not gotten kicked out of school after skipping Jim Sprool's acting class on October 6, 1981, to watch the news that Egyptian president Anwar al-Sadat had been assassinated. The Drama Department told her that acting was "more important than that," and Rosie said, "No, it isn't." With that, she returned to her stand-up career. She was nineteen years old.

**STEPMOTHER** Mary O'Donnell. Rosie gets along with her stepmother "because she wasn't raised in our family and didn't know the rules, so she's communicative."

**SURROGATE MOTHER** When Rosie was three, Jackie Ellard and her family moved in across the street at 22 Rhonda Lane. After the death of Rosie's mother, Bernice Ellard became the closest thing Rosie had to a mother. "They had serving spoons and serving dishes. And gravy, not just at Thanksgiving. Dixie Riddle cups instead of the generic brand. And real Tupperware with lids that matched and 'the burps' instead of margarine containers. They had extras. Four jars of mayonnaise—sealed. Four jars of Seven Seas Italian dressing—sealed. In our house, we always ran out. Our socks didn't match, and our underwear didn't fit—just those little motherly touches that were really missing. I wanted a home like the Ellards'.

"Every Christmas I send a card to Bernice Ellard, Jackie's mom, and I tell her all the Ellardesque things in my house: an electric knife, Tupperware with the right kind of lids, Ziploc bags. I'm so happy to have an Ellard kind of house for my son, because they provided me with safety and the feeling of being nurtured, things I didn't have in my own house."

**SIBLINGS** Eddie (two years older), Danny (one year older), Maureen (one year younger), and Timmy (four years younger). "My sister and I are very close; we were born only fifteen months apart. I'm an active part of her life and her children's lives. I'm more separate from my brothers. I think my career is harder for them. They find my lifestyle a little bit of an oddity. And they are forever being asked if they're related to me, which annoys them. One of my brothers said, 'Every time I open a magazine it's your picture!' with sort of an undertone of discontent.

"[Our mother's death] was an extreme situation—the five of us took care of each other. We're all still close. In our family, any show of emotion was frowned upon, other than humor. You could communicate what you were feeling as long as you could make a joke about it."

**NIECES AND NEPHEWS** Maureen Crimmins and her husband have three children, Katie, Julianne, and Elizabeth. They live in northern New Jersey. Eddie and his wife, Trish, who also live in New Jersey, have two children, Allison and Ryan. Danny, a lawyer and former New York City public defender, lives in Manhattan and is single. He is president of the Broadway Democratic Club, and he serves on Community Board 9 in Manhattan. Danny is reportedly considering a run for the state senate. Youngest brother Timmy lives in Jacksonville, Florida, with his wife and two children.

**CURRENT AND RECENT HOMES** In March 1996, Rosie purchased Pretty Penny, a century-old twenty-two-room mansion that was owned for nearly fifty years by Helen Hayes, the first lady of the American theater. The mansion overlooks the Hudson River in Nyack, New York, and is surrounded by a high stone wall. Madonna had considered buying the house, but she decided the wall wasn't high enough for her needs. She then brought the house to Rosie's attention. Some say it is haunted by the spirit of Mary MacArthur, Hayes's daughter, who died there of polio at age nineteen. After extensive renovations to the house, Rosie took up residence in early in 1997. She had been living on Manhattan's Upper West Side.

About the same time she moved to Nyack, Warner Bros. leased her a penthouse suite in the Grand Millennium, also on Manhattan's Upper West Side, where she and her children stay during the week to be close to work. Proclaimed the first residential CyberBuilding, the Grand Millennium offers a high-tech T1 computer line in every apartment, an in-building fiberoptic network that connects residents to a virtual community, and on-call technicians to help with computer and communications snags. In addition, each apartment at the Grand Millennium has up to twelve digital phone lines, its own E-mail account, and unlimited access to the Internet. Another benefit of the Grand Millennium, its access to the Hudson River, allows Rosie to dock her new twenty-seven-foot yacht there.

Rosie recently gave up the apartment she had near Madonna in Miami, Florida, mainly due to a lack of privacy from the paparazzi. From 1984, when she won $30,000 on *Star Search*, until early 1996, when she moved to New York to create *The Rosie O'Donnell Show*, Rosie lived in Studio City, California, first at 12522 West Moorpark Street, Apartment 109, and then 4116 North Bellingham Avenue.

**ROSIE AS A MOTHER** "I always knew I'd be a mother in the same way I knew I'd be successful. I've always been connected to kids. But I think my capacity to feel love is so increased—exponentially. I don't think I was fully alive before he was in my life. And I didn't go through that thing—I'm gonna be thirty-five in March—I didn't go through that, 'Oh, should I have a kid, should I not . . .' I knew I would be a mom from the time I was twelve, thirteen. I knew it. And I knew I wanted to achieve what I wanted to do in my career first and be ready emotionally and financially, and definitely psychologically. After many, many, and many a month of therapy, I decided I was ready to do it. So, I was prepared. One thing I knew for sure was that I wanted a child, many of them, and I wasn't getting any younger."

❤ ❤ ❤

"I have no genetic investment in a child. Any baby you put in my arms will be my baby; girl or boy, it makes no difference."

❤ ❤ ❤

"Will the next kid be as great [as Parker]? My sister [Maureen] told me you grow a new heart with every child."

❤ ❤ ❤

"I don't really think there is [such a thing as an ideal parent]. I think everybody does the best that they can. . . . I think a benefit of adopting is that I don't have any vested interest in who this child is. I think he's a total, separate entity. I think that if you give birth, you somehow want the kid to be a reflection of you. Adopting a baby, I do feel like I'm able to experience more the joy of who he is separate from me. I think that's probably the biggest challenge, not to put yourself on your kid."

**CHILDREN** Parker Jaren O'Donnell was born on May 25, 1995, and adopted by Rosie two days later. It didn't take long for Rosie to discover that her rising film career would make it difficult to be a full-time mother. "I want to be there when he has his first Little League game. I don't want to be on a set in North Carolina."

❤   ❤   ❤

"I wanted a job that allowed me to spend time with him. I wanted him to sleep in his own bed every night so he'd have consistency and stability in his life. I knew this job [as a daytime talk-show host] would be a lot of hours, but it would also give me the luxury of being a hands-on parent. There's only one hour a day that I need to be totally focused, and that's when I'm on the air. Other than that, he's always with me or nearby. He's just part of the routine here." Rosie is very much a hands-on mother. She gets her children up every morning by 5:00 A.M., feeds and dresses them. Then they leave for the show's studio in Rockefeller Plaza, usually arriving before 8:00 A.M. Originally there was a nursery for Parker adjacent to Rosie's office, but now she's built a complete day-care center down the hall from her office for her kids and those of her show's staff. It is staffed with two certified teachers and has a kitchen, bathroom, a slide, and other facilities.

Rosie does have a part-time nanny–baby-sitter, Kate Fitzgerald, for her kids, for those times when she can't be with them. But she tries to keep those times to a minimum, spending most of her evenings at home with them. "Before my son arrived, I always thought I'd die young, like my mother. Now, for the first time, I think I have something to live for. The dread, fear, doom, and gloom has been replaced by love and sunshine. It's hard to put into words. It's like you grow another heart.

"When I first held my son in my arms, I had that overwhelming connection and feeling of immense love that I never had before."

❤   ❤   ❤

"I have all nieces, so my son was the first boy [in the family]. I have no mom, no one to ask. I'm home. I think, I don't need anyone to help me. I wanna bond with this kid. My mom raised five kids alone before she died. I can do this. I'm totally in a coma the first month. He's up every twenty minutes. I'm changing his diaper. I notice, he's got a baby boner. I freaked out. Because I didn't know. I thought that men, like women, when your period kicks in at thirteen . . . I thought you guys went through the same thing. You know that movie we saw in school about getting your period? I thought you—I had no idea that the equipment functions right from birth. I didn't know what to do. I'm sitting there thinking, Something is wrong with my son. I didn't want to touch it. I thought, Oh, that's a beauty. I took a Q-tip. I'm pointing it down. I put on the Pamper, I made a pouch with the Pamper in case it happened again. I didn't want it to get bent. You know, I was totally unprepared to have a male child."

❤    ❤    ❤

"Parker is not going to be on TV unless he's eighteen and that's what he chooses to do with his life. His mom's on TV; he isn't. This business is very corrupting, and I don't want him to be a part of it. As much as I can keep him away from it, I will. I try to tell the stories on my show about my parenting experience more so than 'Look at the little achievement of my child,' which I think to be a little bit private. Because I don't want him to grow up in front of all of America like Chastity Bono did or Cody and Cassidy [Gifford]. This isn't a judgment about the way that other people do it; it's just that for me, I think that fame really can corrupt you as an adult. It can alter your perspective on the world. I can't imagine what it would do to a child. So I try to keep as much as I can, the private details of our interaction, that— But when you are on a show every day, you talk. . . ."

As the weeks roll on, Rosie's resolve to keep her children's lives private is continuing to erode. Each day now it seems she begins her opening chat with John McDaniel with an anecdote or two about Parker and Chelsea—Parker biting Chelsea, then sending himself to the corner for his punishment, or Parker's penchant for skyscraper construction.

Rosie's second child, Chelsea Belle, was born on September 20, 1997, and adopted one week later. At birth she weighed seven pounds twelve ounces, with green eyes and almost no hair—only a little bit of brownish-blond fuzz. Rosie had been searching for over a year through adoption sources when she suddenly got a call that a baby girl was available. She is currently discussing adopting a third child.

**ADOPTION** "If I was with a man I wanted to have a child with, I would have gotten pregnant, but that was not the case. . . . I really had no ego investment in re-creating myself. . . . Nor did I feel the need to dive into my gene pool or go fishing there, because there is a tremendous amount of illness in my family, a tremendous amount of alcoholism."

❤   ❤   ❤

"I want to adopt another child [she has since adopted Chelsea] . . . and I may want to adopt more after that. I want Parker to be able to look over the bunk bed at his brothers and say, 'Hey, doesn't it suck that Mom's on television?' I want him to have someone who understands. . . . Hopefully his siblings can roll their eyes with him."

Parker and Chelsea were both adopted through a traditional agency, and both adoptions were closed. That means that all contact between Rosie and the birth mothers was done through the agency. This is unusual in today's adoption world, as more and more birth mothers seek greater input in the choice of their baby's adoptive family. And if Parker or Chelsea decide one day to look for their birth mothers? "Then I will totally support them. But I believe they were supposed to be with me and I with them."

**HAIR** Rosie's hair is naturally black, which is what she means when she calls herself "black Irish." She began coloring it for *The Rosie O'Donnell Show* because her hairdresser, David Evangelista, told her it would look better on television. Rosie first went to a dark red with blonde highlights, but now it is simply a reddish-brown without the highlights.

**EYES** Rosie has brown eyes and doesn't wear glasses or contact lenses.

**HEIGHT** Rosie is five feet seven inches tall.

**WEIGHT** "This is the heaviest I've ever been. I'm a junk-food eater. I don't realize when I lose weight or gain it; only my wardrobe tells me. I'm uncomfortable at this weight, especially when I pick up my son or run around, but I'll get it under control again. It doesn't mean I'll be thin by America's standards. I'm like an eighteen now; size ten or twelve is thin for me. I don't hate myself for it, and I don't want to sound like I'm down on myself. Too many kids have eating disorders, and I certainly don't want to feed into that. I just want to be healthy."

❤     ❤     ❤

"As I grew up emotionally, all of the issues surrounding weight that deal with emotions came to the forefront for me. As I became a grown-up, I had to deal with these issues, and with them came weight, because the way that people deal with problems is often with food, which is a symptom of another thing. . . . [W]hen I read in the newspaper that some radio jock says, 'She's so fat and gross,' it hurts my feelings. I sometimes get out of the shower and think, Oh, boy, I have to do something. And then I have to work hard to stand in front of the mirror after that image goes through and say, 'This is who you are, and this is where you are. You're okay in this body, and you're a great, healthy, lovable, and loving person,' and go forward with love. And that's what I try to do. I honestly believe that my weight is a part of my popularity. Thousands of heavy women can identify with me. They see me heavy but enjoying life and having fun."

Rosie was not overweight as a child or even as a teenager. It wasn't until she was on the road as a stand-up comic, eating fast-food meals and sweet snacks, that she gained weight. "If you watch a few years of my VH1 comedy shows, you can watch me go from 140 to 170 in a matter of seconds." "When I did *Grease*, I was 150 pounds, and that was a comfortable weight for me. That's about thirty pounds ago. I'm uncomfortable at this weight, but I don't hate myself for it."

Although she managed to get back down to 150 pounds to film *Exit to Eden*, her normal weight now is probably around 200 pounds. Interestingly, in July 1996 two tabloids had articles about Rosie's weight the same week, one claiming she weighed 185 pounds, the other insisting she was 217. The truth is somewhere in between. Whatever it is, what is important is her emphasis on maintaining one's self-esteem—accept what you are, and then just have fun. "If I'm interested in someone and want to have a romantic relationship with them, I can entice them with my wit, intellect—my essence."

**WHAT ROSIE LIKES TO EAT** First we have to start with Ring Dings, a snack treat made by the Drake's cakes company. These are creme-filled Devil's food cakes coated with chocolate, similar to Hostess's

Ding Dongs (a.k.a. King Dongs). Other Drake's products that Rosie loves include Devil Dogs (two layers of devil's food cake sandwiching a layer of creme) and Yodels (chocolate-covered devil's-food-cake rolls with creme filling). She is not so fond of Yankee Doodles (creme-filled cupcakes), and she doesn't care for Drake's Funny Bones at all (similar to Yodels with a peanut butter–flavored cream filling).

Each audience member of *The Rosie O'Donnell Show* is provided with a package of Ring Dings, Yodels, or Devil Dogs, along with a half-pint carton of milk. This is an idea Rosie borrowed from her close friend Fran Drescher, who does something similar for the audience of her show, *The Nanny*.

Other snack foods that Rosie has mentioned that she likes are bubble gum (she can blow a bubble inside a bubble), M & M's, Snickers, Nutrageous, sugar wafers, and just about anything else chocolate. She's also fond of a tender-cut, medium-rare steak, Chinese chicken-and-spinach salad, and burgers and fries at McDonald's and Burger King. She claims her favorite pizza is California Pizza Kitchen's goat-cheese pie, which is certainly an odd choice for a New Yorker!

**CLOTHES** Rosie has very little interest in style or haute couture. She'd much rather be in sweats or shorts and a T-shirt, with tennis shoes, than just about anything else. She dresses casual for work and doesn't really care what her dresser puts her in for the show as long as it fits. As soon as the show is over, she's back into her casual clothes for the rest of the day. One reason Rosie likes to vacation in Florida and Hawaii is so she can wear casual clothes and beachwear the whole time. "If I could, I would live in Miami and swim in the ocean every day."

**TATTOOS** Rosie has a tattoo of a ring of roses around her right ankle, along with a small cross with a heart on it. One of the roses, under the heart but on top of the cross, is a "side" view instead of a "top" view, like the rest. For her role as the barefoot Betty Rubble in *The Flintstones*, she wore a scarf around her ankle to hide the tattoo.

**CHILDHOOD ROLE MODELS** "Barbra Streisand and Bette Midler. And then as I got older, Carol Burnett, Gilda Radner, and Lucille Ball." She has also mentioned Mary Tyler Moore, Julie Andrews, Merv Griffin, Mike Douglas, Dinah Shore, Luci Arnaz, Liza Minnelli, and Chita Rivera.

## FRIENDS

**Jackie Ellard Elliott** When Rosie was three, Jackie Ellard and her family moved across the street at 22 Rhonda Lane. She and Jackie became instant and lifelong friends. Today Jackie works with Rosie, handling the vast amount of E-mail Rosie receives from her America Online and World Wide Web sites.

**Jeanne Davis** Jeanne has been one of Rosie's best friends since high school, "a model for the Ford Agency. Very tall, very pretty, very Barbie." Actually, Jeanne is a speech pathologist who still lives on Long Island, is divorced, and is raising a child. She says, "Rosie had to be her own parent. She threw herself into everything and became a take-charge person. We used to butt heads all the time because she would try to order dinner for me and then she'd want to pay the bill.

"She was different from the rest of us in so many ways. We'd all go out, and while we'd be drinking with false IDs, she'd be playing video games. Rosie was so isolated. Yet she managed to always be the most popular."

**Madonna** Rosie met Madonna while filming *A League of Their Own*. Rosie watched Madonna at her mother's grave in the documentary *Truth or Dare* and knew they would be friends. Both women were named after their mothers and lost them at a young age. They have remained close friends.

But being a megastar's close friend first showed her something of the price of fame. "Coming to know [Madonna] and love her as a human being brought me to a different awareness of what that kind of media image does to someone." Several years ago Madonna said, "My friendship with Rosie has nothing to do with image. I cannot explain the mystery of what happens when you become friends with someone. I can only say that we are tortured by the same things, we laugh at the same things, and I love her madly."

**Tom Hanks and Rita Wilson** Rosie worked with Tom in *A League of Their Own* and *Sleepless in Seattle* and with Rita, Tom's wife, in *Now* *and Then.* They remain very close friends. It was Rita who pointed out, on the day Rosie brought Parker home from the adoption agency, that he hadn't been circumcised. (He later would be.)

**Penny Marshall** Penny and Rosie met when Rosie auditioned for a part in *A League of Their Own.* Penny, who grew up in the Bronx, New York, and Rosie, from Long Island, quickly became close friends. "I told everyone that the reason I was in that movie so much, it was a little part, [it was because] I was the only one who could understand you."

Penny is a frequent guest because she lives in Manhattan and is available on short notice whenever another guest cancels. For the past three years they have done a series of holiday-season television commercials for Kmart.

**Tom Cruise** Rosie has a "small" crush on Tom Cruise. On September 21, 1996, Rosie hosted the American Cinematheque Moving Picture Ball in Los Angeles, where she met the honored guest of the event, Tom Cruise. Tom planted a kiss or two on her for the cameras. On December 10, 1996, Tom finally appeared on Rosie's show. ("I know that you're just a guy . . . who's an actor, but somehow you make me really happy.") "My crush on him has nothing to do with anything that is adult. It's a prepubescent girl desire to have his picture thumbtacked to my bedroom wall. It doesn't have to do with a thirty-five-year-old woman's adult desire."

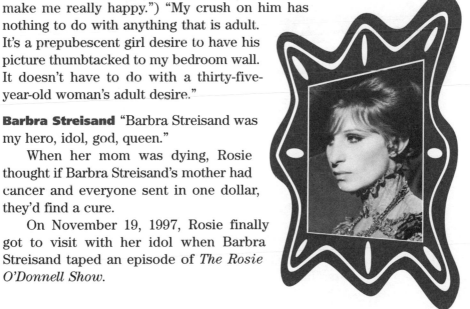

**Barbra Streisand** "Barbra Streisand was my hero, idol, god, queen."

When her mom was dying, Rosie thought if Barbra Streisand's mother had cancer and everyone sent in one dollar, they'd find a cure.

On November 19, 1997, Rosie finally got to visit with her idol when Barbra Streisand taped an episode of *The Rosie O'Donnell Show.*

Rosie was asked if the experience lived up to her expectations. "Oh, and beyond. A lot of people told me, 'You should be careful when you meet someone you idolize, because there's no way they can live up to your expectations.' But I have to say, she exceeded my expectations. She was so warm and nurturing and loving. She was amazing: sisterly and maternal and friendly all in one. You know, it was something I dreamed of as a kid, and I had lived that moment for, like, twenty years in my head."

**Bette Midler** "Bette Midler is the reason I'm in entertainment today. I owe her my life! I was twelve years old when I saw her on Broadway in *Clams on the Half-Shell*. I stole ten dollars out of my father's wallet to buy a ticket. . . . I remember watching her up there onstage and thinking, That's what I want to do."

**Roseanne** "We have both learned a lot from our childhood. I look up to her. She faces her demons. Maybe a little too publicly for my level of comfort. But she has done a tremendous service [by discussing her troubled childhood] for many, myself included."

**Linda Richman** Linda Richman is the mother-in-law of Mike Myers and the model for his "Coffee Talk" character on *Saturday Night Live*. Linda, who is Jewish, calls Rosie her "lawst dawta [lost daughter]."

**ON CELEBRITY** "There was some magazine wanted to give me "Single Parent of the Year" and I thought, Why? You know, there's a woman somewhere in the South Bronx with four kids living on welfare, and those kids are going to school every day and have good grades and are not in gangs. That's the woman who deserves the award. Look at me. I get a private plane here and a limo and a bazillion of those Nikes that are eighty dollars; they send me every size. I have a really privileged life. And I'm not stupid enough to deny it. People have said, too, with the adoption, Did it help being a celebrity? You know what? I don't know how much it helped, but I can tell you this: Being a celebrity helps in every aspect of your life in this culture. You can get a baby quicker, you can kill your wife and get away with it. You can do a lot of things in this culture being a celebrity. And so I don't think that we as celebrities deserve awards in that way."

**AUTOGRAPH POLICY** "I never give autographs to adults, only kids. If you're thirty-five years old and asking for an autograph on a napkin, you gotta get a life."

**PETS** Rosie owns three dogs: two long-haired Chihuahuas named Buster and Valentine and a German shepherd guard dog named Donna that would rather urinate on the carpet than defend its domicile. Her home in Nyack is often visited by assorted squirrels, skunks, birds, and other critters.

**POLITICS** Democrat. "I said this on my show and I thought Uh-oh. I guess there's a reason Dave and Jay never get into their political affiliations; I'm gonna get letters from Republicans about this. Then I realized: What Republicans are watching daytime television? They're too busy tryin' to make more money than anybody else."

**ON BREAST CANCER** In 1993, Rosie discovered a lump in her left breast while doing a self-examination. "I was horrified. I thought history was repeating itself. You can imagine how devastated I was. I was practically the same age as my mom when she was diagnosed. I made an urgent appointment to see my doctor, who told me they'd have to do a biopsy. It was terrifying. But the result came back almost instantly, and thank God, the lump was benign. I was given the all-clear."

Rosie vowed to be a leader in the fight against breast cancer. During October 1997 she used her show to educate millions during National Breast Cancer Awareness Month. Her show's visit to Los Angeles in February 1998 was also used to raise money for Concept: Cure, another breast-cancer charity. "I know that with fame comes the power to cure diseases and help people. I still carry out regular self-examinations and go for regular mammograms. But there are many women out there who have lumps in their breasts and don't even know it. To all the women out there I say: Please, please, please listen to your doctor's advice and help us fight this killer disease. Don't wait until it's too late."

**HOBBIES** Rosie likes to play board games like Scrabble, attend Broadway shows, and collect fast-food kids' meal toys. She has thousands of toys from McDonald's and Burger King, which she displays on custom shelves in her home. Says her sister, Maureen, "She knows exactly where each toy goes. Sometimes I'll move one just to see how long it takes her to notice." She also collects *Playbills* and memorabilia from her favorite stage shows, television shows, and films. Her collections include dolls, action figures, lunch pails, records, and other toys.

She's still active in sports, too. "I'm in a bowling league, basketball league, and a softball league. I go to the batting cages. I throw the football around with my friends and my brothers sometimes. And chasing after my son seems like a big athletic event lately."

**MUSICAL SKILLS** Rosie took lessons on the drums as a preteen and played with a rock band in junior high school, doing occasional gigs at the neighborhood roller rink. She is still quite accomplished. She and Parker have matching trap sets in the basement of their home in Nyack. Sadly, what she cannot do musically is sing well, and she knows it. "I love to sing. I sing in the shower. I sing to my baby every day. I know I'm not a great singer, but it's fun."

**BOOK** When Rosie O'Donnell first asked kids to send her their best jokes, thousands of young viewers all across the country immediately flooded the show's mailbox with drawings, letters, and of course, great puns and riddles. Soon Rosie was sharing the funniest jokes and pictures with her audience, and a much-loved feature on *The Rosie O'Donnell Show* was born. For her first book, *Kids Are Punny*, she has collected her favorites.

FEATURE ARTICLE

# "Rosie's Big (and Little) New Plans"

From REDBOOK,
October 1997

*With both her "babies" (son
Parker and her hit talk show)
well into their terrific twos,
an unusually candid Rosie
O'Donnell talks about the
changes she'll be making on TV and in her family.*

## BY MARTHA FRANKEL

As Rosie O'Donnell opens the door to her spacious home in suburban
New York, it's hard not to stare at the random Magic Marker lines that
snake across her arms, her legs, even her neck. O'Donnell laughs. "Hey,"
she says in that famous New York voice, "I'm one of those mothers who
says it is perfectly all right to draw on me. I actually encourage it. Come
in, meet the artist." With that, O'Donnell's bright and sunny blond 2½
year-old son, Parker, comes racing around the corner, stopping only
long enough to mumble, "Hi, Mommy." The look on O'Donnell's face
says it all: These are the words she's waited her whole life to hear.

Her story is a bit of a dream come true. One of five kids raised on
Long Island, Rosie was ten when her mother died of cancer—the defin-
ing moment in her life. Her father, an electrical engineer, was emotionally distant; although O'Donnell's grandmother lived with the
family, the children were pretty much left to raise themselves and to
find role models where they could. For O'Donnell, the screen and stage

provided plenty—Barbra Streisand, Dinah Shore, Bette Midler, and Merv Griffin were some of her idols—and eventually offered her a clear career path in entertainment. The rest, of course, is history. After a successful run in comedy and film, O'Donnell eventually decided the role she was really hungry for was that of mom. In 1995 she adopted a son, a decision that eventually pushed her to redirect her career and pursue a daytime talk show so she could spend more time with him. Now heading into its second year, *The Rosie O'Donnell Show* is in for some changes, and Rosie O'Donnell, whose gig as a mom is in its third year, is in for some changes herself.

**THE VOID HER BABY FILLED** Home for the O'Donnells is a turn-of-the-century house that once belonged to the actress Helen Hayes. O'Donnell happily points out the rose garden, the pool, and the view of the Hudson River. *Not bad*, O'Donnell's manner says, *for a girl who never had anything.*

Before settling on the veranda, which looks out over a dozen bird feeders ("Every morning, Parker races out here to show me which ones need more feed," O'Donnell says proudly), she makes sure that Parker is well entertained by his nanny until she gets back to him. He looks so cute that she grabs the camera and snaps a photo. This will be just one more of thousands that O'Donnell has already taken to document his life. They line the refrigerator and walls, and cram dozens of photo albums.

"I'm 35 now," says O'Donnell, "and my mother was 39 when she died. I want to make sure that if something happens to me, Parker knows how much he is loved. I want that to be a clear, tangible thing he can hold, and say, 'Look, she loved me.'"

The death of her mother was very confusing (O'Donnell wasn't allowed to attend the funeral or see her mother's body because the family thought it would be too traumatic), so she began living in her own fantasy world. Convinced that her mother wasn't actually dead, she spent hours talking to her spirit. Her fifteen years of ongoing therapy have helped to make her ready to raise a child of her own. Close pal Madonna once explained to her, "When you surpass the age your mother was when she died, you're freed." Madonna, who also lost her mom as a child, has now passed that age. Rosie is approaching it. "I think all motherless children feel that having their own children will fill that hole in their lives. And Parker has done that for me," she says, "I feel like an adult for the first time."

As a kid, O'Donnell dreamed of being the next Barbra Streisand. And although her mother pointed out that Rosie didn't have the same kind of voice as her idol, the daughter was confident. "I'll learn," she answered. After high school, O'Donnell realized that stand-up comedy, not music, was her strength. From there she was cast in her first movie, Penny Marshall's women's baseball film, *A League of Their Own.* That led to her friendship with Madonna, more movies (including *Now and Then, Harriet the Spy,* and the new children's movie, *Wide Awake*), more friendships with the very famous, a role in the Broadway version of *Grease!* In 1994, those zany Kmart commercials with Marshall, and then her talk show. And no, she still doesn't have Streisand's voice, but she more than makes do with what she's got.

Now O'Donnell grabs Parker and flings him into the air. The squeals of delight from both of them prove that mother and son are a perfect match. And it's Parker who is teaching O'Donnell about her own mother. "When he looks at me, I can finally see my own mother as a woman, not just as my mom. I feel closer to her than I have in a long time. I finally understand just how much she loved me. I realize that she felt, for me, the things I feel for him.

**FAMOUS FRIENDS, SURPRISING NEWS** Unlike women who spend years waiting to adopt a baby, O'Donnell admits that her celebrity helped her get Parker quickly (she adopted him when he was a few days old). "But this is one time that I'm not going to beat myself up over being famous," she says. When O'Donnell first started the adoption process, she decided not to ask for a specific gender. "You get what you need in life. I guess I needed a boy," she says now. She doesn't worry about Parker lacking male role models: "Parker will have men in his life; I'm very close with my brothers, and they're great with him."

O'Donnell throws back her head and laughs. "But I'll tell you—I was singularly unprepared for a son. I read all these books on adoption and I didn't have any help, because I wanted it to be just him and me.

But one day Rita Wilson [the actress married to Tom Hanks] and Kate Capshaw [the actress married to Steven Spielberg] came over [to her rented house in Los Angeles] to help. Rita went to change his diaper. She said, 'Why didn't you have him circumcised?' I said, 'I did.' She goes, 'Rosie, you didn't.' I said, 'Look, here are the adoption papers, they say he's circumcised.' And Rita holds up the baby and says, 'Well, look at this . . . he's *not* circumcised.' Now I know this sounds crazy, because I grew up with three brothers. But I never saw my brothers naked when we were kids. And because my mom died when I was young, she was never around to talk to us about those things. Call me silly. I became hysterical, uncontrollable. But Rita and Kate took care of it. They called a doctor friend who is also a mohel [a specially trained Jewish figure who performs ceremonial circumcisions]. He came over the next day and circumcised the baby. Kate brought bagels and lox—we had a little party!" Without missing a beat, O'Donnell belts out, "I did it my way."

**THE GIFT SHE GAVE HER SON** O'Donnell does most things her own way. She taught Parker to swim by throwing him into the pool with water wings on when he was ten months old. "Much to the chagrin of my friends who were mothers," she says now with a laugh. But Parker thrived and is now a terrific swimmer.

Downstairs in the basement are mother-and-child drum sets. O'Donnell, who is a proficient and exuberant drummer, encourages Parker to beat along on his own set, noise levels be damned. For the most part, O'Donnell tries to make Parker's life as normal as possible: playing in his sandbox, basketball with Mom, walks into town for ice cream, 25¢ mechanical horse rides at the local toy store, bath and bed by eight-thirty. But it almost didn't turn out that way.

Although her movie career was thriving, in 1995, at the time she adopted Parker, O'Donnell soon found that going on location with a little baby was sheer craziness. "I was tired of trying to play with him between takes, and having to make sure he didn't throw up on my costumes," O'Donnell says.

So she decided that the manageable schedule of a TV talk show would be perfect for her. She had grown up enthralled by the Merv

Griffin and Mike Douglas shows, and thought that daytime TV needed a lift. She came up with a variety format that was an instantaneous hit. During her first year, guests included Hillary Clinton, Tom Cruise, Elton John, and pal Madonna, who now often brings her baby daughter, Lourdes (whom O'Donnell refers to as Lola), up to O'Donnell's house to swim with Parker.

The one film she'd like to do, however, is the screen version of the play *Chicago*, with Madonna and Goldie Hawn. For a woman who grew up listening to cast albums, the chance to be in a movie musical might be too much to pass up. For three to four weeks she'd be running between the New York sets of her show and the film. And although she is still trying to work out the details, O'Donnell says, "I'd get to sing two numbers. Are you kidding me? It doesn't get better than that!"

**NEW FORMAT, FUNKY CLOTHES** With the kind of success that *The Rosie O'Donnell Show* has enjoyed, you'd think O'Donnell would stick with the same winning format in year two. But that's not her style. She has introduced two animated series (one based on funny adventures of four kids, one based on the life of a single mom) that run for a minute or so each, and offbeat comedian Paula Poundstone is a monthly correspondent, going to different places and interviewing real people. For Poundstone's first piece, O'Donnell gave her a video camera and told her to "go film her summer vacation."

Another change: O'Donnell's wardrobe, which leaned toward conservative suits the first season. O'Donnell points to her own outfit—bicycle shorts and a T-shirt. "These are the sorts of clothes I like: younger, funkier, more fun. The suits got a little stuffy." The change in her clothes might also reflect O'Donnell's comfort with her looks and her weight. She explains, "I feel like it's the ebb and flow of my life, and I don't think I'm any less appealing or sexy or funny because of it. I see these shows on anorexia, and women look in the mirror and think they're fat. I am kind of fat, and I look in the mirror and I don't think I'm as fat as I am. But I don't have self-loathing because of it."

It's that kind of naked honesty that has brought *The Rosie O'Donnell Show* the kind of ratings to make a second season possible (Warner Brothers has given her a four-year contract). And it really *has* turned out to be the perfect job for a mom. "When Parker was a baby it was easier, because you just threw him in the Snugli and off we went. Now I have to wake him up so he can come with me. But I'm not complaining. I am so lucky. The good part is that we're out of the studio by one or two in the afternoon. We can get back here and be on the swing set by three!"

Although Parker is now at the age conventionally called "the terrible twos," O'Donnell isn't experiencing the difficulty that many parents have. "They say it's terrible, but it's not," she confides. "I think it's because I'm more relaxed about the things other mothers say are no good. He wants to draw on me—so I let him. If I was going to fight with him about it, it could get terrible real quick."

But it's not always easy being Rosie O'Donnell the Mom. Aside from the difficulties of raising a child alone and in the spotlight, O'Donnell faces special issues because Parker was adopted. While most mothers are looking for their own characteristics in their children by age 2, O'Donnell can't do that. "I watch him become who he is as opposed to trying to mold him into a reflection of me." (The adoption was closed, so O'Donnell didn't meet the birth mother. She would have been open to it, but the birth mother, who is not aware that O'Donnell is the adoptive mother, chose not to.) Most of all, the stigma of "adopted" is what bothers O'Donnell. "When George Burns died," she explains, "he was 100 years old, and at his bedside was his 60-year-old son. In the obituary it read, 'the adopted son.' After 60 years you'd think, Oh my Lord, when does that adjective become non-applicable?"

**HER HOPES FOR ANOTHER CHILD** It's children for whom O'Donnell feels the most affinity. She will only sign autographs for them—not their parents—and even at that, she downplays her celebrity, especially in the small town where she lives. "When Parker and I are walking through town and a little kid comes over and asks for an autograph, I say, 'What's your name?' I say, 'Hi, Mindy, you know what? I live in this town and you're gonna see me a lot. You're gonna see me at Little League, and at the school plays. So I'm not gonna be Rosie O'Donnell in this town. I'm just gonna be Rosie, Parker's mommy, okay?' And they always understand. I hear them as I walk past, telling each other, 'She's not a star here, she's just Parker's mommy.' And I feel so good."

And the clomping of tiny feet will get louder in the near future if O'Donnell has her way. She admits, "I want to adopt another child, perhaps as early as next summer, and I may want to adopt more after that. I want Parker to be able to look over the bunk bed at his brothers and say, 'Hey, doesn't it suck that Mom's on television?' I want him to have someone who understands. I mean, whenever we walk down the street, everyone knows his name. He has to think that's crazy as he gets older. So, hopefully, his siblings can roll their eyes with him."

With that, O'Donnell picks up the drumsticks and says, "Watch this." She hits the high hat twice and the patter of Parker's feet is barely audible as he runs into the room. He rushes to get behind his drums before his mother gets too far ahead. "Are you ready, Parker?" O'Donnell asks. "And-a-one, and-a-two, and-a-three, and-a-four," says the mom as the son just starts banging away. The only thing louder than the drums is their laughter.

You know just what O'Donnell means when she says, "This is the best time in my life."

Martha Frankel is a freelance entertainment journalist who lives in upstate New York.

# Rosie Stands Up

R osie got her first chance at stand-up while she was in high school. The brother of a classmate owned a comedy club and asked her to give it a try. That *wasn't* what she'd dreamed about, so she turned down the offer. But he kept asking, and she finally gave in. At sixteen she performed her first stand-up date by memorizing a Jerry Seinfeld routine she'd seen Jerry perform on *The Merv Griffin Show*. When she was told that you couldn't steal another comic's work, Rosie thought they were idiots because "when you're an actress, they don't ask you to write the movie."

Regardless, she began writing her own routines and began working steadily at the club while going to school. But her first paying job as a comic didn't come until after she'd left Boston University. She talked her way into a gig at Plums in Worcester, Massachusetts, and shared the bill with Dennis Leary. She didn't do very well, but they paid her sixty dollars anyway. She hung around the Boston comedy scene for a few months before returning to Long Island to work in the catalog department at Sears. She spent her nights emceeing around the area while she created an act for herself.

**DEVELOPING AN ACT** After her "Jerry Seinfeld" incident, she decided instead to work as an emcee and introduced other comedians while she listened to the various acts and learned the ropes. "Even when people would tell me I'm too heavy, too tough, or not pretty enough to succeed, I knew they were wrong. You have to believe in yourself."

**THE ROAD** At twenty she took her act on the road. There wasn't much money to be made doing stand-up in those days, and she often slept in filthy "communal condos" with the other comics on the bill—mostly male. "You'd arrive in town and they'd have a kid come pick you up in a used Vega with a door that didn't close. You'd have to get in on the driver's side and climb over his lunch from Hardee's. All of us would be scrunched in the backseat, and he'd take us to this filthy condo, where we would all live for days.

"The other comics were much older. They'd pick up women at the bars, bring them home, and have sex in the rooms next to mine. I was like twenty and totally freaked out from hearing these noises through the wall. I put the dresser up against the door. Everybody was doing drugs and drinking."

**OTHER FEMALE COMICS** In the early eighties, Rosie estimates she was one of about six women doing stand-up at the time. "It was such a rarity to have a female comic performing at all in a comedy club that it helped me to get noticed. There were about six women working the circuit when I started.

"When I started, some women comics were jealous of other women comics. . . . My philosophy always was, 'If she did, I can, too.' All of us who are working are already in the all-you-can-eat buffet. If you get to the table and there's no shrimp, wait one minute and they'll come out with more. There is no need to push people down."

**ON DRINKING** "When I was a young comic I used to drink a lot. . . . Instead of going back to the motel to be awake and afraid, I would stay and drink with the waitresses after the show and try to get sleepy. Then, when I moved to L.A. and got on a sitcom [*Gimme a Break*], a friend of mine said, 'You drink too much, and you've had a lot of alcoholism in your family.' I was so mad. I said, 'Are you implying that I'm an alcoholic?' She was a therapist, this friend, and she said, 'I just think you have a problem.' So I stopped drinking totally for five years just to show her I could. And I think it's good that I did, because if I had continued along the way that I was, I seriously feel that it would have become a problem for me."

Still, Rosie is not a teetotaler. She prefers an occasional Sam Adams beer over wine or cocktails.

**OPENING ACT** One step up from playing the comedy clubs is getting to open for other entertainers, either on the road or in cities like Las Vegas or Atlantic City. By 1985 she was the opening act for illusionist David Copperfield at Caesars Palace in Las Vegas. She went on to tour with country stars Dolly Parton and Wynonna Judd. Dolly remembers that her fans loved Rosie, even though she was a New Yorker, because "she was so real and so down-home and they understood her comedy. We made a good team." And Rosie credits Wynonna with coining her signature line, "You rock, sister friend."

# Highlights of Rosie's HBO Special

**APRIL 1995**

**ROSIE ON MAKING *A LEAGUE OF THEIR OWN*** It was so much fun. . . . I was very nervous 'cause I had to meet Penny Marshall, Laverne. Schlemiel, Schlemazle, Hossenfeffer Incorporated." I was so nervous. I was in the little waiting area thinking, Don't call her Laverne, don't call her Laverne. . . . She comes out and says, "Hi, I'm Penny." I go, "Hi, I'm Laverne." F**k, f**k! Luckily, she thought I was kidding; she laughed. [*Imitating Penny's laugh*] Ha . . . ha . . . ha. . . . [*Audience laughter*]

So I went in and auditioned, and she said to me [imitating Penny's voice], "Okay, Rosie, you're gonna play Doris. Tomorrow Madonna's gonna come in. . . . She likes you, she likes me, she'll do the movie. Try to be funny, don't be nervous." Don't be nervous? I had diarrhea for twelve hours. I thought, What could I possibly say to Madonna? How do you connect to her? How do you make a bond with her? I said, "Hello, I have a vibrator." She said "Panasonic?" I said "No, Black and Decker." We were like *this*. [*Rosie crosses her fingers*]

I actually ended up being in the film a lot more than I was supposed to. . . . It was a tiny part. It ended up a much bigger part, not because I'm a great actress but because I was from New York City and I was the only one who could understand Penny. All the women in the movie would be in the dugout waiting for her. She'd come over [*imitating Penny*]: "Oh kay . . . I need somebady to go ovah to tird base . . . do something there with a bat or whatevah . . . you know, pick it up . . . play wid da ball . . . film dis up dand down . . . who wants to volunteer to do da little scene dere at tird base. Anybody wanna?" "I'll do it Penny" "*Rosie again?* . . . all the time . . . don't you girls wanna be in the movee?" [*Audience laughter*]

**ROSIE ON DIETING** I've been on every diet in the world. I'm a yo-yo dieter. I go up and down. It's very sad. I've been on SlimFast, yeah, for breakfast you have . . . a shake. For lunch you have [*someone in audience yells "a shake"*] . . . a shake, that's right. And for dinner you kill anyone in the room with food in their plate 'cause you're starving by this point. But that condescending commercial—what do they say? For dinner have a sensible meal. *Oh*, a *sensible* meal! If I could have a sensible meal, I wouldn't need f**king SlimFast to begin with. That's so rude. A sensible meal. Honey, put down the Ding Dongs; let's have some carrots. I never thought of that . . . that's sensible. A sensible meal, damnit. [*Audience laughter*]

My favorite diet is the Richard Simmons Deal-a-Meal. I've never been on the diet, but I love the commercial. Have you ever watched that show? Three in the morning, you're sitting at home, eating Doritos, drinking a Yoo Hoo. There he is, in his pink shorts, happy as can be. . . . [*Imitating Richard Simmons*] "I'm Richard Simmons, and today we're gonna go meet Jennifer, who lost a hundred and forty pounds. . . . Jennifer! Surprise!" [*Imitates crying, wiping tears away, imitates Jennifer's voice*] "Richard Simmons! Richard, before I was on the Deal-a-Meal program, I was three hundred pounds. I was sitting home . . . eating Doritos, drinking a Yoo Hoo. I Love you Richard!" [*Imitates Richard*] "I love you, Jennifer". . . . I'm at home going, "I love both of you!" [*Mimes grabbing Doritos out of a bag; audience laughs*]

Weight Watchers . . . a lot of people have been on that, right? Remember Lynn Redgrave for Weight Watchers . . . This Is Living? Lying sack of s**t. I'm gonna kick her ass if I ever meet her. You ever see her? [*In a British accent*] "If you're hungry, don't have ice cream or anything like that. Simply have a lovely German Chocolate Cake from Weight Watchers. It's fabulous. Simply pop it in the oven and pop it in your mouth and you're full for the whole day." It's the size of a goddamn coin, all right? I'm surprised they can get icing on something so small. There must be a little Weight Watchers factory somewhere with little Oompa Loompas working there. . . . [*Sings*] "Oompa Loompa doobidy do . . . I have some more cake for the fat you." [*Laughter*]

**ROSIE ON HER DAD** I am Irish. My father is from Ireland. He's got a thick brogue. [*Pointing to someone in the audience*] You're Irish, I could tell. You could sneak into one of my family reunions. He's got a thick brogue, and when I was a kid my friends used to make fun of him. He never knew it. They'd call my house, he'd answer the phone. [*In a thick Irish accent*] "Hello, who'd you want to speak to?" and my friends would say, "Ro was after me Lucky Charms. The frosted-oat cereal with sweet surprises." [*Audience laughter*] And he never knew. . . . He'd write it all down. [*Mimes writing a note*] "Slow down, sweetheart, I'm trying to get it all. The frosted-oat cereal. . . ." I'd come home, there'd be messages on the refrigerator. "Ro, Jackie called, said mainly yes, but I like it, too." I got older and he started to think this was a code. I was like, fifteen years old, I'd come home, he's grilling me. [*Irish accent*] "Your friends called again, sweetheart. Lucky Charms, Irish Spring. You're taking pot, aren't ya? I figured it out, the whole lot of you pot takers. You don't be taking the pot in my house." [*Audience laughter*]

He was very concerned with that in my adolescence, that I was taking pot. I don't know where he thought I was taking it to. But the transportation of marijuana was paramount in his mind. I bought him a phone-answering machine for Christmas. He still hasn't figured out how to leave [an outgoing] message. You call my father's house . . . ring . . . ring . . . click . . . [*In her father's voice*] "God damn it, Mary, how in the hell do you use this stupid piece of s**t? Come over here and look and see if you can help me with the . . ." Beep! [*Audience laughter*]

About once a year, when I know he's not home, I'll call his house and leave a message. "Hi. I hope this is the right number. This is Rosie. I'm looking for Donna. I'm trying to buy some pot." He still doesn't get it. He calls me, screaming, "Now I've got you on tape, you pot taker. Calling your pot dealer on me phone. Pot taker!" [*Audience laughter*]

**ROSIE ON HER USELESS KNOWLEDGE** I was good shopping in the cereal aisle last month. For no apparent reason, I started singing "Honeycombs big, yeah, yeah, yeah. It's not small, no, no, no." I didn't even know I knew that song. I ran into the cookie aisle thinking, I'm safe, I don't know any cook. . . . [*Singing*] "Oh, you never would believe where those Keebler cookies come from. They're baked by little elves in a hollow tree." Frozen Food: "Oh, Poppin' Fresh dough . . . bake it up hot!" Canned goods: "Yum, yum, Bumblebee, Bumblebee tuna." Candy: "Sometimes you feel like a nut. Sometimes you don't. Peter Paul Almond Joy's got nuts. Peter Paul Mounds don't because . . ." First aid: "I am stuck on Band-Aids 'cause Band-Aid's stuck on me. 'Cause they hold on tight in the bathtub and they cling in soapy suds." [*Audience laughter and applause*]

That's useless s**t, stuck in my brain. I don't know why I know it. It's a waste. It's never gonna be a category on *Jeopardy*. You're never gonna hear, "Yeah, Alex, I'll take useless s**t for five hundred, please." [*Mimics Alex Trebek*] "The answer is . . . George Glass." Ding! "Who was Jan's imaginary boyfriend?" [*Audience laughter and applause*]

## Rosie List: FAVORITE TV COMMERCIAL JINGLES

| | |
|---|---|
| Alka-Seltzer | "Plop, plop, fizz, fizz, oh what a relief it is!" |
| Band-Aid | "I am stuck on Band-Aid, and Band-Aid's stuck on me." |
| Bumble Bee Tuna | "Yum, yum Bumble Bee, Bumble Bee Tuna, I love Bumble Bee, Bumble Bee Tuna . . ." |
| Campbell's Soup | "Mm! Mm! Good! Mm! Mm! Good! That's what Campbell's Soups are, Mm! Mm! Good." |
| Coca-Cola | "I'd like to teach the world to sing . . ." |
| Dr. Pepper | "Wouldn't you like to be a Pepper, too?" |
| Mounds/ Almond Joy | "Sometimes you feel like a nut, sometimes you don't . . ." |
| Oscar Mayer | "My bologna has a first name. It's O-S-C-A-R . . ." |
| Tic Tac | "Put a Tic Tac in your mouth and get a bang out of life." |
| Toys'R'Us | "I don't want to grow up, I'm a Toys'R'Us kid!" |

# Highlights of Rosie's Chat on America Online

**SEPTEMBER 13, 1995**

© Copyright 1995 Oldsmobile; licensed to America Online, Inc.

**CelebCircL:** Rosie! Welcome to Oldsmobile's Celebrity Circle!

**Rosie:** Hello and sorry I am so late. My son had a doctor's appointment and it took forever.

**Question:** Is the motherhood "thing" harder or easier than you expected?

**Rosie:** It is harder and more wonderful than I ever expected. Last night he slept for 7 hours straight. Yippeeee!

**Question:** Now that you are a mother, has your stand-up material changed a lot? I saw your last HBO special & it was really good.

**Rosie:** Many thanks Laurie. I am doing a bunch of stand-up dates in the next few months and I hope to use some new baby material.

**Question:** Ili Rosie. Any more HBO specials planned?

**Rosie:** I hope to do another next year, there is a 16-month waiting period imposed by HBO, the new material should be ready by then. I hope.

**Question:** Congrats on being a mother. Who did your name your child after?

**Rosie:** Hi Gil, I didn't name him after anyone in particular, I wanted a name that would work if he were a surfer, or a supreme court judge. So Parker it is.

**Question:** Which work is more fulfilling for you, your stand-up work or the musicals you have been in?

**Rosie:** I loved doing Broadway, but after 6 months, it got old. I like doing stand-up because you have total control over what you say, how you say it, and how it is perceived, stand-up is more satisfying.

**Question:** Rosie, I know you're big on the old "Honeycomb" cereal commercial, but how about a few lines from the theme of the old "Magic Garden" show?

**Rosie:** Come along, sing a song, join our happily family, the two of us together happy as a feather, swinging round and up and down, is where we will be.

**Question:** Rosie—have you done much reading about adoption? AOL has an adoption forum—have you visited there?

**Rosie:** No I haven't, how do I get there, I still haven't mastered the nooks and crannies of AOL. I have been in the pet forum. I would love to visit there, so let me know. I did a lot of reading on adoption, and I hope to adopt another child next year.

**Question:** Hi Rosie. I hope you don't mind me asking a personal question. I heard you recently adopted a baby. Do you think it is easier for a celebrity to adopt a child than it is for "ordinary" people?

**Rosie:** I think it is easier for a celebrity to do most things, except maybe go to the mall, so although I do not know how much it helped me, I would be lying to say it had no effect.

**Question:** I am a big fan!! I'm 14-year-old boy and I have seen all of your movies (*Exit to Eden* being my favorite). I am also a comedian in the making. Do you have any advice?

**Rosie:** First of all, 14 and you saw *EXIT TO EDEN!* Freshbone, that was a very R movie!! As for advice, believe in yourself and never quit.

The more you do stand-up, the better you are. So get started.

**Question:** What's the best job you ever had?

**Rosie:** I never really had a normal job. I did work at SEARS one summer when I was 17. That was fun on the whole, all my jobs in the entertainment field have been fun.

**Question:** Who has been your favorite person to work with and why?

**Rosie:** Emilio Estevez. He is the nicest guy and we have the same strange sense of humor. We laughed the whole time.

**Question:** Are you currently dating anyone?

**Rosie:** No, not at the moment.

**Question:** Rosie darling, we were wondering what your next Broadway production was going to be. Love you, mean it. Two of your gay friends in Florida.

**Question:** Lol, well Dolls, are you in Miami? I am working there Thursday night. As for Broadway, well Honey Bunch, buy the CD, my days as a singer are over, did they ever begin? I ain't no Patti Lupone.

**Question:** Where do you find all your jokes?

**Rosie:** Just from my life experiences, from observing friends and family and myself.

**Question:** How about your thoughts on Madonna at the recent MTV music awards?

**Rosie:** I thought she looked great, seemed calm, and only cursed once, which is an improvement.

**Question:** Rosie—How was working with Tom Hanks?

**Rosie:** He is the best, very family oriented, professional and prepared, the crew loves him, that is always a good way to tell who is OK.

**Question:** Did you enjoy the Betty character in *The Flintstones* and will there be a sequel?

**Rosie:** I really hope so, I had so much fun filming it, and little kids love it, which is reason enough to make another. We are supposed to shoot it next summer when John is on vacation from *Roseanne*.

**Question:** Hey Rosie, what kind of music do u listen to?

**Rosie:** Well, Annie Lennox is my favorite and Elton John and Tori Amos and Bruce Hornsby. Like that.

**Question:** What's the best part & worst part of being an actress?

**Rosie:** The best part is creative fulfillment and tons of cash and fun, fun, fun. The worst part is always worrying if you will ever work again.

**Question:** Rosie, are you content with your status as a celebrity?

**Rosie:** Do I have a status? Hmmm! Well, I guess so, it makes life interesting, I can say that. It is oftentimes quite odd.

**Question:** Rosie, were you an athlete in high school? You were a natural in *League*.

**Rosie:** Yes, I played softball and volleyball and tennis and basketball. A regular tomboy jock girl and proud of it.

**Question:** I'd like to know if you enjoyed playing the role of Rizzo on Broadway, (you were great, by the way), Brooke just wasn't cut out for it!

**Rosie:** Well, I saw Brooke and thought she was pretty good, really. It isn't a tough role to master, especially for me, I grew up playing Rizzo in my backyard, my sister always got to be Sandy.

**Question:** How is the baby? I'm so proud of you and glad you've become a success—great comedienne from 53-yr.-old grandma.

**Rosie:** Well thanks nana, he is wonderful, almost 4 months old, smiling and laughing and sleeping thru the night, finally. I am madly in love with him.

**Question:** Rosie, rumor has it you are going to host the AIDS walk in Miami again this year, is it true?

**Rosie:** I hope I can. Last year I flew in an hour after it started. So I hope I can do it this year.

**Question:** When can we expect *Exit to Eden* part two?

**Rosie:** No way, Jose. That movie was slammed by every critic, and made no money at all. So I doubt it.

**Question:** Congratulations on your new son. I'm a single adoptive and exhausted mother of 3 preschool boys. Is yours an open adoption? What did you think of the process?

**Rosie:** Mine is a closed adoption, with full disclosure at the age of 18. I think the process is wonderful and I hope to get the word out about the many children who are in need of a home. Congrats to you. 3 boys, Lord, you must be tired and thrilled.

**Question:** Hi Rosie, remember me? Just wanted to know if you are as fed up with the O. J. thing as I am.

**Rosie:** O. J., uugghhhhhhh! Thanks to moron Furman, Mr. Simpson will be vacationing in Hawaii for the holidays, which is tragic, as he is so obviously GUILTY.

**Question:** Rosie, if you were a fruit, would you rather be perched on Carmen Miranda's head, or mixed into a jar of Frutopia?

**Rosie:** Mixed, dear Bradley, oh pen pal from the west. How is college, kid?

**Question:** What is Madonna like?

**Rosie:** Well, like you think and then not at all. It is hard do describe what anyone is "LIKE." I love her, she is not nearly as provocative as she seems.

**Question:** Of the movies you have been featured in, which one was your favorite?

**Rosie:** *Sleepless in Seattle.*

**Question:** So how did you enjoy the Emmys?

**Rosie:** It was kinda hot and a tad long. There in the theater, I had front row seats, so I had to smile for 3 hours straight.

**Question:** Did you enjoy wearing "the leather" in that undercover cop movie with Dan Akroyd?

**Rosie:** Well, at first I was freaked out and scared and embarrassed, but then I kinda got used to it, and I did rather enjoy it.

**Question:** Do you prefer talking to fans online, or in person? And why?

**Rosie:** Well online is easier, cause I usually have free time, and am not with someone else, being interrupted which is always weird. I have an account on AOL, ROSIE OH O, and I answer all my mail myself. So feel free to write and ask any question you have.

**Question:** Rosie, was that bauble around your neck at the Emmys real?

**Rosie:** Yes, 400gs for the necklace, 90 for the ear bobs. Wild huh!

**Question:** What is Letterman like REALLY?

**Rosie:** I don't really know him, I only speak to him when I am on his show. I think he is the best talk show host around, following in Johnny's footsteps. I enjoy him and his show.

**Question:** Hello Rosie. What's the last good tennis match you saw? Catch any of the US Open?

**Rosie:** Finals women, Monica and Steffi. I loved every minute of it. I wish I could have seen it live.

**Question:** Rosie, how did you get those EXCELLENT seats at the EMMYS? Way to Go, Girl!

**Rosie:** I wish I knew! I think someone must have canceled at the last minute.

**CelebCircl:** Rosie, thanks for joining us tonight. Is there anything you would like to say to our audience before you go?

**Rosie:** Once again, sorry for being late and thanks for sticking around. See you all online.

# TV Series Appearances

**STAR SEARCH** Remember, Rosie wanted to be on television like Mary Tyler Moore. She wanted to do Broadway and films, like Bette Midler, Barbra Streisand, and Julie Andrews. Stand-up was simply a means to an end, a road that might just take her to the top. Rosie got a big break in that regard when she appeared on *Star Search* and won five times. She lost only in the finals, to comic John Kassir. But the $35,000 she won allowed her to have her front teeth crowned and move to the West Coast, into an apartment in Studio City ("in the valley").

"I thought that after I did *Star Search*, Spielberg would be at home going, 'She's the next girl in *E.T. 2*.'" But it did not result in any other offers, so she continued to spend most of her time on the road doing stand-up comedy.

**GIMME A BREAK** In 1986, Brandon Tartikoff, then head of entertainment at NBC-TV, came to a Los Angeles comedy club to see Dana Carvey. A waitress Rosie had befriended refused to bring the table of NBC executives their check until they'd seen Rosie's act. As a result of that exposure, she was offered a role in the sitcom *Gimme a Break*, which had been on the air since 1981. Rosie joined the cast in the middle of its last season, playing Maggie O'Brien. Appearing in the last eleven episodes of the show (November 19, 1986–May 12, 1987), Rosie was a dental technician and upstairs neighbor to Nell Harper, played by Nell Carter.

Although Nell Carter's visit to *The Rosie O'Donnell Show* in December 1996 was all hugs and kisses, Rosie was less kind describing Carter a few years earlier, right after the series ended. Apparently they hadn't gotten along too well, with Carter calling Rosie "Maggie" both onstage and off.

The series ended in the spring of 1987, and Rosie was back on the road doing stand-up. But her exposure on television did help to get her a job as a video jockey (VJ) at cable music channel VH1.

**VH1 STAND-UP SPOTLIGHT** On a tip from a comedy-club owner, Rosie auditioned for a VJ (video jockey) job on MTV in early 1988. Although she was turned down for the job, she followed up the interview with a really nice thank-you letter. That unusual response made an impression on the producer at MTV, and as soon as a VJ spot opened up at their sister music cable channel, VH1, he hooked her up. Being a VH1 VJ consisted of writing and performing twenty-four three-minute comedy segments each day as breaks between the music videos. "The hardest part was not having an audience. I never know if I'm going over."

She said at the time, "VH1 is perfect for me right now. I get to talk about my life, my weight—whatever pops into my head. It certainly beats working for a living." Eventually, though, VH1 decided to phase out all of its VJs. Rather than accept that, Rosie proposed a stand-up show that would spotlight established comics and newcomers and give Rosie a chance to be both host and producer. The network had nothing to lose, so it agreed. *Stand-Up Spotlight* ended up being VH1's highest-rated show for several years.

"I've spent years developing my own act, and now producing *Stand-Up Spotlight* lets me cultivate new talent and help other people develop their careers."

**STAND BY YOUR MAN** In early 1992 Rosie starred in a short-lived Fox sitcom, *Stand by Your Man*, along with Melissa Gilbert (*Little House on the Prairie*). They played two New Jersey sisters, Lorraine and Rochelle, who decide to live together after their husbands are put in jail for bank robbery. Rosie (as LORRAINE): "I'm thrilled. Artie's in prison with a tattoo that says, 'Rap Sucks.'" The show was based on the British comedy series *Birds of a Feather*.

The pilot, originally part of CBS's development slate, was filmed a year earlier, in April 1991. Rosie had suggested Fran Drescher to play her sister Rochelle, but the CBS executives said they sounded too much alike. ("Helloooo, we're sisters!") Christine Ebersole and Leila Kenzle were also considered for the role before it was given to Melissa Gilbert-Brinkman. Rich Hall and Sam McMurray played their wayward husbands, and Miriam Flynn was a coworker at the Bargain Circus department store where the sisters worked. When CBS passed on the series, it was picked up by the fledgling Fox Network.

The series only lasted seven episodes in the spring of 1992, airing on April 5, 12, 19, and 26 and May 3, 10, and 17.

# Other TV Series Appearances

| SERIES | EPISODE | ROLE | AIR DATE |
|---|---|---|---|
| **Suddenly Susan** | | herself | February 1997 |
| **The Nanny** | | herself | October 9, 1996 |

The Nanny is in the audience at *The Rosie O'Donnell Show* and yells out a comment. Rosie has her come up and join her onstage, then asks her to do regular segments about being a nanny.

| | | | |
|---|---|---|---|
| **All My Children** | | Naomi, Adam Chandler's maid | July 30, 1996 |

Rosie won the award for Best Guest Appearance from *Soap Opera Digest*.

| | | | |
|---|---|---|---|
| **The Nanny** | "Where's the Pearls?" | Cozette | February 26, 1996 |
| **The Larry Sanders Show** | "Eight" | herself | November 15, 1995 |

Rosie received a 1996 Emmy nomination for Outstanding Guest Actress in a Comedy Series.

| | | | |
|---|---|---|---|
| **Bless This House** | "I Am Not My Sister's Keeper" | Sister Peggy | October 11, 1995 |
| **Night Stand** | "Breast Augmentation" | herself | 1995 |

| SERIES | EPISODE | ROLE | AIR DATE |
|---|---|---|---|
| **Living Single** | "There's No Ship Like Kinship" | Sheri | December 15, 1994 |
| **Beverly Hills, 90210** | "Destiny Rides Again" | herself | November 4, 1992 |

**OTHER TV APPEARANCES**

| | | |
|---|---|---|
| **Say It Fight It Cure It** | | October 5, 1997 |
| **The 51st Annual Tony Awards** | host | June 1, 1997 |
| **The 24th Annual Daytime Emmy Awards** | presenter | May 21, 1997 |
| **I Am Your Child** | | April 28, 1997 |
| **10th Annual Kids' Choice Awards** | host | April 19, 1997 |
| **Happy Birthday, Elizabeth—A Celebration of Life** | guest | February 26, 1997 |
| **Saturday Night Live** | (cohost with Penny Marshall) | December 14, 1996 |
| **Barbara Walters Presents the 10 Most Fascinating People of 1996** | honoree | December 6, 1996 |

| SERIES | EPISODE | ROLE | AIR DATE |
| --- | --- | --- | --- |
| **Late Show With David Letterman** | | guest | October 22, 1996 |
| **Dateline NBC** | | guest | October 22, 1996 |
| **E! Uncut** | | subject | September 13, 1996 |
| **MTV Music Video Awards** | | presenter | September 4, 1996 |
| **Nick News Special Edition: The Body Trap (with Linda Ellerbee)** | | cohost | May 29, 1996 |
| **The 23rd Annual Daytime Emmy Awards** | | presenter | May 19, 1996 |
| **9th Annual Kids' Choice Awards** | | cohost | May 11, 1996 |
| **Catch a Rising Star 50th Anniversary . . . Give or Take 26 Years** | | host | April 24, 1996 |

(Filmed at the Second Annual U.S. Comedy Arts Festival in Aspen, Colorado, on February 28, 1996)

| SERIES | EPISODE | ROLE | AIR DATE |
| --- | --- | --- | --- |
| **The Good, the Bad and the Beautiful** | TBS Special | cohost | March 17, 1996 |
| **Kmart Commercials** | | (with Penny Marshall) | November 12, 1995, to present |
| **8th Annual Kids' Choice Awards** | | presenter | May 20, 1995 |

| SERIES | EPISODE | ROLE | AIR DATE |
|---|---|---|---|
| Rosie O'Donnell HBO Comedy Special | (from Faneuil Hall) | | April 29, 1995 |

Outstanding Individual Performance in a Variety or Music Program. [See the excerpts of this performance elsewhere in this book.]

| SERIES | EPISODE | ROLE | AIR DATE |
|---|---|---|---|
| In a New Light '94 | | | July 9, 1994 |
| Sesame Street's All-Star 25th Birthday | | guest | May 18, 1994 |
| The 48th Annual Tony Awards | | presenter | June 12, 1994 |
| The Cindy Crawford Special MTV | | guest | May 18, 1994 |
| The Flintstones: Best of Bedrock | | host | May 8, 1994 |
| The 66th Annual Academy Awards Presentation | | presenter— short films | March 12, 1994 |

"Look at me, I'm on the Academy Awards. Can you believe it? I've got the dress. I've got the jewels. I've got the breasts. And they all have to be back by midnight."

| SERIES | EPISODE | ROLE | AIR DATE |
|---|---|---|---|
| A Gala For the President at Ford's Theatre | | guest | November 24, 1993 |
| Saturday Night Live | | host | November 13, 1993 |
| MTV Movie Awards | | presenter | June 9, 1993 |
| Hurricane Relief | | comic | October 16, 1992 |

| SERIES | EPISODE | ROLE | AIR DATE |
|---|---|---|---|
| **Back to School '92** | | | September 8, 1992 |
| **The 44th Annual Primetime Emmy Awards** | | presenter | August 30, 1992 |
| **Women Aloud** | | guest | July 13, 1992 |
| **A Pair of Jokers: Bill Engvall & Rosie O'Donnell** | | | June 2, 1990 |

As a contestant in the mock Miss America Pageant: "I have the IQ of toast. My talent is eyeliner."

| SERIES | EPISODE | ROLE | AIR DATE |
|---|---|---|---|
| **Showtime Comedy Club All-Stars** | | comic | March 26, 1988 |

She tells about getting $8,000 worth of crowns on her front teeth. "Eight thousand dollars! It's a car! Okay, it's a Hyundai with a slutty radio, but it's a car."

**ROSIE LIST: VEHICLES ROSIE OWNS/HAS OWNED**

Chevrolet Chevette
Plymouth Volare
Mazda Miata
Honda motorcycle
Suzuki motorcycle
Assorted Jet-Skis
Ford Explorer
Volvo Station Wagon
Cadillac (bought at the Cystic Fibrosis Charity Auction)
Chevrolet Venture Mini-Van
A 27-foot yacht

# Highlights of Rosie's Chat on AOLive

**JULY 3, 1996**

**AOLiveMC14:** Welcome, Rosie O'Donnell. We are very happy to have you here.

**Rosie:** Hello Nick fans. Ask away.

**Question:** You've had Elmo and Miss Piggy on your show. So, do you like Muppets or what?

**Rosie:** I love the Muppets. Always had. Always will. And I'm going to be on *Muppets Tonight* sometime in August.

**Question:** Do you ever have time to do stand-up comedy anymore?

**Rosie:** Not very much. Sometimes I work weekends in Las Vegas but I'm mostly just doing the TV show now.

**Question:** Will you ever take your TV show to different cities for live audiences?

**Rosie:** I hope so. We've only been on three weeks but should we stay on for a long time, we hope to go to different places.

**Question:** Was it fun making a movie with Nickelodeon?

**Rosie:** It was great. I got free "gak." And everyone tried to slime me.

**Question:** Rosie, what big musical guest would you like on your show?

**Rosie:** Barbra Streisand.

**Question:** Rosie, do you have a photographic memory? I never saw someone who could remember so many lyrics!

**Rosie:** Sadly, I do. I can't get the songs out of my head even when I try.

**Question:** What would you want to be if you were not a "star?"

**Rosie:** A teacher because teachers taught me a lot when I was a kid and I think that it's the most important job in the world. The most important job in this country is to be a teacher and a parent.

**Question:** Is it hard doing a live TV show?

**Rosie:** It's not hard but it's very tiring and I'm having a lot of fun.

**Question:** Hi Rosie! I love your new show, especially how all the guests think they need to give you a gift. What has been the most outrageous gift and who was it from?

**Rosie:** I got corn on the cob from Erika Slezak and it was really good. And I ate it all, myself.

**Question:** Who would you most like to be stuck in elevator with?

**Rosie:** My son.

**Question:** Rosie, did Harriet wear a red sweatshirt during *Harriet the Spy* like in the book? Did you read the book when you were a kid?

**Rosie:** Yes, I read the book when I was ten years old. I loved it. And yes, Harriet wore a red sweatshirt.

**Question:** Have you spied on anyone, lately, yourself?

**Rosie:** I live in New York City and I do have binoculars near my window. Sometimes I look across the street and I see other people looking at me with their binoculars.

**Question:** Have you ever had to kiss someone in a movie? What was it like?

**Question:** You are so funny. You finally brought laughter to daytime. Whose idea was the format for your show?

**Rosie:** Oh, it was Merv Griffin's idea and I stole it.

**Question:** What was it like working on *The Flintstones*?

**Rosie:** It was the best job that I ever had in the movies. I got to have bare feet and I only had one dress in the whole movie.

**Question:** Hi Rosie! I love your show. Has your own talk show changed your life?

**Rosie:** Not too much yet. It's only been three weeks. I go to sleep a lot earlier because I have to get up very early but besides that things are the same and I'm having a lot of fun.

**Question:** What has been your worst show business experience?

**Rosie:** My first movie I ever did, *Car 54, Where Are You*?

**Question:** How does it feel to be a TV host and movie star on top of being a new mother?

**Rosie:** Well, the best part is being a Mom and the other two are pretty good too.

**Question:** Rosie, Will your show remain live?

**Rosie:** Yes, always live.

**Question:** If you could have three wishes, what would they be?

**Rosie:** A cure for AIDS. That every kid in our country was safe. And that there was no more pollution.

**Question:** Rosie, first of all love, love, love your show. Second, when do you do the *All My Children* stint?

**Rosie:** The week of July 8th. It'll air the middle of July. I'm playing a maid in the Tyler mansion.

**Question:** Rosie, do you watch the "soaps" yourself?

**Rosie:** Yes, all the ABC soaps.

**Question:** What do you do for fun?

**Rosie:** I play with my kid and I go to the movies. I saw *Independence Day*. It was great.

**Question:** Are you going to have Madonna on your show?

**Rosie:** Yes, in November when she's promoting *Evita*.

**Question:** Any famous people you would like to meet that you haven't already met?

**Rosie:** Sure, there are a lot of them; Princess Diana, Barbara Streisand, Tom Cruise.

**Question:** Rosie, I love the way you sing! You have a terrific Broadway voice! Are there any other Broadway musicals you would like to be in and which parts?

**Rosie:** *They're Playing Our Song.* I'd love to play Sonya which is the role that Lucie Arnaz played on Broadway.

**Question:** Rosie, do you enjoy the show as much as you seem to?

**Rosie:** Yes, I'm having a great time. It's a lot of fun.

**Question:** Hi! I was wondering what was the funniest thing that happened on the set of *Harriet the Spy*?

**Rosie:** I had a cherry pit fight with Michelle, Gregory and Vanessa and I won.

**Question:** Rosie, how are you handling all this terrific fame and success?

**Rosie:** Well, I feel the same as I always did. So I guess I'm handling it okay.

**AOLiveMC14:** Thanks, Rosie O'Donnell for being with us this evening. It is too bad we couldn't get to all the questions. Thanks.

**Rosie:** Thanks for chatting with me online. I hope you had as much fun as I did. See ya on Nick.

# Broadway

**GREASE** (1994–95) After previews first at the Orange County Performing Arts Center in Costa Mesa and then in Boston, Rosie O'Donnell opened on Broadway in the role of Rizzo in a revival of *Grease* on May 11, 1994. "They were looking for a 'name' to be one of the leads, and when I said I had wanted to do Rizzo, they thought that would probably work."

She had dreamed of being on Broadway since she was a child, and here was her big chance. "I was never a singer. . . . But I always wanted to do it because to me there is nothing like the thrill of going to a Broadway show. . . . It's the reason I went into show business in the first place."

She played Rizzo for one year, and it was a time when she made many friends, such as with musical director John McDaniel. But she also found the experience tedious and frankly quite boring. "I found myself mouthing whole conversations with my friends in the audience, 'Hey, you wanna go over to Joe Allen's for dinner after the show?' "

Rosie joked about her *Grease* stint during her 1995 HBO Special: "Let me tell ya. It was a childhood dream of mine. And childhood dreams are to be dreamed and not lived. Not that I didn't have fun, but I had no idea what it would take to do the same thing every night of my life for a year. To do the same thing every night of my life for a year. To do the same thing every night of my life. . . . It was like living in the movie *Groundhog Day*. Without Andie MacDowell to make it appealing."

# Highlights of Rosie's Chat on AOLive

**AUGUST 13, 1996**

**Question:** Rosie, you mentioned on your show that doing kissing scenes in movies gave you the tingles. Were you speaking of your "Slave Man, Tommy" from ETE by any chance? ; )

**TheROSIE:** Well, Tommy was my only on screen kiss. I did get to make out during *Grease* on Broadway. I think you do feel the tingles, camera or not.

**AOLiveMC1:** Here's a nice comment:

**Question:** Rosie, I am a mom of three, a teacher, a technology guru, an author. I sing for fun, and I cannot thank you enough for what you are doing for the children around the world. You are fun and witty! You are giving dignity to your profession and to authors. I could go on and on. Diann.

**TheROSIE:** Thanks, Di. I do feel honored to be given the opportunity to address so many. Mostly our kids and I am having fun. The fact that you all are enjoying it is an added plus. Thanks.

**Question:** Being in the public eye, what keeps you from becoming like other Hollywood actresses and staying so normal and down to earth? That is your success line!

**TheROSIE:** I don't know. I have always felt more like an audience member than a performer. I don't know how or why, but it is my truth. And I think it is a blessing in many ways.

**Question:** Rosie, would you like to adopt more children?

**TheROSIE:** Yes, I would. Many more.

**Question:** Hey, Rosie! Just a quick question. The boards have been a buzz about you having Lucy Lawless on your Friday, Aug. 16 show. Is it true? I couldn't find her listed on your scheduled list of guests. Thanks and keep up the good work! MSnaring@AOL.

**TheROSIE:** Yes, Lucy Lawless is on but will not be in costume. :) This Fri.

**Question:** I am here with a 5-year-old girl and a four year-old boy. They would like to tell you that they really like your singing. And could you please sing "Old MacDonald Had a Farm" on your show some time? Also they would like to know your favorite color is.

**TheROSIE:** Favorite color is blue. I will sing "Old Mac" tomorrow.

**Question:** Rosie, I was wondering if you are going to the Clintons' birthday party?

**TheROSIE:** Yes, I am going to the president's birthday bash. I will be performing along with Whoopi and Tony Bennett.

**Question:** Do you love doing what you do?

**TheROSIE:** Yes, I do. I am lucky in that way.

**Question:** Rosie, how do I get to be a guest on your show? Can we sing a Streisand duet together?

**TheROSIE:** Well, we are gonna have a write-in contest, "Why I should be a guest." If you win, we can sing Babs.

**Question:** You are a remarkable person. almost a super hero! How do you juggle being a mother, having a career, see Broadway shows, read books, travel, and still be so funny, lovable, and down-to-earth! (I'm exhausted just thinking about it!) Don't ever change.

**TheROSIE:** Well, thanks. If you saw me in an off moment, you wouldn't think so. I am lucky, I think, to have this beautiful boy and a job that I love that lets me be with him. Reading is my passion, and juggling is possible with practice.

**Question:** I look like you at 12. Can I play you in a TV movie about your life?

**TheROSIE:** Sure, if they ever make one. Do you like Drake's cakes? It is a requirement, and you may have to grow a chin hair.

**Question:** I'm not sure if this is too personal, but I was wondering if the ring you wear used to be your mom's. If you choose not to answer, I understand.

**TheROSIE:** No, I had a ring of my mom's, and it was stolen when I went skiing 6 years ago. I got this one instead.

**Question:** Have you talked to Meatloaf since the show? What did you do with the tickets?

**TheROSIE:** Didn't talk to Meat. Didn't go to his show. He is a wild guy. That was our weirdest show, by far. He's an okay guy. Just a bit wacky that day. [See Show Companion for the details.]

**Question:** Hi, Rosie, it was great to see you in *Another Stakeout*. You are my favorite, and I feel about Richard Dreyfuss the way you feel about Tom Cruise. I was wondering if he's fun to work with and a nice guy.

**TheROSIE:** Richard is the nicest and the smartest guy I have ever worked with. He is a dedicated dad and a remarkable friend. I adore him.

**Question:** Rosie, did you ever meet Lucille Ball in person?

**TheROSIE:** One time in passing, and I didn't get to speak with her. She was doing that series that only lasted 4 weeks, 1989, I think. She was the best.

**Question:** If you could have any three guests from the history of the world on your show, who would they be and why?

**TheROSIE:** Hello, everyone. Not getting a question in? Jesus Christ, Martin Luther King, and George Burns.

**Question:** Rosie, what is your favorite toy? Mine is Buzz Lightyear.

**TheROSIE:** When I was a kid, it was Ker Plunk. Now that I am an adult, Happy Meal toys.

**Question:** How much time do you spend on AOL a week?

**TheROSIE:** About an hour a day.

**Question:** Will you ever have a Rosie-look-a-like contest?

**TheROSIE:** Yes, and folks can send in photos. We will pick 10, and the audience will decide the winner in November.

**Question:** Are you still going to be doing films or is it too much with your schedule, the show and your son? If so, will you miss doing films?

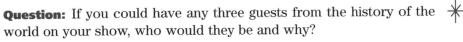

**Rosie List:**
**FAVORITE SINGERS**
Julie Andrews
Neil Diamond
Elton John
Madonna
Barry Manilow
Bette Midler
Dolly Parton
Bonnie Raitt
Barbra Streisand
Wynonna

**TheROSIE:** I will miss doing movies. I will only do small parts like *Harriet the Spy* or *Now and Then* or *Wide Awake* (out in December) cause of my schedule.

**Question:** What would advice be to someone like me (age 15/f) who has a strong desire to go into comedy/acting?

**TheROSIE:** Ta dah! I advise to go to college and get a degree cause no one wants a dumb actress. And then never give up. Study, watch, listen, and believe in you.

**Question:** Do you really ride a motorcycle?

**TheROSIE:** Yes, I have 2. One Suzuki (in Fla.). One Honda (in NY).

**Question:** Rosie, do you like Robin Williams?

**TheROSIE:** I love him. He's brilliant. Never met him though.

**Question:** What was the movie you made that you dislike the most and why?

**TheROSIE:** *Car 54, Where Are You?* My 1st film. It was a bad movie and not a lot of fun to do. At least I had a good time doing *Exit to Eden,* Also not a great film.

**Question:** Do you have a favorite basketball team? If so, will you have any of the members of the team as guests on your show?

**TheROSIE:** Love the Knicks. Not a huge basketball fan.

**Question:** When can we expect a book from you?

**TheROSIE:** No, I had a deal to write one, but I will put it off for a while cause the prospect is a bit daunting for now.

**Question:** Is Letterman ever going to be a guest on the show?

**TheROSIE:** I hope so.

**Question:** Why did you change your hairdo? I liked it.

**TheROSIE:** Who knows? I have a hair guy, David. He makes all the decisions.

**Question:** So, how much French do you really speak?

**TheROSIE:** None.

**Question:** Rosie, you are so wonderful with children. You don't talk down to them. I see a lot of posts on your message board from children saying how much they love you. Are you aware of how special you are with children? Love ya Rosie! Betsy.

**TheROSIE:** I love kids. Always have. It means so much to me to brighten up a kid's day.

**Question:** I am a surgeon who was on vacation last week and fell in love with your show. It is intelligent and hilarious. Do you have any suggestions on how to deal with "Rosie Withdrawal?"

**TheROSIE:** Have a Yodel and call me in the morning.

**Question:** Rosie, I would like to make you a grilled cheese sandwich too! That little girl was precious on your show today! Do you plan on having a lot of children on? You have the most interesting things happening on your show! Betsy.

**TheROSIE:** Betsy, I love grilled cheese. She was adorable, wasn't she? I love having kids on. We have a kid frog jumping contest this week.

**Question:** I loved watching you on *Star Search*. What did you do with the 100 grand? Did you meet Madonna on *A League of Their Own?* Will you be my best friend?

**TheROSIE:** Sure. I will be your pal. I met Madonna on *League*. I lost the 100 grand on *Star Search*.

**Question:** Rosie, will Donny [Osmond] be back on your show?

**TheROSIE:** I hope so. He was a good sport. [See Show Companion for all the details.]

**Question:** Rosie, what is your work day like now? You had said that you wanted Kathie Lee's hours! Is it getting close to that? Betsy.

**TheROSIE:** I work a lot of hours. Would like to leave at 1 PM, but it hasn't worked that way yet.

**Question:** Hey, Rosie. One of my favorite stars is Barbra Streisand too. Any hope of getting her on your show? Msnaring.

**TheROSIE:** That would be a dream come true. I adore her. She is the reason I am an entertainer. She has a film out in December. Maybe.

**Question:** If you could have three wishes, what would you wish for?

**TheROSIE:** That all kids were safe and loved. That we had a cure for all diseases and for 3 more wishes.

**Question:** How does it feel to be a talk show host?

**TheROSIE:** It's fun and a thrill to meet my childhood idols.

**Question:** Rosie, can you please have the Beatles on your show before September 4th? My friends and I and also my family are huge fans. Thanks. I love ya.

**TheROSIE:** The Beatles? I doubt it. Maybe one at a time, if we are lucky, but not together. They don't do that.

**Question:** Would you ever consider visiting a university as a guest speaker about women and children's rights?

**TheROSIE:** Sure. But time is a problem right now. I have spoken at event, "The Stand for Children Rally" in DC. Women's conferences, etc. I always will.

**Question:** Do you think you will be a little harder on the next Republican politician (if any) you have on the show? You showed a lot more restraint w/Molinari than I could have. I would have bombarded her w/questions, especially concerning the new welfare regs.

**TheROSIE:** I know, but we are an entertainment show, not *Crossfire*. I had to be civil and not bombard her with pointed accusations about her party. It was tough.

**AOLiveMC1:** Thanks for being such a great guest, Rosie. Any closing remarks?

**TheROSIE:** I had a lot of fun. See you all online, keyword: Rosie. I cruise the rooms daily. Thanks. Sorry I didn't get to all the questions. See ya.

# Major Film Work

## CAR 54, WHERE ARE YOU? (1994)

| | |
|---|---|
| David Johansen | Gunther Toody |
| John C. McGinley | Francis Muldoon |
| Fran Drescher | Velma Velour |
| Rosie O'Donnell | Lucille Toody |

*Director:* Bill Fishman; *screenwriters:* Erik Tarloff, Ebbe Roe Smith, Peter McCarthy, and Peter Crabbe. *Running time:* 89 min. Rated PG.

Filmed in 1991 but not released until 1994, *Car 54*, based on the popular television sitcom of the same name, was Rosie's first film. Rosie costarred with David Johansen as Gunther Toody's brash wife, Lucille.

Lucille Toody: Are you cheating on me?
Gunther Toody: Cheating? Are you crazy? You would kill me.
Lucille Toody: Worse. I would grab your scrotum, I would stretch it over your head, and I would use you as a punching bag.

## A LEAGUE OF THEIR OWN (1992)

| | |
|---|---|
| Tom Hanks | Jimmy Dugan |
| Geena Davis | Dottie Hinson |
| Lori Petty | Kit Keller |
| Madonna | Mae Morabito |
| Rosie O'Donnell | Doris Murphy |

*Director:* Penny Marshall; *screenwriters:* Lowell Ganz and Babaloo Mandel, based on a story by Kim Wilson and Kelly Candaele; *composer:* Hans Zimmer. *Running time:* 124 min. Rated PG.

Everything came together for Rosie in this film, in which she was partnered with fellow New Yorker Madonna. "I never expected to be Meryl Streep. I don't have the talent to inhabit other characters and do accents. I'm sort of myself in every movie." Rosie's ability to play baseball allowed Penny to expand her Doris Murphy role from a bit part to a major character. "They put me at third base because I was the only one on the set who could throw the ball from third to first."

"There was a scene in *A League of Their Own* where I had to catch a baseball and lean over into the stands and grab a hot dog with my mouth. I had to do that twenty times to get it just right."

Much of the film was shot during the summer of 1991 in Evansville, Indiana. While some of the other cast members complained ("They don't even get MTV!"), Rosie loved it there. There was a mall, a movie theater, and a McDonald's. What else could a girl who'd been on the road for the past ten years ask for?

Mae Morabito: What if my bosoms, you know, fall out?
Doris Murphy: You think there ain't no man in America what ain't seen your bosoms?

## SLEEPLESS IN SEATTLE (1993)

| | |
|---|---|
| Tom Hanks | Sam Baldwin |
| Meg Ryan | Annie Reed |
| Ross Malinger | Jonah Baldwin |
| Rosie O'Donnell | Becky |

*Director:* Nora Ephron; *screenwriters:* Jeff Arch, Nora Ephron, and David S. Ward, from a story by Jeff Arch. *Running time:* 100 min. Rated PG.

Playing another sidekick, this time opposite Meg Ryan, Rosie gives advice and shares a tearful evening watching *An Affair to Remember.*

Annie: Now that was when people knew how to be in love. They knew it! Time, distance . . . nothing could separate them because they knew. It was right. It was real. It was . . .

Becky: A movie! That's your problem! You don't want to be in love. You want to be in love in a movie.

Becky: Verbal ability is a highly overrated thing in a guy, and it's our pathetic need for it that gets us into so much trouble.


## ANOTHER STAKEOUT (1993)

| | |
|---|---|
| Richard Dreyfuss | Chris Lecce |
| Emilio Estevez | Bill Reimers |
| Rosie O'Donnell | Gina Garrett |

*Director:* John Badham; *screenwriter:* Jim Kouf. *Running time:* 109 min. Rated PG-13.

This is a surprisingly entertaining sequel to *Stakeout*. The highlight of the film is a dinner party for which Rosie's character makes appetizers out of boiled eggs and black olives, combined to look like a lot of little penguins standing around. The dinner party goes from bad to worse to absolutely hysterical.

Roger Ebert: "The relationship between Estevez and Dreyfuss is exasperated and affectionate, O'Donnell is good at standing her ground and speaking her mind, and the plot makes just enough sense to hang the gags on. . . . Movies like this are chewing gum for the mind. This one holds its flavor better than most."

Gina: Cover me! I'm taking a bath.

Bill [*to Gina*]: I've had this mustache for thirteen years. How long have you had yours?

### THE FLINTSTONES (1994)

John Goodman............................Fred Flintstone
Elizabeth Perkins .......................Wilma Flintstone
Rick Moranis..............................Barney Rubble
Rosie O'Donnell..........................Betty Rubble

*Director:* Brian Levant; *screenwriters:* Steven E. De Souza, Jim Jennewein, and Tom S. Parker, based on the animated series by Hanna-Barbera. *Running time:* 92 min. Rated PG.

*The Flintstones* captures the spirit of the cartoon with the genuine love of an ardent fan. The sets, costumes, and fanciful critters are true to the original and pleasing to the eye. Goodman was a stroke of casting genius: his delivery is perfectly positioned between Alan Reed's original Fred and Jackie Gleason's Ralph Kramden (*The Honeymooners* sitcom was, of course, the inspiration for the TV cartoon). Moranis does a fair impression of Mel Blanc, the original voice of Barney, and Rosie O'Donnell perfectly imitates Betty's titter.

Roger Ebert: "The parts of the movie you'd think would have been the trickiest are the ones that work best. Led by John Goodman, the actors successfully impersonate the classic cartoon characters, and look and sound convincing. And the world they inhabit is just right."

Betty Rubble: Wilma, how did you get rid of ring-around-the-collar?
Wilma Flintstone: I just started washing Fred's neck.

## EXIT TO EDEN (1994)

Dana Delaney..............................Lisa
Paul Mercurio .............................Elliot
Rosie O'Donnell..........................Sheila
Dan Aykroyd ..............................Fred

*Director:* Garry Marshall; *screenwriters:* Deborah Amelon, Bob Brunner, and Anne Rice (as Anne Rampling), based on the novel by Anne Rice. *Running time:* 113 min. Rated R.

Rosie List:
**FAVORITE FILMS**

*Beauty and the Beast*
*Funny Girl*
*Good Will Hunting*
*Jerry Maguire*
*The Lion King*
*Manny & Lo*
*The Sound of Music*
*The Way We Were*

Why does Rosie dislike Roger Ebert? See for yourself:

"You know me. I'm easy on actors. These are real people with real feelings. When I see a bad performance, I'm inclined to blame anyone but the actors. In the case of *Exit to Eden* I'm inclined to blame the actors.

"Starting with Rosie O'Donnell. I'm sorry, but I just don't get Rosie O'Donnell. I've seen her in three or four movies now, and she has generally had the same effect on me as fingernails on a blackboard. She's harsh and abrupt and staccato and doesn't seem to be having any fun. She looks mean."

## NOW AND THEN (1995)

| | |
|---|---|
| Rosie O'Donnell | Roberta Martin |
| Christina Ricci | Young Roberta |
| Melanie Griffith | Tina Tercell |
| Thora Birch | Young Teeny |
| Demi Moore | Samantha Albertson |
| Gaby Hoffmann | Young Samantha |
| Rita Wilson | Christina Dewitt |
| Ashleigh Aston Moore | Young Chrissy |

*Director:* Lesli Linka Glatter; *screenwriter:* I. Marlene King. *Running time:* 102 min. Rated PG-13.

*Now and Then* is a coming-of-age story of four girls just entering their teens. The adult roles are used as a brief wrapper at the beginning and end of the film. Rosie, who plays a doctor, is on-screen for less than ten minutes after the opening credits.

## BEAUTIFUL GIRLS (1996)

| | |
|---|---|
| Matt Dillon | Tommy Rowland |
| Noah Emmerich | Michael Morris |
| Tim Hutton | Willie Conway |
| Natalie Portman | Marty |
| Annabeth Gish | Tracy Stover |
| Lauren Holly | Darian Smalls |
| Rosie O'Donnell | Gina Barrisano |

*Director:* Ted Demme; *screenwriter:* Scott Rosenberg. *Running time:* 117 min. Rated R.

"After working with Dennis Leary and realizing how much fun it is to work with a comic actor that can think on his feet and bring a character to life, the idea of working with Rosie O'Donnell was exciting to me," said director Ted Demme. "And she's such a great improvisational actress. Gina's got two really great speeches in the movie, and I knew that Rosie'd kill them.

"The thing about Gina that's great is that I really wanted her to be the guys' best friend and the girls' best friend. She grew up with all these guys, knows everything about all of them, and has really great insights into the girls. And Rosie definitely brought that to the role."

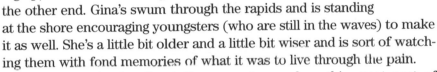

Rosie said about her character, Gina: "My character has an overview of breaking up; she has lived through it and is now at the other end. Gina's swum through the rapids and is standing at the shore encouraging youngsters (who are still in the waves) to make it as well. She's a little bit older and a little bit wiser and is sort of watching them with fond memories of what it was to live through the pain.

"I'm lucky in that I get these great speeches, this great sort of Gloria Steinemesque rhetoric that I love. The women are the voice of reason in this movie (or at least my character is the voice of reason). And they sort of get to say everything that most women have thought but never have found the words for. It was easy to do and to memorize because it's sort of how I feel, so it wasn't such offbeat casting."

Even Roger Ebert liked this one: "There is a scene in *Beautiful Girls* where a small-town feminist [Rosie O'Donnell] grabs a copy of *Penthouse* from a magazine stand and uses it as a prop while lecturing some of her sheepish male friends on the realities of womanhood. It is not common, she points out, for women to have small hips and large breasts. 'Small hips—small breasts. Big breasts—big hips,' she explains. By holding on to an unrealistic image of the dream girl they might somehow, someday, be able to meet, the guys are denying themselves a good relationship with a real flesh-and-blood woman right here in their hometown."

Gina [*to Tommy and Willie*]: I'm finished speaking to both of you, okay? You're both f**king insane. You wanna know what your problem is? MTV, *Playboy*, and Madison f**king Avenue. Yes, let me explain something to you, okay? Girls with big tits have big asses—girls with little tits have little asses—that's the way it goes. God doesn't f**k around— He's a fair guy. He gave the fatties big, beautiful tits and the skinnies little tiny niddlers. It's not my rule; if you don't like it, call Him. . . . Get over yourself. No matter how perfect the nipple, how supple the thigh, unless there's some other s**t going on in the relationship besides the physical, it's gonna get old, okay? And you guys as a gender have got to get a grip. Otherwise, the future of the human race is in jeopardy.

### HARRIET THE SPY (1996)

Michelle Trachtenberg...............Harriet
Rosie O'Donnell..........................Ole Golly
Vanessa Lee Chester .................Janie Gibbs
J. Smith-Cameron.......................Mrs. Welsch
Robert Joy ..................................Mr. Welsch
Eartha Kitt..................................Agatha K. Plummer

*Director:* Bronwen Hughes; *screenwriters:* Douglas Petrie and Theresa Rebeck, based on the novel by Louise Fitzhugh. *Running time:* 102 min. Rated PG.

A couple of years ago, Rosie went to Disney executives and told them she wanted to be their next Dean Jones and remake all those juvenile sixties movies like *That Darn Cat.* They turned her down. But Nickelodeon, the cable television network aimed at children, cast her in its first foray into feature films. Rosie plays Ole Golly, a cross between Mary Poppins and Hazel, in this version of the popular children's book.

Ole Golly: There are as many ways to live as there are people in this world, and each one deserves a closer look.
Ole Golly: Sometimes a really small lie can be a really big help.

## WIDE AWAKE (1998)

*Wide Awake* finished filming in November 1995 and stars Dennis Leary, Rosie, and Robert Loggia. It's about a ten-year-old boy who searches for God after his grandfather's death. Rosie plays a nun, Sister Terry. After being scheduled and postponed at least five times, *Wide Awake* was released by Miramax Films on March 20, 1998.

## TARZAN (Animated—1998)

Rosie provides the voice of Terk in Disney's animated *Tarzan*, due out in late 1998. Alex D. Linz (*Home Alone 3*) is the voice of Tarzan as a child, while Tony Goldwyn is the voice of the adult Tarzan. Wayne Knight, Glenn Close, and Minnie Driver provide other voices.

Rosie recorded her part as Terk during *The Rosie O'Donnell Show*'s stay in Los Angeles in February 1998. Many takes of her screaming while being chased by cartoon elephants left her hoarse and squeaky-voiced for several days afterward.

## TOTIE

Rosie has asked to play Totie Fields in an upcoming television movie about this pioneering comedienne. She loves the script by Susan Rice for ABC-TV, and producer Craig Anderson says they're trying to work out the schedule during *The Rosie O'Donnell Show*'s 1998 summer hiatus.

Other films that Rosie has expressed a desire to appear in include *Angela's Ashes* and *Double Wish*. She had also wanted to be in the film version of the hit Broadway revival of *Chicago*, with Madonna and Goldie Hawn, but the adoption of her second child will probably prevent that from happening.

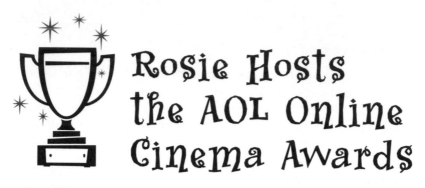

# Rosie Hosts the AOL Online Cinema Awards

**MARCH 20, 1996**

**OnlineHost:** AOL's Entertainment Channel welcomes you to the first-ever Online Cinema Awards! We're live at Planet Hollywood Beverly Hills with host Rosie O'Donnell!

**Rosie:** I am eating the Captain Crunch chicken. Yummy.

**Rosie:** So folks, this is it. We are gonna start. No one is sure what we are doing, but hell, we are gonna do our best.

**OnlineHost:** Rosie! We are really happy to have you on AOL again! How are your fingers doing? They warmed up for tonight?

**Rosie:** I am online every night, so I am ready. I am a cruddy typer and speller.

**OCA MC:** Very cool! FYI everyone, the LIVE event here at Planet Hollywood is really happening!

**Rosie:** Anyone have a question? Can questions get through? They turned off my IM's. Boo hoo. So this is almost as much fun as the Oscars.

**OCA MC:** Except you don't have to dress.

**Rosie:** Only we don't have annoying opening numbers.

**OCA MC:** Christina Ricci is here with us now!

**OCA MC:** Hey everyone, Christina Ricci is on the phone!

**OCA MC:** Rosie, do you have a question for her?

**Rosie:** I played the grown-up Christina in a flick last summer [i.e., *Now and Then*]. How is high school?

**Christina:** Real interesting!

**Rosie:** Sure it is. Are you doing any new movies?

**Christina:** Yes, I just started a movie called *Ice Storm.*

**Question:** Christina, are you friends with Rosie?

**Christina:** I would say we're friends. I don't know how Rosie feels about that.

**Rosie:** How old are you now, Christina? We are closer than Lucy and Ethel.

**Christina:** I'm 16.

**Question:** Christina, how old were you when you started acting?

**Rosie:** We hang. We play Twister.

**Christina:** Rosie, I like that! I was 8 years old.

**Question:** Christina, who do you look up to in terms of your career?

**Rosie:** Besides me. LOL.

**Christina:** I don't really know.

**Question:** Christina, are most of your friends actors?

**Rosie:** No one comes to mind? (Hint)

**Christina:** I don't really have that many friends. My best is an actress.

**Rosie:** Oh, you made me blush. Stop. Which actress? That one from *Now and Then?*

**Christina:** Rosie, are you having fun typing?

**Rosie:** I don't want you robbing any liquor stores like that chick from *Different Strokes.* I worry about the kids.

**Christina:** Rosie, we're through with that phase.

**Rosie:** Kinda. It is better than changing diapers, which is what I would be doing now. And I get free appetizers.

**Christina:** Rosie, oh yeah! How's your son?

**Rosie:** He is the best. Walking and talking and saying "Ma ma" to me and everyone else he sees.

**Christina:** LOL.

**Rosie:** But still, it is mama.

**Question:** Christina, are you online much?

**Christina:** No, I'm a computer illiterate. I wouldn't be able to find my way through!

**Rosie:** Get a Mac. It is simple.

**Christina:** LOL.

**Rosie:** I love mine. Can teach you in 10 minutes. Then you will be addicted, like moi.

**Question:** Hey, do you have a boyfriend now?

**Christina:** No!

**Rosie:** She is 16. She probably has many. How many chicken wings can a human eat in one sitting? I think I am breaking some sort of record.

**OlineHost:** Let's get going with the first set of original categories—we call them the OCA Bests!

**OlineHost:** Your nominees for the Best Movie Soundtrack are: *Batman Forever*; *Clueless*; *Dangerous Minds*; *Mr. Holland's Opus*; *Waiting to Exhale*.

**Rosie:** Spam rules. Shoop, shoop a doop. Who will it be? Well, hello Skyler in Florida, now you have—the winner is . . .

**Rosie:** *DANGEROUS MINDS*

**Rosie:** Hip hip hooray!

**OCA MC:** I loved that movie! Michelle Pfeiffer did a great job!

**Rosie:** Coolio is in da house. Swear. And I am kinda nervous to meet him, 'cause I love him.

**OCA MC:** He's here! I'm looking at him!

**Rosie:** He rules.

**Rosie:** Been spending most my life living in a gangster paradise . . .

**Question:** What does Coolio think of Weird Al's song "Amish Paradise."

**Rosie:** Well, he isn't here now. He is getting his prize thingy.

**OCA MC:** Coolio is accepting his award now. He'll be with us in a sec.

**Rosie:** It's kinda nice, like a crystal sphere thing. Cool, as I call him, said Weird Al's song is an aberration, and I agree. We are sharing chicken.

**Question:** Coolio, what is next for you?

**OCA MC:** Rosie and Coolio are also sharing a keyboard.

**Rosie:** More chicken for Coolio.

**OCA MC:** Coolio, so what do you think of this event?

**Rosie:** Cool is gonna be a dad again in about 2 weeks. He thinks it is good—at least the winning part, 'cause it is voted on by the people.

**OCA MC:** Coolio, you out recording now?

**Rosie:** Yes, he just finished a song for a new movie called *Eddie,* starring Whoopi.

**Question:** Are you online a lot, Coolio?

**Rosie:** The song is called "All the Way Live." Movie comes out in May. Yes, he is online quite a bit—won't give ya his secret code name. Can't blame ya on that one.

**OCA MC:** I'll throw you a fiver to tell, Rosie.

**Question:** Coolio, what was your favorite flick of '95?

**Coolio:** *The Prophesy* was the favorite film, and *When Nature Calls.*

**Question:** Are you planning to work on any more movie soundtracks?

**OCA MC:** A Jim Carrey fan, eh?

**Rosie:** Christopher Walken was in that (he scares me.) He says he likes Jim a lot—makes him laugh. I like Jim Carrey, too.

**OCA MC:** Hey Coolio, how does it feel to win one of the first OCAs?

**Coolio:** Feels good, 'cause it is a real award by the people, for the people, of the people.

**Question:** Coolio, where do you see yourself in 10 years?

**Rosie:** People—people who need people.

**OCA MC:** Event update: Planet Hollywood is jammin'! Rosie and Coolio are sharing a keyboard.

**OCA MC:** Rosie and Coolio, do you two think you'll ever work together on anything? Would you like to?

**Coolio:** We are doing it right now—the first of many, I am sure.

**Rosie:** Tomorrow is my birthday!

**OCA MC:** Happy birthday, Rosie!

**Rosie:** Everyone sing for me. Now at home, in unison. Ah, thanks.

**OCA MC:** So, may I ask how old? Nah . . .

**LIVEONAOL:** Happy Birthday to you, Happy Birthday to you, Happy Birthday from AOL; Happy Birthday to you! (That was supposed to be singing.)

**Rosie:** 34. With gray hair to prove it.

**OnlineHost:** Now, for OCA Best Onscreen Duo. Your nominees are: Sandra Bullock & Bill Pullman, Casper & Kat (Christina Ricci), Clint Eastwood & Meryl Streep, Meg Ryan & Kevin Kline, and Al Pacino & Robert DeNiro.

**OCA MC:** Did you see *Toy Story*, Rosie? What'd you think?

**Rosie:** I loved *Toy Story* but I didn't think they had to make the neighbor kid so demonic. He could have been a nerd, but he was so mean and scary. I didn't like that.

**OCA MC:** I agree. Reminded me of an agent.

**Rosie:** I thought it was inventive. Oh, now the duos, Hmmmmmm. Al and Bob get my vote, but we shall see. The winner is . . .

**Rosie:** SANDY B and BILLY P

**Rosie:** Hip hip hooray! I like them. I worked with Bill in 2 movies—*League* and *Sleepless*. He is awful sweet.

**Rosie:** I never met her, but I hear she is a doll.

**OnlineHost:** Your nominees for the Best Picture in the Comedy category are: *Babe*; *Billy Madison*; *Clueless*; *Toy Story*; *While You Were Sleeping*.

**OCA MC:** Uh-oh. What's your personal fave, Rosie?

**Rosie:** I gotta vote for the pig, but whatta I know? I loved that movie. I haven't had bacon since, and I love BLT's. The woman who was the voice of Babe is here—Christine Cavanaugh.

**OCA MC:** She's sitting down with Rosie now.

**Rosie:** So, she is here sitting next to me. She is much better looking than the pig.

**OnlineHost:** Send in your questions for Christine Cavanaugh now!

**Rosie:** I asked Chris if this was her first voice. Nope, she was Chucky on *Rug Rats*, Oblina on *The Monsters*.

**Question:** What is the world like through a pig's eyes?

**Rosie:** Dexter on *Dexter's Lab*. In other words, she has done a bundle of 'em—and she is a real live actress, as well.

**Question:** What's it like being "anonymous"—easier?

**Rosie:** Yeah! I can go to the mall in my slippers.

**OCA MC:** LOL!

**Rosie:** Best Comedy Online Picture winner is *Toy Story*.

**OnlineHost:** Your nominees for the Best Picture in the Horror/Sci-Fi category are: *Outbreak*; *Dolores Claiborne*; *From Dusk Til Dawn*; *Seven*; *12 Monkeys*.

**OCA MC:** :::whispering *12 Monkeys, 12 Monkeys*:::

**Rosie:** Rosie "Almost 34" O'Donnell.

**OCA MC:** LOL!

**Rosie:** It has to be *12 Monkeys*. *Seven* was dull, dull, dull. And please, could they have used a little lighting? I couldn't even see any of the gross dead dismembered bodies in that dim light. *Seven* was icky.

**OCA MC:** So true, Rosie. Although, I could digest at least a small part of my popcorn having been spared the gross details.

**Rosie:** *Outbreak* was OK.

**OCA MC:** *Outbreak* was pretty good.

**Rosie:** The monkey was cute. And the winner is . . .

**OCA MC:** I loved the monkey.

**Rosie:** Suspense . . .

**OCA MC:** :::drumroll:::

**Rosie:** *OUTBREAK*

**Rosie:** The crowd went wild.

**OCA MC:** :::bravo bravo::::

**Rosie:** They are screaming, *Outbreak, Outbreak!*

**Rosie:** Nutso.

**OnlineHost:** Your nominees for Best Actor in a Comedy film are: Jim

Carrey (*Ace Ventura 2*); Chris Farley (*Tommy Boy*); Adam Sandler (*Billy Madison*); John Travolta (*Get Shorty*); Robin Williams (*Jumanji*).

**Rosie:** Best actor in a comedy.

**OCA MC:** Anticipation building . . .

**Rosie:** Gotta go with Jimmy C. Whatta ya think?

**OCA MC:** Yeah, but Travolta was so good.

**Rosie:** Didn't see it. The winner is . . .

**OCA MC:** It's that Tarantino blend of humor.

**Rosie:** Welcome back, Kotter . . .

**Rosie:** JOHN TRAVOLTA

**OCA MC:** Yes!

**OnlineHost:** The next OCA is for Best Actor in a Drama.

**OCA MC:** :::::even more thunderous applause:::::

**Rosie:** John isn't here—he is at a Sweathog reunion being held at L. Ron Hubbard's house.

**OnlineHost:** Your nominees for Best Actor in the Drama category are: Nicholas Cage (*Leaving Las Vegas*); Richard Dreyfuss (*Mr. Holland's Opus*); Mel Gibson (*Braveheart*); Tom Hanks (*Apollo 13*); Brad Pitt (*12 Monkeys*).

**Rosie:** LOL. Cracking myself up. Drama actor.

**OCA MC:** Rosie, did you see the *Mad TV* version of Tarantino's *Welcome Back, Kotter?*

**Rosie:** No, missed it. Was it funny?

**OCA MC:** 'Twas a hoot.

**Rosie:** Send it to me. NOW.

**OCA MC:** You bet.

**Rosie:** And the winner is . . .

**Rosie:** A man in a league of his own, *Forrest Gump*, *Apollo*.

**Rosie:** TOMMY HANKS

**OCA MC:** Well, what'd you expect? Mr. Wonderful.

**Rosie:** Tom could not be here tonight—he is trying to save John Travolta from the claws of L. Ron Hubbard. It is a full-time job.

**OCA MC:** ROFL!

**OnlineHost:** And the next OCA category is for Best Actor in a Villain role.

**Rosie:** Best villain actor—Woody Allen, hands down.

**OnlineHost:** The nominees for the Best Actor in a Villain Role are: Jim Carrey (*Batman Returns*); Tommy Lee Jones (*Batman Returns*); Tim Roth (*Rob Roy*); Kevin Spacey (*Seven*); Kevin Spacey (*The Usual Suspects*).

**OCA MC:** LOL! No comment.

**Rosie:** Wimp. Jim Carrey, I think. But I need the e-mail, please.

**OCA MC:** I can't afford the lawsuit.

**Rosie:** "Welcome. You've got mail." And the mean guy trophy goes to . . .

**Rosie:** Help, my screen froze, screen froze, screen froze. Oops, fixed. I love the Escape key. The winner is . . .

**OCA MC:** :::::Rosie's now famous virtual drumroll::::

**Rosie:** Tommy Lee from Motley Crew. Oops . . .

**Rosie:** TOMMY LEE JONES

**OCA MC:** He's got my vote! ;)

**OnlineHost:** The next OCA category is for Best Dinner Date/Actor!

**OCA MC:** :::::REALLY long drumroll::::::

**Rosie:** Best dinner date/actor. They should have this on the Oscars.

**OnlineHost:** The nominees for the Best Actor to go out on a Dinner Date with are: Harrison Ford; Chris O'Donnell; Brad Pitt; Keanu Reeves; Christian Slater.

**Rosie:** O'Donnell, of course. He is my second cousin, twice removed. And I am full of it. Don't know him. He does look good in tights.

**OCA MC:** Does that mean you two . . . forget it.

**Rosie:** Forgotten.

**OCA MC:** Good.

**Rosie:** The winner is . . . in tights . . .

**Rosie:** HARRY FORD

**OnlineHost:** The next Online Cinema Award will go out to the best actress in a comedy.

**OnlineHost:** The nominees for the Best Actress in a Comedy are: Sandra Bullock (*While You Were Sleeping*); Nicole Kidman (*To Die For*); Christina Ricci (*Now & Then*); Meg Ryan (*French Kiss*); Alicia Silverstone (*Clueless*).

**Rosie:** Best funny gal. I vote for Nicky Cruise. She rocked in that.

**OCA MC:** Christina Ricci was adorable.

**OnlineHost:** Before we announce the winner of this category, we wanted to share a quote from Alicia regarding her nomination: "It feels so nice knowing that so many people online have responded not only to the film but also my work in *CLUELESS*. Thank you so much for considering me and therefore nominating me for Best Actress in a Comedy."

**Rosie:** Bet that Alicia chick could snag it.

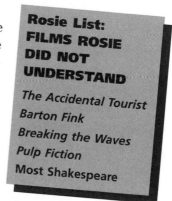

Rosie List:
FILMS ROSIE
DID NOT
UNDERSTAND

*The Accidental Tourist*
*Barton Fink*
*Breaking the Waves*
*Pulp Fiction*
Most Shakespeare

**OCA MC:** This is true.

**Rosie:** Well Alicia, all I have to say is AS IF . . . The winner is . . .

**Rosie:** SANDY B

**OnlineHost:** The next Online Cinema Award category is for Best Actress in a Drama.

**Rosie:** Drama actress. Well, OK.

**OnlineHost:** The nominees for Best Actress in a Drama are: Sandra Bullock (*The Net*); Michelle Pfeiffer (*Dangerous Minds*); Susan Sarandon (*Dead Man Walking*); Elisabeth Shue (*Leaving Las Vegas*); Emma Thompson (*Sense and Sensibility*).

**Rosie:** Who are they? Lizzy Shue, that's what I think, although Susan Sarandon rules all.

**OCA MC:** Susan Sarandon gets my vote.

**Rosie:** OK, so wouldn't it be nice if the gal from *Cocktail* won? The queen of all things . . .

**Rosie:** SUSAN SARANDON

**Rosie:** Super actor/mom/human. Congrats to her! Guess who is on the phone!

**OCA MC:** Hey everyone! We've got Dustin Hoffman on the phone!

**Rosie:** Oh my God!

**OnlineHost:** Send in your questions for Dustin Hoffman now!

**Rosie:** I am nervous.

**Dustin:** Rosie, oh yeah?

**Rosie:** So Dust, can I call you Dust?

**Dustin:** Of course.

**Rosie:** Still watch *The People's Court?*

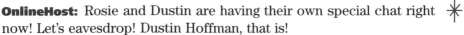

**OnlineHost:** Rosie and Dustin are having their own special chat right now! Let's eavesdrop! Dustin Hoffman, that is!

**Rosie:** Well, he is on the phone, and someone other than me gets to chat with him.

**Dustin:** This will all improve in years to come.

**Rosie:** I just have to type.

**OCA MC:** Rosie, would you like to talk with him?

**Rosie:** Of course! How are your kids?

**Dustin:** They're crazy about you!

**Rosie:** Awwww, that is sweet. I am the queen of *Sesame Street*.

**Dustin:** They were very excited when they heard you were online. They want to have you over for dinner.

**Rosie:** Tell them I said hello, and it is too late to be up in New York. They have to go to bed.

**Dustin:** Hey, they're insulted! They're too old for *Sesame Street!*

**Rosie:** Ouch! Sorry.

**Dustin:** They're 8, 11, 12, and 16.

**Rosie:** They are adults. My baby is 10 months. He thinks anyone who can walk is cool.

**Dustin:** They understand your sophisticated humor.

**Rosie:** Intelligent children you have.

**Dustin:** Bring your baby to my house.

**Rosie:** Will do. Built-in baby-sitters.

**OnlineHost:** If you've just tuned in, we've got Rosie O'Donnell talking to Dustin Hoffman!

**Dustin:** They would love it if you brought your baby over!

**Rosie:** I heard a rumor that you were doing *The Mayor of Castro Street* and that I was gonna be your assistant. Dream on, Rosie—right?

**Dustin:** I wanted to, but they haven't been able to get a director. I love the documentary.

**Rosie:** Well, let's get one, bring the kids, rent a big house, and ba-boom, all is well. Are you online, Dust?

**Dustin:** Oh, I want to talk to you about a movie!

**Rosie:** I am available—whatever, whenever.

**Dustin:** Nope.

**Rosie:** I have no commitments, other than to you.

**Dustin:** I'm too old for that ****.

**Rosie:** Damn.

**Dustin:** We'll meet!

**Rosie:** OK.

**Dustin:** Break bread!

**Rosie:** You bring the bibs.

**Dustin:** The Knicks beat Indiana tonight, so I'm very happy.

**Rosie:** Thank God. About time. Who do you like in the NCAA?

**Dustin:** Rosie, it's your birthday?

**Rosie:** Tomorrow. 34.

**Dustin:** It's Jake's birthday.

**Rosie:** Ouch. Wow! Joint parties! Joint, as in together, not as in . . . well, you know.

**OnlineHost:** The nominees for the Best Actress Portraying a Villainess are: Natasha Henstridge (*Species*); Famke Janssen (*Goldeneye*); Nicole Kidman (*To Die For*); Sam Phillips (*Die Hard 3*); Sharon Stone (*Casino*).

**Rosie:** Girl villain. Nicky Cruise. Gotta go there. She was mean. Ooh, she scared me. And the winner is . . .

**Rosie:** Basically, ummmmmm, my instinct says . . .

**Rosie:** SHARON STONE

**Rosie:** Sharon was unable to accept tonight; she is kneeling in St. Pat's, praying for Monday Night. I will accept it for her—and she will never see it.

**OnlineHost:** The next is for Best Actress who you'd like to take on a Dinner Date!

**OnlineHost:** And, the nominees for Best Actress to go out on a Dinner Date with are: Sandra Bullock; Rosie O'Donnell; Michelle Pfeiffer; Christina Ricci; Alicia Silverstone.

**Rosie:** Actress on a dinner date. Hmmmm, gotta be me. Me. Me. Me. Me. Me. Me. Me. The winner is ME. Yes, it is ME. Me me me me me me me me. What? What? Who? I thought you said it was . . . Oh, OK. Ummmm, well . . .

**Rosie:** SANDRA BULLOCK

**Rosie:** Ouch! Boo hoo. Hurt me. (Crying.) Calling my shrink. Wanting your love, approval. Hmmmmmm. Sadness, pain. :( ;0(

**Rosie:** Oh, Sandy, Sandy, why would you hurt me so? Boo hoo. And I always liked her—till now. That skinny, good-for-nothing . . . I must go. I am no longer able to move my pained fingers. Even my digits hurt. Ugh.

**OnlineHost:** Rosie's finished for the night, but we want to thank her so much!

**OCA MC:** Rosie is leaving the building. This place is really happening.

# The Rosie O'Donnell Show

**R**osie's adoption of Parker is the primary reason Rosie decided to suddenly veer her career from film and Broadway to daytime television. "I wanted a job that allowed me to spend time with him. I wanted him to sleep in his own bed every night so he'd have consistency and stability in his life. I knew this job would be a lot of hours, but it would also give me the luxury of being a hands-on parent. There's only one hour a day that I

**Above: Rosie with the author's son, Evan**

need to be totally focused, and that's when I'm on the air. Other than that, he's always with me or nearby. He's just part of the routine here."

"You know, people thought I was kidding when I said I want to do a Merv Griffin/Mike Douglas show. They're, like, 'You're kidding, right?' and I'm, like, 'No.' I love that show. I used to run home and watch it with my grandmother and my sister. I loved . . . Steve and Eydie were my heroes. I'm a big nerd, you know? . . . I tried to make a show that an eight-year-old kid could watch with his mother and grandma that would entertain everyone."

Says coexecutive producer Hillary Estey McLaughlin, "Rosie has the rare combination of a keen self-awareness, confidence, and honesty that people universally respond to."

"You know when you go on a roller coaster and it clicks up and then right after the last click before you go into the whoosh? That's what I feel [the moment before she walks onstage for the show]. It's almost like when the audience member is doing the opening announcement, I hear the click and then I just go for the ride. It's the one hour I don't have to think in the day. It's like free time, like a kid in nursery school where you get a one-hour nap. The one hour I'm there, I don't have to think of anything else. I just have to be in the moment."

Rosie admits to borrowing a lot from Merv Griffin, Mike Douglas, and Dinah Shore. She also follows in the footsteps of Johnny Carson, David Letterman, and Jay Leno. During practice shows in early June she even tried doing an opening stand-up monologue, like many of her predecessors. But Rosie just didn't feel comfortable with it. She and her staff came up with the idea of jokes taped inside a newspaper and magazine and "to the desk," but even that was done less and less until she felt comfortable with a purely ad-libbed opening segment. Rosie's at her best when she just takes a topic and wings it, so she's spends most mornings now telling personal anecdotes.

Unlike most of her talk-show counterparts, O'Donnell is not one to bring up any subject that might cause her guests to squirm in their seats. "There are issues that celebrities don't want to bring up, and I can understand why. And I won't do it, in the same way that I wouldn't want an interviewer to do it to me. But then there are certain situations, for example . . . if you book O. J. Simpson, you're not going to talk about his football career. But you know what? I would never book those people, so I don't get into that problem."

But that doesn't mean she's always nice to everyone. Writes Ken Tucker, television critic for *Entertainment Weekly*: "I find that she can be kind of snappy and sarcastic and disagree with the guests in a completely polite, we're-just-here-talking kind of thing without devolving it into a shouting match." When Whitney Houston canceled her appearance on the show (October 30, 1997) at the very last minute, Tucker says Rosie "certainly for days on end ragged on Whitney Houston for canceling and was clearly irritated and didn't let her feelings be hidden about that."

As an interviewer, Rosie has become a master of guiding the conversation, particularly when there is a book or movie to promote. When the time is right, she smoothly holds up the book or mentions the clip that needs to be shown.

When she needs to stir things up a bit or when she's running low on things to talk about, Rosie has several topics that she routinely falls back on. She often brings up a guest's children, something few other talk-show hosts ever discussed until Rosie started doing it. If she learns that a guest who is not a singer has ever sung before, as in a school musical production, then she will try to get them to sing something on her show. When Rosie prodded Lucy "Xena" Lawless to sing, it resulted in an offer from the producers of *Grease* for Lucy to appear in the show on Broadway. If the conversation turns to food, Rosie is quick to ask the guest's preference for snack foods and whether they like Drake's Ring Dings, Yodels, and other products. Finally, if the guest has ever

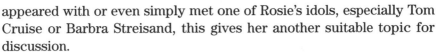

appeared with or even simply met one of Rosie's idols, especially Tom Cruise or Barbra Streisand, this gives her another suitable topic for discussion.

Rosie and her writers are continually trying to find themes and gimmicks that utilize recurring guests or members of her staff. Early on, there was "Listen to Iman" and Florida restaurant reviews from Mort and Sylvia Drescher. Then came hair-care tips from David Evangelista, which was soon followed by household tips from Lenny [Wechsler], the cameraman. None of these lasted very long. Iman and the Dreschers did their shtick three or four times and then were rarely heard from again. David's and Lenny's bits were placed in the time capsule Rosie used at the start of the second season to retire things her fans had grown tired of.

Before the start of the second season, it was announced with great fanfare that Paula Poundstone would be a "roving reporter," providing videotaped segments which would be featured on the show. Rosie outfitted Paula with a camera, and for her September appearance, she showed a funky cross-country travelogue, reminiscent of a schoolgirl's "what I did last summer" essay. Then she traveled to Dallas in October, where she attempted to capture the magnitude of the State Fair of Texas. Poundstone's December report (she did not appear during November sweeps) took her to Atlanta, with all of its many Peachtree Streets.

Response to Paula's segments must have been dismal, because she hasn't been heard from much since. While all of this harks back to Steve Allen's man-on-the-street interviews with regulars Tom Poston, Louie Nye, and Don Knotts on Allen's TV shows, it seems that Rosie is still trying to figure out exactly what is right for her show.

### SHOW-DEVELOPMENT TIME LINE

**November 21, 1995:**
Comedienne and actress Rosie O'Donnell joins the talk-show wars. O'Donnell has signed a deal with Warner Brothers Television for a daytime chat fest. *Daily Variety* reports that several other television studios are bidding for O'Donnell's services.

**December 1, 1995:**
Warner Bros. Television is expected to replace Carnie Wilson's talk show with a new offering by Rosie O'Donnell. And rather than waiting until next fall, many believe O'Donnell will be pinch-hitting this summer.

**January 12, 1996:**
Rosie O'Donnell's talk show is getting the green light. *Daily Variety* reports that the show has been sold to ABC and NBC stations in four of the top five markets in the country, which means it can be seen by more than 50 percent of television viewers in the United States. *Rosie* is set to debut in mid-June.

**May 28, 1996:**
Two weeks of practice shows begin. These shows are done with the clock as if they are the real thing, with guests, audiences, commercials, etc. (At least two of these shows have been shown in reruns.)

**June 10, 1996:**
*The Rosie O'Donnell Show* premieres in syndication with an approximate 90 percent U.S. coverage. However, many markets get the show on hard-to-find UHF stations and at hard-to-find times. The Philadelphia station, for example, airs the show around 2:00 A.M., after the late movie.

**June 13, 1996:**
Just when you thought talk shows were dead, Rosie O'Donnell comes along. The actress's talk show premiered Monday with a 4.4 rating and a 16 share. That's the highest first-day rating for any talk show in the last ten years.

**A DAY AT THE ROSIE O'DONNELL SHOW** I went to see *The Rosie O'Donnell Show* with my ten-year-old son, Evan, on March 23, 1997. I was working at the time as a consultant for IBM Credit Corporation in Westchester County, New York. Our day began at 6:00 A.M. as we dressed quickly and drove to the commuter train station in White Plains, a busy place even at that hour in this affluent suburb of New York City. Although the train looked nearly full, I spied a couple of empty middle seats, so Evan and I eased our way closer and asked the commuters if they would move their briefcases so we could sit. What did we know; we're not from New York.

The daytime view from the commuter trains is repugnant, to say the least. People have been dumping their trash along the transit ditches for decades, apparently unaware that there are people on those trains who look out the windows at all the rubbish. Not just in New York City but through prosperous White Plains, Scarsdale, Tuckahoe, and Mount Vernon, too.

Eventually the train drops underground, where there is nothing but blackness out the windows. Then, as we approach Grand Central Terminal, the view opens out again, with train tracks and support pilings as far as you can see in either direction. It almost looks like there's room for another city down here, beneath the skyscrapers of midtown Manhattan.

Not knowing which direction to go, we followed the commuters off the train and up the stairs into the terminal. (Heaven forbid we should ask for directions.) Anxious to get to Rockefeller Center, we didn't stop to admire the art and architecture of this enormous transit hub, probably the most famous train terminal in the world. Finding our way outside through all the construction that is a constant in this city, we worked our way northwest up Madison and Fifth Avenues.

It was two days after Rosie O'Donnell's birthday, which falls on the first full day of spring, but the sky was overcast, and it was cold enough to see our breath as we hurried along with everyone else to catch each "walk" light.

We turned left on Forty-ninth Street and headed into the cavernous Rockefeller Center. Just before we reached the Forty-ninth Street entrance to the NBC Building at 30 Rock, we could see a small crowd of people standing outside NBC's *Today Show* Studio, peering through the glass, hoping to get picked up by the cameras.

We hurried into 30 Rock and found two lines waiting for *The Rosie O'Donnell Show*, one for ticket holders, the other for stand-by. We were not exactly either, being the personal guests of Tracy Wormworth, the bass player in the McDLTs. Not knowing where we were supposed to be, we got in the ticket holders' line and waited for a page or someone else we could ask. That was about 7:15 A.M., and there were already over 100 people with tickets waiting in that line. (Rosie's studio has seats for only 180–200 guests.)

About 8:30 A.M. a couple of NBC pages came along with clipboards, so we asked where we were supposed to be. They escorted us out of the ticket holders' line, straight through the airport-style metal detector, and into a waiting elevator to the ninth floor. There we were escorted to a waiting area at the back of another studio, where we stood waiting with a dozen other personal guests for nearly forty minutes.

Finally, we were quickly taken, two and three people at a time, into Rosie's studio. We entered the studio at the back. About a dozen chairs in various locations in the audience area had duct tape across the arms designating the seating locations for each of the personal guests. We were taken down to our seats, on the aisle, about four rows back, just across from the corner where the show's band, the McDLTs, squeeze in. Beneath our seats we each found an Equal sweetener T-shirt, a package of Drake's Ring Dings, and a half-pint carton of skim milk.

The studio, which is on the eighth floor, is really quite cozy. To the right of center stage is the blue curtain where Rosie makes her daily entrance and where visiting bands set up. At other times you'll see a door there, where surprise guests come knocking. To the left is Rosie's desk and three maroon guest chairs, all raised two steps up. Behind Rosie and her guests is artwork of a roller coaster and other amuse-ment-park features. At the far left is the corridor where guests enter, which runs behind the amusement-park artwork, making a ninety-degree turn to the left just before it opens onto two steps down to the stage. To the left of that is where musical director John McDaniel and the other band members are shoehorned into a small area carved out of the audience. Also carved out of the audience, front and center, is a space for the director, segment producer, stage manager, and a cue-card person to stand unseen by the cameras. You can sometimes see Rosie's hairstylist, David Evangelista, there, too.

On the stage are two large main cameras mounted on dollies for flexible movement. There are also two handheld cameras, which can be placed on long booms, to reach into odd corners of the studio.

The audience area steps up to the point where the back is on the building's ninth floor. The ceiling is painted flat black and is filled with a crazy mass of lights, cables, and wires, mostly painted black, extending up to the tenth floor and streaming off in all directions.

After the personal guests were seated, they began seating the regular ticket holders, a few at a time. We really didn't pay much attention to that, since we were scarfing down our Ring Dings, along with those of some nearby women who claimed to be allergic to chocolate. Also, Joey Kola, the human tornado, began his daily warm up of the audience.

After all the ticket holders were seated, a few empty chairs were filled by stand-bys. In the rare event that there are still empty seats left or should someone get sick or leave for any other reason, people are pulled from anywhere to fill the seats—writers, clerks, pages, any warm body. On camera, there are *never* any empty seats.

Until airtime, Joey Kola is in charge of the audience, and he works extremely hard—physically harder than anyone else on the show—to be sure that the audience is filled with high energy. First he explains the rules:

➤ You cannot take pictures during the show or they'll confiscate your camera. You can take pictures after the show, and sometimes before, if you are seated early enough.
➤ Signs and posters are forbidden.
➤ And they ask you not to yell to Rosie or the guests during the show.

Then Joey tells jokes and "works" the audience, with the help of John McDaniel and the McDLTs. Joey will often pull audience members out of their chairs to dance with him. He drills the audience in some of the responses that they might have to make, as when they used to respond, "Taped to the desk!" He also interviews people to do the opening announcement if there is no special guest to do it. The day we were there, the opening announcer was Dr. Lorraine Hale, from Hale House, a children's charity.

Assuming ours was a typical day at *The Rosie O'Donnell Show,* Rosie never addresses the studio audience before the show, even when she is at her desk. Just before airtime, Rosie steps backstage, David

Evangelista primps her hair, and Joey gets the audience to start clapping. The opening announcement is made, and when the announcer says, "Hit it, John," what we really get is taped music during the opening cartoon credits. The band jumps in live right after Rosie's little rhyme. ("Today's show is a killer 'cuz we got Phyllis Diller.") Then Rosie appears, doing her little "baby step" entrance dance—she only walks a few feet from the curtain to her mark.

Rosie sits behind a desk, which is cluttered with small toys, Koosh balls, and a couple of Koosh shooters. Behind her is a DigiCard machine, sort of a digital jukebox. She keeps the DigiCard loaded with songs appropriate to her guests. And like the McDLTs and the musical guests, the DigiCard sounds much richer and fuller in person than it does on television—an indictment of the poor sound quality found on most TV sets.

On the air and off, Rosie is totally focused on her job at hand. She handles the guests with amazing poise while keeping one eye on her stage manager, Rose Riggins, who keeps her aware of the time until the next commercial. Because of all the cameras and behind-the-camera staff, the studio audience isn't forced to focus on Rosie and her guest, so the interviews are more distant, and often less compelling, than when seen at home on television. But it is fascinating to get to see what else is going on during the show.

Rosie is all business during commercial breaks, too. David Evangelista, her hairdresser, comes out at every break to add more spray to her hair, while her makeup person, Mariella Smith Masters, touches up her face and neck as needed. Sometimes she also consults with the director or one of the segment producers. Each guests wears a wireless lavaliere microphone, which includes a transmitter the size of a cigarette pack, which is usually attached in back to the guest's belt. For good measure Rosie wears two mikes.

The band does not play during the commercial breaks. As soon as the commercial starts, the music abruptly stops. Hillary Estey-McLaughlin, the executive producer, makes it a point to thank each guest after his or her segment. For upcoming music segments, the crew scrambles to get the instruments and microphones set. Near the end of each break, on cue from Rose, the band picks up the song it was playing, usually near the end of the song, and Rosie begins shooting Koosh balls at the crowd.

After the regular show, Rosie sometimes tapes segments with certain guests for later use, such as for "Listen to Iman" or the "Twelve Days of Christmas" which aired on Christmas, 1996. If they have an afternoon taping—most "Friday" shows are taped on Wednesday afternoons—they bring in a whole new audience. If you attend a morning taping, don't try to join the stand-by line for the second show. The staff wants as many people to get to see the show as possible, and they frown on "double-dippers." You can always get in line for *Conan O'Brien* or walk over to the Ed Sullivan Theater and try to catch Letterman.

Once all the taping is done, Rosie asks the people with kids sixteen and under to stay seated, dismissing everyone else. Then the kids line up for a personally autographed five-by-seven photo of Rosie. Rosie usually takes time to talk with each kid while she autographs the photos. If their parents want to take a picture of Rosie with their child, she is happy to oblige. If the parent doesn't have a camera, an assistant takes a Polaroid of the moment for him or her to take home. When we were there, Rosie even took an adorable little redhead child to her desk for picture taking (at the mom's request) after all the other kids had gotten their autographed photos.

But the highlight of our visit came next, as we were able to meet and talk with all the members of Rosie's band—John McDaniel and the McDLTs. There was another taping that afternoon, so the pages kept hurrying us to leave, but Evan and I had about ten minutes to shake hands and chat with Tracy Wormworth (bass), along with Rodney Jones (guitar), Mo Goldberg (sax), Ray Marchica (drums) and, of course, John McDaniel. That is ten minutes that I will remember all of my life. I'd like to say thanks to each of them, and most of all, to Tracy Wormworth, a very special friend.

**TICKET TRICKS** With the incredible popularity of *The Rosie O'Donnell Show*, it is practically impossible to get tickets. Don't be afraid to try stand-by, because a few people manage to get in nearly every day that way. I know of many fans who have gotten to see a show by getting a stand-by seat. Just be aware that to be one of the first in line, you have to get to 30 Rockefeller Plaza before 5:30 A.M. for the 10:00 A.M. show.

Anyone who gets a chance to attend *The Rosie O'Donnell Show* should do so. It's really a once-in-a-lifetime experience. Just remember to tape the show you attend, too, so that you can see what you might have missed by being there in person. Also, if you can, take a kid with you. You'll enjoy it more, and you'll get to stay after the show and interact with Rosie more than you would otherwise.

**JOHN McDANIEL AND THE McDLTS** When it came time for Rosie O'Donnell to find a band for *The Rosie O'Donnell Show*, she knew exactly where to begin—John McDaniel, musical director of *Grease* during her Broadway run. John jumped at the chance and set to work determining the size and style of their new band.

John and Rosie wanted a band big enough to back anyone who might perform on her show, but not as big as the *Late Show* or *Tonight Show* bands. They settled on a five-person band, similar to the Posse on *The Arsenio Hall Show*. And rather than hiring his pals from previous gigs, John "wanted to surround myself with 'new blood,' as it were. I did hold auditions, and I'm so pleased with the way it's all worked out! I hadn't worked with any of them [before]."

John wrote the music for the show's theme song, with Randy Cohen, the show's first head writer, providing the lyrics. John also arranged and recorded the theme, using singers from *Grease* for the backing vocals. The lyrics for the second season were written by John and Judy Gold. With that behind him, John and the band set to work developing a repertoire of show tunes, movie themes, and pop and rock songs to play during commercial breaks. How does John decide what the band should play as they go to commercial? "I like to surprise Rosie with the music to commercial. Sometimes it has to do with something that just happened or something coming up, but many times it's just something I like to play!" The show's research department also helps John find appropriate songs for certain guests.

During the first week of the show, Rosie suggested she might have a contest to name the band, but in the meantime began calling them the McDLTs. The name stuck, and there's been no discussion of any need to change it.

With Rosie signed through the 1999–2000 season, the band has settled in for the long haul. There are "no plans for any changes; I love them all!" claims a very pleased John McDaniel.

**John McDaniel—Leader and Pianist** John has a long history as music director, band leader, and pianist for many Broadway shows, including *Grease*, for which he has conducted two cast albums (one with Rosie as Rizzo, the other with Brooke Shields). Even with *The Rosie O'Donnell Show*, John still has his hand in the Broadway world. He conducted *Chicago* for a week during the first season's December break, and he still supervises *Grease* on Broadway and on tour. He was Patti LuPone's director and pianist on her last tour and on her *Patti LuPone Live* album, recorded June 8, 1993, for RCA Victor.

He has directed and played piano for many musicals both in New York and around the country. John's E-mail address is TheR0McD@aol.com.

**Morris "Mo" Goldberg—Alto Sax, Penny Whistle** Known for his expert playing of the penny whistle as well as alto saxophone, Mo has appeared on three albums by Paul Simon (including *Graceland*, 1986) and with Hugh Masekela (*Beatin' Aroun De Bus*, 1992), Hans Theessink (*Call Me*, 1993), Tony Bird (*Sorry Africa*, 1990) and Philip Tabane (*Unh!*, 1989) to name a few. You can write to Mo at TheR0Sax@aol.com.

**Rodney Jones—Guitar** Rodney is musical director for, and frequently tours with, blues singer Ruth Brown (*Songs of My Life*, which Rodney produced, arranged, and directed, *Fine and Mellow*; and *Blues on Broadway*). In addition, he is producing Lena Horne's next album for Blue Note and working on his own next album.

Rodney has already recorded several albums of his own, the most recent a jazz-and-blues album on BMG/Musicmasters called *X Field*, for which he wrote nine of the ten tracks. His earlier albums are *Articulation* and *When You Feel Love*.

As an accompanist, Rodney has also appeared on albums with Dizzy Gillespie (1976's live *Dizzy's Party*), organist Jimmy McGriff (*Right Turn on the Blues*, *McGriff's Blues*), former James Brown alto sax player Maceo Parker (*Life on Planet Groove*, *Roots Revisited*), and the two-volume *Tribute to Wes Montgomery*.

You can write to Rodney online at TheR0Gtr@aol.com.

**Ray "Boom-Boom" Marchica—Drums** Ray has played perfect paradiddles in the pits for many Broadway shows, including *Damn Yankees* and *The Will Rogers Follies*, for both of which he can also be heard on original cast albums. He has also recorded with Earl Klugh and Craig Peyton (*Tropical Escape*, 1994). He also appeared in the 1987 Woody Allen film *Radio Days* as a USO musician. Ray's hobby is collecting baseball cards. You can reach Ray at rpmbeat@aol.com.

**Tracy Wormworth—Bass** "I had just completed a European tour with Wayne Shorter before I started playing on *The Rosie O'Donnell Show*." Tracy spent two years in the early eighties with The Waitresses (two albums), toured with Sting on his *Nothing Like the Sun* tour, and has provided the bottom line with the B-52s (*Good Stuff*, 1992), Paula Abdul, Toshi Reagon, Special EFX, Rachell Ferrell, and Wayne Shorter. "I have also recorded with David Lee Roth, pop vocalist Des'ree, jazz violinist Regina Carter, R & B/pop group The Family Stand, jazz pianist Rachel Z, Lena Horne, and I've played on jingles for AT&T, HBO, Domino's Pizza, and others. Outside of the show I play gigs locally, and I still do recording sessions when my schedule permits."

Tracy's e-mail address is TheR0Bass@aol.com.

**FEATURE ARTICLE** How

# the Heartbreak of her Childhood Made Rosie O'Donnell the Nicest Person on Tv

**LADIES' HOME JOURNAL, February 1997**

**BY MELINA GEROSA**

Rosie O'Donnell is plopped in an overstuffed chair in her colorful suite of offices overlooking New York City's Rockefeller Center. She is a renegade in a Yankees T-shirt, shorts, and high-tops, and she is telling a story, although loud giggles from her twenty-month-old son, Parker, keep interrupting her. "I'm sitting on the plane, and who walks on but Burt Bacharach," says O'Donnell, her eyes wide and her Long Island accent thick. "I turn to the lady next to me and say, 'Oh my God, that's Burt Bacharach!" And she turns to me and says, 'Oh my God, it's you!' "

What exactly does "being you" mean for someone like Rosie O'Donnell? For one thing, it means pulling down a cool $4 million to have her childhood idols—Mary Tyler Moore, Liza Minnelli, Elton John—take turns in the guest chair of *The Rosie O'Donnell Show.*

It means being best buddies with folks like Madonna or Tom Hanks and his wife, Rita Wilson.

It means craving motherhood keenly enough to submit to the rigors of single-parent adoption.

But, more than anything, being Rosie O'Donnell means having a drive born of a sadness so deep that it permeates every aspect of her adult life.

Once upon a time, O'Donnell sang Barbra Streisand songs to her mother, Roseanne, as she cooked dinner every night. Then, when Rosie O'Donnell was ten, her mother died from breast cancer. "My whole life revolves around my mother's death," says the thirty-four-year-old star. "It changed who I was as a person. I don't know who I would be if my mother had lived. But I would trade it all in to see."

Perhaps she never recovered from the tragedy because her family never dealt with it. "It wasn't spoken about in our house. All of my mother's things were removed," recalls O'Donnell. Her father, she says, became "emotionally absent," leaving her and her four brothers and sisters to be raised by neighbors. One neighborhood mom took the pre-teen to buy her first bra. "It was traumatic," she recalls quietly. "When a girl gets her period and her mom is not there to comfort her, it's incredibly painful."

To fill that void, O'Donnell relied upon the television shows *Eight Is Enough*, *The Brady Bunch*, and *The Partridge Family*. "I would watch these shows hoping that my father would meet a Julie Andrews type who would bring love and life back to our home," she says.

She also took her search for surrogate parents to school, where her popularity (she was voted homecoming queen) had a purpose. "I didn't care about the kids," she says. "I wanted to make the adults laugh."

O'Donnell had always loved to perform, from the time she was in kindergarten. "For show-and-tell, kids are bringing in Barbie dolls, and I'm singing 'Oklahoma,'" she says now with a chuckle. "In 1973 I saw Bette Midler on Broadway, and I thought, That's what I want to do. I'd watch Barbra Streisand and think, I want to be her. Carol Burnett, Lucille Ball—I wanted to be the funny women, and when I saw characters like Ethel and Rhoda, I knew, Now there's a role for me."

Her mother's death infused a single-minded sense of purpose in the daughter left behind. "I remember thinking at ten years old, if I was going to die in my thirties, what would I want to have achieved?" says O'Donnell. "It made me strive for my goals with a fervent passion."

The goal she chose—to make people laugh—was a well-worn survival tactic in her family. "After our mother died, if you wanted to express something painful, you could only do it couched in comedy," she explains. Comedy was also a way of emulating her late mother. "One night I was watching my mother at a PTA meeting making everyone laugh," says O'Donnell, with a twinkle in her eye. "I was about five, and I remember thinking, Wow, that's a good thing."

While still a teenager, O'Donnell took her act—personal observations about her life and family—on the road. For a decade she worked the clubs until some TV roles led to her first major break, a plum role in *A League of Their Own*. Director Penny Marshall says O'Donnell worked hard both on-screen and off: "You could see the thousands of extras getting restless, and she would take the microphone and do her stand-up and imitate Madonna singing 'Like a Virgin.'"

Still, O'Donnell says that she was terrified to meet Madonna. "Totally. Had diarrhea," she admits. But she had just seen *Truth or Dare*, and caught a glimpse of a kindred spirit. At their first meeting, O'Donnell recalls, "I looked her in the eye and said, 'My mom died when I was ten, too. Your movie reminded me a lot of my life.' And that was it. We became friends right then."

O'Donnell met another friend for life, Nora Ephron, when the director cast her in *Sleepless in Seattle*. O'Donnell's appeal, according to Ephron, is that "the audience looks at her and thinks, I wish that could be my best friend," says Ephron. "Rosie had that in *Sleepless*, and it's why her show works. She's a fantastically open person." And Ephron should know. Says O'Donnell, "Nora's a mother to me. She's the one I go to when I have questions."

> **Rosie List:**
> **FAVORITE CHILDHOOD TV SHOWS**
>
> The Mary Tyler Moore Show
> Ryan's Hope
> The Partridge Family
> The Brady Bunch
> Laverne & Shirley
> The Carol Burnett Show
> The Merv Griffin Show
> The Mike Douglas Show
> The Dinah Shore Show
> Saturday Night Live

If there's one thing O'Donnell has never questioned, it's her wrenching desire to become a mother herself. "The same way I knew that I would be an entertainer, I knew that I would be a mother," she says. So, at the age of thirty, she started the two-and-a-half-year procedure of interviews and counseling to adopt. "I would be open to giving birth, but it wasn't in the near future when I started the process," she says, adding, "I have no investment in having a miniature me running around."

Nor did O'Donnell have a gender preference, although she has a theory about why she wound up with a son. "I have a lot of issues to work out about men," she explains carefully. "I had some stuff with my dad that was never really resolved. I think that [the adoption] helps me to connect in a way that I wasn't able to before. I'm so in love with this child, who is a male and his own person."

While O'Donnell has always been a doting aunt for her nieces, her inexperience with boys manifested itself early on. "I told Rosie [that] Parker hadn't been circumcised, even though she insisted that he had," laughs friend Rita Wilson.

"I just thought, Wow it really healed good in two days," remembers O'Donnell, who burst into tears when she realized the mistake (due to a mix-up in the hospital records). Friend Kate Capshaw, the wife of Steven Spielberg, arranged to have the circumcision performed the next day.

Parker has provided a joyful priority in O'Donnell's life. "He's taught me to value my time with him more than anything else," she says. "I leave work by three o'clock every day and turn the phones off until he goes to bed." Not that every moment of motherhood has been, well, delicious. "I picked him up and was like, 'Hi!'" she says, opening her mouth wide to demonstrate, "and he vomited an entire jar of baby squash right in my mouth!"

Still, it's all because of Parker that *The Rosie O'Donnell Show* even exists. When O'Donnell was filming *Harriet the Spy*, she came home to a little boy who hadn't seen her in so long, he wouldn't go near her. The

**Rosie List:
FAVORITE
ACTRESSES**
Julie Andrews
Carol Burnett
Madonna
Mary Tyler Moore
Barbra Streisand

next day, O'Donnell called her agent and said, "That's my last movie." That was when the comedian came up with the idea for a chat show that would be "a Merv Griffin for the nineties," she says. "And I knew it could work because I used to watch Merv and Dinah every day after school with my grandmother."

To say the show works is an understatement—its success is, in fact, unprecedented. Just four months after its debut, the show's one-year contract was renewed until the year 2000 for the largest fee increase in television history. O'Donnell has certain ironclad rules to make it work so well. First of all, *The Rosie O'Donnell Show* is friendly to the famous. Rule number two: O'Donnell keeps Parker out of the act. "I don't want him to become like Chastity Bono or Cody Gifford where his name and experiences are public record." Rule number three: She will not willingly compete with Oprah. "People say to me, 'How do you feel that Barbra Streisand is doing Oprah and you can't get her booked?' I say, 'If I were Barbra, I'd do Oprah, too,'" she explains.

> **Rosie List:**
> **FAVORITE CDS**
>
> *Greatest Hits,*
> Elton John
>
> *Nick of Time,*
> Bonnie Raitt
>
> *Higher Ground,*
> Barbra Streisand
>
> *The Sound of Music,*
> Soundtrack

The admiration is mutual. "I adore Rosie," says Winfrey. "She and I have the same gift, which is the ability to be ourselves in front of the camera. The truth of who we are comes through, and that's what people like."

Critics agree that *The Rosie O'Donnell Show*'s success has everything to do with the down-to-earth host, who really is as big a fan of her guests as any audience member. Take her on-air obsession with Streisand. "When my father removed my mother's things, her records were the one thing he left," says O'Donnell. "So Streisand was a connection to my mom."

O'Donnell's fun-loving spirit is also reflected in her home, which is decorated in Big Kid chic—primary colors and toys. "It's like a kid's playroom, except adult size," says Rita Wilson. "She has her collection of McDonald's Happy Meal toys on the shelves of her living room. Her enthusiasm comes from creating a fun childhood in her adult life."

Despite the accolades, it does not seem likely that success will spoil this star. "I still wear Gap," says O'Donnell, whose reaction to her *Newsweek* "Queen of Nice" cover story seems typical Rosie. "You know how you can get your picture on a fake magazine cover?" she says. "Every time I saw [the magazine] on a newsstand, I thought they'd put out a fake *Newsweek* that week."

Oddly, the star feels just as disconnected from her physique. "Whenever anyone tells me to lose weight, I always laugh, like I could, but I'm just keeping it on because I like to!" she cracks. "But when I'm at my thinnest, I never really feel thin, and when I'm at my heaviest, I'm always surprised at how I got there. So I'm disconnected from my career and my physical self. Two things I have to work on. Like Oprah's book says, make the connection. I have not made the connection."

If there is one area where O'Donnell needs no fine-tuning, though, it's her principles. Some examples: She will never work with Woody Allen because of his relationship with his stepdaughter Soon-Yi. She declined to be photographed for Madonna's 1992 book, *Sex*. On the set of *Now and Then*, she gave her food money to a homeless mother. "I said, 'Great, now she's going to find drugs,' " says Wilson, one of the films co-stars. "And Rosie said, 'Maybe. But maybe this will change her life.' " And now O'Donnell is setting up a foundation to help working moms. "Basically, I'm going to ask rich women to give one million dollars each to subsidize day-care centers in inner cities," she says. Adds Wilson, "If the Celestine Prophecy ever had a human manifestation, it's Rosie. The more she gives away of herself, the more it just comes back to her."

Sometimes those huge returns come in pint-sized packages, like the one scampering around O'Donnell's office. "Before him, I was a little depressed and I didn't know it. I knew I wasn't as happy as I thought I should be, based on my success," she says as Parker comes to rest his head on her knee. "But when I'm with him, I feel true joy."

O'Donnell seems in no rush to wrap up the interview, but the tuckered-out tyke has his own agenda. Leveling his gaze at the visitor, he yells one of the few words he knows, "Bye-bye!" cutting off the conversation with comedic timing that even his old lady couldn't beat.

## ROSIE'S RULES: HOW THIS NICE GIRL FINISHED FIRST

**Be Friendly to Everyone**—She landed her first acting job, a role on the sitcom *Gimme a Break*, with the help of a cocktail waitress she befriended at one of her regular comedy gigs. Because O'Donnell had always been nice to her, the waitress refused to give a table of NBC executives their check until they'd seen O'Donnell's act.

**Mind Your Manners.** After her VJ audition tape was rejected by MTV, O'Donnell still wrote the producer a nice note. He was so impressed by the gesture that he hooked her up at VH1, where she landed a coveted VJ job. "A thank-you note got me that job," she says.

**Play Nice.** The comedian will only tell jokes about somebody that she would feel comfortable saying to them—exceptions being O. J. Simpson and Woody Allen. "If I'm morally offended by somebody—if your accused of murder or you sleep with your stepdaughter—you're open game," she says. "But I've never been interested in mean-spirited comedy." An audience-pleasing move, considering her show is the highest-rated debut of daytime talk shows in the last decade.

**Forgive and Forget.** When Donny Osmond made a fat joke on her show, he was booed off the stage. Still, the host invited him back to apologize. "I made him put on a puppy-dog suit and sing 'Puppy Love,'" she says. "It was the highest-rated show ever."

# The Rosie O'Donnell Show Companion

## SEASON ONE

### Monday, June 10, 1996
Actor George Clooney (TV's *ER*; *Batman and Robin*)
Soap star Susan Lucci (TV's *All My Children*)
Singer Toni Braxton

ROSIE: This show is unique, original, unlike anything you've ever seen on TV. And today's program is brought to you by the letter L and the number 3.

For Rosie's first show, George brought roses and champagne. At the end of the show George opened the champagne, and Rosie took Polaroids of her guests.

### Tuesday, June 11, 1996
The fabulous Penny Marshall (actress and director)
*Good Morning America*'s Joan Lunden
Broadway's Savion Glover and the cast of *Bring in 'Da Noise Bring in 'Da Funk*

ROSIE: I told everyone that the reason I was in that movie [*A League of Their Own*] so much, it was a little part, I was the only one who could understand you.

PENNY [*laughing*]: That's true.

ROSIE: Remember, when you'd come over, you'd go [*imitating Penny*], I need somebady ta go ovah to t'ird base . . . do somethin' dare wid a bat or whatevah . . . [*In normal voice*] They didn't have a clue. . . .

ROSIE: The Kmart thing—what happened?

PENNY: I don't know. They called me and said you would do it if I would do it.

ROSIE: And they called me and said that you would do it if I would do it.

PENNY: So we're stupid. We're doing it!

Joan made the mistake of promoting two things on one show—her interest in mountain climbing and her new cookbook. For the cooking segment, Rosie showed up wearing climbing gear and carrying an ice ax.

**Wednesday, June 12, 1996**
Actor Dennis Franz (TV's *NYPD Blue*)
Actress Fran Drescher (TV's *The Nanny*, Rosie's *Car 54* costar, and author of the bestselling book *Enter Whining*)
Restaurant reviews from Fran's parents Mort and Sylvia Drescher
Comedienne Wendy Liebman

Oddly, stand-up comedy didn't go over well on the show. Fans preferred the synergy between the comics and Rosie when she interviewed them. Wendy would be one of the few to do a stand-up routine on the show.

Mort and Sylvia are the parents of Fran (*The Nanny*) Drescher and good friends of Rosie's. They have retired to Florida, from where they occasionally provide "early-bird" restaurant reviews—complete dinners for two for under twenty dollars.

**Thursday, June 13, 1996**
Singer Gloria Estefan
Actor and comedian John Henton (*Living Single*)

ROSIE: No other family was as obsessed with TV in my neighborhood as mine was. We were allowed to watch TV twenty-four hours a day. And we did. My favorite shows were Merv Griffin and Mike Douglas. I would literally run home from school every day and switch them on. I hope we can bring back that kind of show to television.

### Friday, June 14, 1996
Actor Nathan Lane (*The Birdcage*)
Singer and songwriter Joan Armatrading
Geography-bee winner Seyi Fayanju
Teen idol Donny Osmond

"It was the first week of the show, and I don't think he had seen it before. He's on the road doing *Joseph and the Amazing Technicolor Dreamcoat.* I believe that when he came out and saw my albums and my Donny Osmond doll, he thought I was going to ridicule him. I don't think if he were booked on the show now, after it's been on for forty-five days, that he would ever do what he did. Instead of seeing what I was doing as a reverential tribute—which it was, because I honestly do like Donny Osmond and his music and I did have the doll—I think he thought I was going to be aggressively poking fun at him. So what happened was, I was saying, 'Oh, Donny, you have to go and do this dangerous stunt out in Utah, and God, I'm worried about you. You know what, don't you go on that helicopter. I'll go and be your stuntperson. I'll be your double, and I'll do it for you.' And he said, 'I don't think the helicopter can handle that much weight.' So I took a moment and I went, 'Whoooa!' For a moment I thought, Does he mean me and him together on the helicopter? Or does he mean me separately? That comment became the bane of his existence, because everywhere he went, people were saying, 'How could you?' And I didn't let up on it. The next day, I did the show and I said, 'Can you believe that Donny Osmond called me fat?'

"I went out to L.A. that weekend for a funeral, and there were a lot of people there who had seen the show. One of them was Roseanne, who said, 'I can't believe he said that. I saw your face.' I think anyone who has ever had weight be an issue in their life felt the pain of having lived through that. He did apologize profusely during the commercial and afterwards. I don't believe it was necessarily malicious; it was just stupid of him. I think he thought that this would be his shot and that because I'm a comic I could take it. He came back on the show because we were getting so many letters, literally thousands of them, saying, 'I'm burning my albums.' He was getting booed onstage, apparently, and I didn't want it for him, either. I mean, one stupid comment shouldn't end your career. So we had him come back, and I thought he was a real sport to play along. In the end, it was okay. I don't think he was mean-spirited in the sense of somebody like a Howard Stern, whose agenda it is to be mean and hurtful. I don't think that's Donny Osmond's agenda. I think he was just a little nervous and defensive, and he didn't think."

**Monday, June 17, 1996**
From the gold medal–winning U.S. Olympic basketball team, Rebecca Lobo
Comedian Martin Short
Country singer Shania Twain performs from her album *No One Needs to Know*
Actress Lela Rochon (*Waiting to Exhale*; the upcoming movie *The Chamber*)

**Tuesday, June 18, 1996**
Actress and comedian Janeane Garofalo (*The Truth About Cats and Dogs*)
The very funny Dana Carvey
Country singer Roseanne Cash
Bestselling author Terry McMillan (*Waiting to Exhale*)

**Wednesday, June 19, 1996**
Actor Tony Danza (*Taxi*; *Who's the Boss*)
R & B singer Monica performs from her album *Miss Thang*.

**Thursday, June 20, 1996**
Actor Matthew Broderick (*The Cable Guy*)

For whatever reason, Matthew wouldn't open up and talk, and Rosie couldn't find anything to bring him out. Possibly one of the worst interviews in the show's history.

### Friday, June 21, 1996—Day of Compassion
Actress and singer Vanessa Williams (*Eraser*)
Actress Morgan Fairchild
AIDS speaker and author Mary Fisher
A performance from the Tony Award–winning cast of the Broadway
   phenomenon *Rent*

### Monday, June 24, 1996
Actor Harvey Keitel (*Pulp Fiction; From Dusk Till Dawn*)
Hip-hop band The Fugees perform from their album *The Score.*
Broadway legend Carol Channing
Comedian and *Politically Incorrect* correspondent Chris Rock

Contrary to popular belief, Rosie did not mention to Harvey that she saw his penis, but if he caught her HBO stand-up act, he already knew that!

### Tuesday, June 25, 1996
Actress Christine Lahti (*Chicago Hope*)
Actress Jada Pinkett (*The Nutty Professor*)
Musician and former *ET* anchor John Tesh performs his song for the
   Summer Olympics.

### Wednesday, June 26, 1996
From NBC's *Dateline*, Jane Pauley
Actress Vanessa Marcil (*The Rock*; TV's *General Hospital*)
High school student and NBA draftee Kobe Bryant

ROSIE TO JANE PAULEY: It is sick that I know all these words [to TV show themes and commercial jingles]! Imagine what diseases I could cure if I could empty the useless crap from my brain! It's like a high-speed computer, but it only doodles, ya know what I mean?

Rosie loves to shoot hoops, so she often has basketball stars on her show.

**Thursday, June 27, 1996**
Singer Liza Minnelli
Bestselling author Pat Conroy (*Beach Music; The Prince of Tides*)
Supermodel Tyson

**Friday, June 28, 1996**
Talk-show host Regis Philbin
From *Sesame Street*, Elmo
Soap star Erika Slezak (*One Life to Live*)
A performance from the cast of the Broadway play *Seven Guitars*

During the interview with Regis Philbin, Rosie brought out his daughter, Joanna, who is a talent assistant on *The Rosie O'Donnell Show*.

**Monday, July 1, 1996**
*Today Show* coanchor Katie Couric
Muppet "actress" Miss Piggy
From TV's *Blossom* and *Brotherly Love* Joey
    Lawrence with brothers Matthew and Andy
Seventies singing sensations Captain & Ten-
    nille perform one of their classics.

**Tuesday, July 2, 1996**
Actor Michael Keaton (*Multiplicity*)
Actress Victoria Principal (Lifetime's original
    movie *The Abduction*)
Actress Sheryl Lee Ralph performs from
    Broadway's *Dreamgirls* (currently seen on TV's
    *Moesha*)
Comedian Dave Chapelle (*The Nutty Professor*)

A year after this show, Rosie spotted Victoria on an airplane and gushed like any ordinary fan would, completely forgetting that they had met.

**Wednesday, July 3, 1996**
Singer Tony Bennett performs one of his timeless classics.
Actor James Caan (*Eraser*)
Plus a special Fourth of July pie-eating contest

**Thursday, July 4, 1996—a show taped during
the "practice" weeks, before June 10, 1996**
Actress Teri Garr
Actor, director, and author Garry Marshall (*Murphy Brown*; director
   of *Exit to Eden*; and author of *Wake Me When It's Funny*)
A performance by entertainer Lainie Kazan
Comedian Joe Yannetty

ROSIE: I went to seven colleges. I was a professional transfer student.
   I had to drop out 'cause I couldn't see out the back window.

Rosie did two weeks of practice shows before the premier on June
10th. It was during the practices that she decided she did not want to
do an opening stand-up routine, similar to what Jay Leno and David
Letterman do. Instead, she and her staff came up with Rosie at her
desk reading regional newspapers and magazines, with jokes on blue 5-
by-7 cards. As she got more comfortable with her instincts, she eventually dropped that and today just ad-libs about whatever interests her
each day.

**Friday, July 5, 1996**
Actor Peter Berg (*Chicago Hope*)
Singer Linda Ronstadt performs from her latest CD, *Dedicated to the
   One I Love.*
Cajun chef Emeril Lagasse, host of the TV Food Network's *Essence of
   Emeril*
Soap star Ruth Warrick (*All My Children*)

**Monday, July 8, 1996**
Singer and Oscar-winning actress Cher
Actor Malcolm Gets (*Caroline in the City*)
Actress Katie Schlossberg (*Multiplicity*)

A Pots 'N' Pans perfomance from the Broadway sensation *Bring in 'Da Noise Bring in 'Da Funk*

Rosie displayed her skills as a drummer by joining the cast in an encore. She flailed away earnestly on an upturned plastic paint bucket, never missing a beat.

**Tuesday, July 9, 1996**
Emmy Award–winning actress Christine Baranski (*Cybill*)
Boxer George Foreman
Actress Michelle Trachtenberg (Rosie's costar in *Harriet the Spy*)
Seed art with Lillian Colton

**Wednesday, July 10, 1996**
Legendary talk-show host Mike Douglas
Soap star Deirdre Hall (*Days of Our Lives*)
Singer Oleta Adams performs from her latest album *Moving On.*

Rosie shared with Mike Douglas how her show is modeled after talk shows like his and Merv Griffin's.

**Thursday, July 11, 1996**
Actor Richard Dreyfuss (*Mr. Holland's Opus* and Rosie's *Another Stakeout* costar)
Country trio Pam Tillis, Lorrie Morgan, and Carlene Carter
Twin actresses Tia and Tamara Mowry (*Sister, Sister*)

**Friday, July 12, 1996—**
**Elton John Suck-up Day!**
Actress Meg Ryan (*Courage Under Fire*)
Actor Richard Karn (*Home Improvement*)
Actress and singer Jennifer Holliday performs her classic song from the Broadway musical *Dream Girls.*

Rosie declared todays show "Elton John Suck-up Day." Throughout the show she begs and pleads for Elton to contact her and agree to be a guest on her show. She even has astronaut Buzz Aldrin perform a dramatic reading of the words to Elton's hit song "Rocket Man." The ploy is successful, and Elton appears on the show November 15, 1996.

### Monday, July 15, 1996
Singer and actor Harry Connick Jr (*Independence Day*) performs from his latest album *Star Turtle*.
Actress Andie MacDowell (*Multiplicity*)
NBA and Olympic basketball star and actor Shaquille O'Neal (*Kazaam*)

### Tuesday, July 16, 1996
Actor and comedian Garry Shandling (*The Larry Sanders Show*)
Gospel singer Ce Ce Winans
Actress Margaret Colin
Former voice of New York taxi cabs Victoria Drakoulis

Victoria's voice was heard in New York taxis speaking various public service messages like "Don't leave any personal belongings when you leave." They replaced Victoria with the voices of famous New Yorkers like Joan Rivers and Jackie Mason.

### Wednesday, July 17, 1996
Talk-show host Geraldo Rivera
Singer and songwriter Jewel performs her song *Who Will Save Your Soul*.
Actor and director Paul Michael Glaser (*Starsky & Hutch;* director of *Kazaam*)
Dance performance by the children's African dance troupe Batoto Yetu

### Thursday, July 18, 1996
Actor David Duchovny (*The X-Files*)
Author Delia Ephron (*Hanging Up*)
The Boys Choir of Harlem
Snapple lady Wendy Kaufman

The Snapple Pitch lady was on because people kept telling Rosie that they looked alike.

Rosie's popularity has made her the cover girl on many magazines. (Author's collection)

With on-screen husband David Johansen in *Car 54, Where Are You?* (Photofest)

Rosie's portrayal of Lucille in *Car 54, Where Are You?* was one of the film's too-few highlights. (Photofest)

Rosie names *A League of Their Own* her favorite filmmaking experience. (Photofest)

Rosie and Madonna became friends during the filming of *A League of Their Own*. (Photofest)

*Sleepless in Seattle:* Becky (Rosie) and Annie (Meg Ryan), two hopeless romantics  (Photofest)

The stone-age friends: The Flintstones (John Goodman and Elizabeth Perkins) and the Rubbles (Rosie and Rick Moranis)  (Photofest)

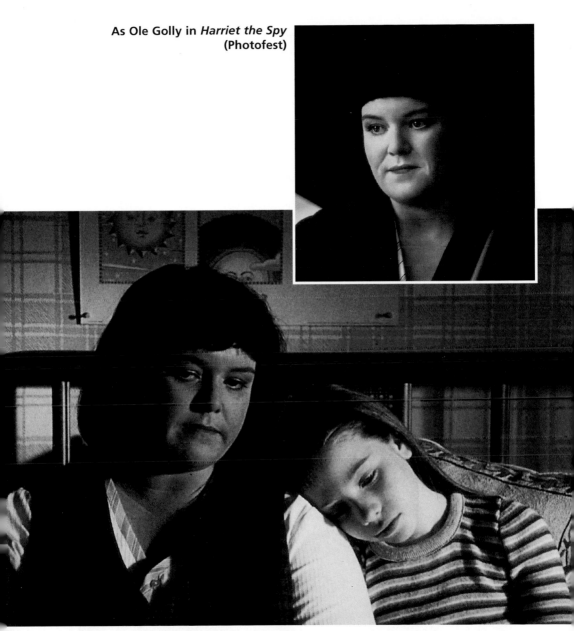

**As Ole Golly in *Harriet the Spy*** (Photofest)

**With Michelle Trachtenberg, who had the title role in Nickelodeon's *Harriet the Spy*** (Photofest)

*Wide Awake:* **With young costar Joseph Cross  (Photofest)**

**As Sister Terry in *Wide Awake*  (Photofest)**

**After being rescheduled at least five times, *Wide Awake* was finally released in 1998. (Photofest)**

Rosie (seen here with frequent guest Elmo) has redefined the TV talk-show format. (Photofest)

**Friday, July 19, 1996**
Actor and *Saturday Night Live* alum Mike Myers
From Broadway's *Sunset Boulevard*, actress Betty Buckley
Actress Catherine Keener (*Walking and Talking*)
The cast of the off-Broadway sensation *Stomp*

Rosie again showed her rhythmic abilities by joining the *Stomp* cast in an encore, this time keeping time with a long wooden pole.

**Monday, July 22, 1996**
Martial arts star Jackie Chan (*Supercop*)
Soap star Genie Francis (*General Hospital*)
Singing legend Wayne Newton

**Tuesday, July 23, 1996**
Actress Rita Wilson (Rosie's *Now and Then* costar)
Comedian Lisa Ann Walter (*Life's Work*)
Singer Dee Angelo

**Wednesday, July 24, 1996**
The Monkees!
Actress Linda Dano (*Another World*)
Actor Jonathon Taylor Thomas (*Home Improvement*)
Actress and martial artist Michelle Khan (*Supercop*)

**Thursday, July 25, 1996**
Actor Lou Diamond Phillips (*Courage Under Fire*)
Actor Jon Cryer
Singer L L Cool J
Ten-year-old painter Alexandria Nechita
Restaurant reviews from Mort and Sylvia Drescher

**Friday, July 26, 1996**
Singers Donny and Marie Osmond reunited
From MTV's *Singled Out*, Jenny McCarthy
R & B act Maxwell performs from the album *Maxwell's Urban Hang Suite.*

After Marie shares her own stories of Donny's insensitive nature, Rosie forces Donny to don a dog suit and sing "Puppy Love" to her as retribution for his comments on the June 13th show. Donny tries to sway and swoon Rosie, but they both end up on the floor, playing and laughing. All is forgiven.

**Monday, July 29, 1996**—a show taped during the "practice" weeks, before June 10, 1996

Rosie welcomes actress Valerie Harper (TV's *Rhoda*).
*All My Children's* Michael Knight
Singer Jann Arden performs her hit "Insensitive."
Actress Bitty Schram (*Caught*)

**Tuesday, July 30, 1996**—Repeat from June 10, 1996—a rebroadcast of the very first show!

**Wednesday, July 31, 1996**—A show taped during the "practice" weeks, before June 10, 1996

Actress Joely Fisher (*Ellen*)
Rap artist Coolio
Comedian David Brenner
New York Yankees' groundskeeper Brian Cooney

**Thursday, August 1, 1996**—repeat from June 11, 1996
**Friday, August 2, 1996**—repeat from June 12, 1996
**Monday, August 5, 1996**
U.S. Olympians Mia Hamm and Jackie Joyner-Kersee
Actress Gwyneth Paltrow (*Emma*)
R & B sensation Keith Sweat performs from his chart-topping, self-titled CD.
From the movie *The Usual Suspects*, actor Kevin Pollak

**Tuesday, August 6, 1996**

U.S. Olympian Amy Van Dyken

Actor Kurt Russell (*Escape From LA*)

Author Anne Rice (*Interview with the Vampire*)

Young singer Tatiana Bolanos

**Wednesday, August 7, 1996—Barbra Streisand Suck-Up Day!**

Fitness guru Richard Simmons

Rocker Meatloaf

Comedian Vickie Vivrette

Rosie presents another suck-up day, this time to entice Barbra Streisand to be a guest on her show. This one is less successful than her Elton John Suck-up Day. It would be another fifteen months before Barbra finally appeared on the show (November 21, 1997).

Meatloaf proved himself to be a very disruptive guest. He missed his cue for a song that he was supposed to sing with Rosie. Then he kept talking while John McDaniel repeatedly played the song introduction. And at the end, he grabbed Rosie in a big bear hug and French-kissed her. While it shocked and upset Rosie at the time (and for several days after), it did make for good live television.

**Thursday, August 8, 1996**

U.S. Olympian Keri Strug

Republican National Convention keynote speaker U.S. representative Susan Molinari

Actor Patrick Muldoon (*Melrose Place*)

Actress and former Harlette (i.e. Bette Midler backup performer) Linda Hart (*Tin Cup*)

ROSIE: We made a rule: None of the guests are allowed to French-kiss the host. It's just the rule! From now on. Richard Simmons tried to do it, Meatloaf. I can't blame them—everyone wants to!

**Friday, August 9, 1996**

Rosie interviews comedian and actor Dennis Miller from *Bordello of Blood*.

Soul and gospel legend Al Green
From Broadway's *Grace and Glorie,* actress Lucie Arnaz
Actress Ellen Burstyn (*Spitfire Grill*)

ROSIE: *They're Playing Our Song* on Broadway, which you starred with
   Robert Klein originally, and then Tony Roberts took over the role
   after Robert left. Hello, useless shit stuck in my brain, and, um,
   oops, did I just say, boy, we'll edit that, don't worry, oh, boy, hello,
   there we go, we just lost all of the South.
LUCIE: That's all right, wait'll I French-kiss you; then
   you'll lose the rest of 'em.

This show was especially rewarding to Rosie
because of her idolization of Lucie Arnaz. As a
teenager, Rosie had written Lucie, then appearing
on Broadway, a fan letter. Lucie wrote back with
kindness and encouragement, something that Rosie
always remembered.

### Monday, August 12, 1996
Actress Kyra Sedgwick (*Phenomenon*)
Comic actor Mark Curry (*Hangin' with Mr Cooper*)
Actress and pop-culture icon Maureen McCormick (TV's original
   Marcia Brady)
A performance from Grammy Award–winning singer Emmylou Harris

### Tuesday, August 13, 1996
Actor and director Danny DeVito and actress Rhea Perlman (*Matilda*)
Pop stars Hootie and the Blowfish perform from their album *Fair-
   weather Johnson.*
Actress and singer Vicki Lawrence

### Wednesday, August 14, 1996
Actor and legendary singer Harry Belafonte (Robert Altman's film
   *Kansas City*)
Critically acclaimed singing sensation Me'Shell Ndegeocello performs
   from her new album *Peace Beyond Passion.*

Former Charlie's angel Kate Jackson
The one-and-only Phyllis Diller

**Thursday, August 15, 1996**
New York Knicks' cocaptain Patrick Ewing
Actress Ellen Barkin (*The Fan*)
Actress Thora Birch (*Alaska; Now and Then*)

**Friday, August 16, 1996**
Tipper Gore, wife of Vice President Al Gore
Actress Lucy Lawless (*Xena: Warrior Princess*)
Actress Mariette Hartley
Country singer George Jones performs from his album *I Live to Tell It All.*

**Monday, August 19, 1996**—repeat from June 14, 1996
**Tuesday, August 20, 1996**—repeat from June 17, 1996
**Wednesday, August 21, 1996**—repeat from June 28, 1996
**Thursday, August 22, 1996**—repeat from June 18, 1996
**Friday, August 23, 1996**—repeat from July 10, 1996
**Monday, August 26, 1996**—repeat from July 8, 1996
**Tuesday, August 27, 1996**—repeat from July 1, 1996
**Wednesday, August 28, 1996**—repeat from July 16, 1996
**Thursday, August 29, 1996**—repeat from July 12, 1996
**Friday, August 30, 1996**—repeat from July 18, 1996

**Monday, September 2, 1996**
Action hero Chuck Norris (*Walker: Texas Ranger*)
Actress Yasmine Bleeth
Singer Donna Lewis performs from her CD *Now in a Minute.*
Comedian Henriette Mantel (*A Very Brady Sequel*)
Heather, an audience member, gets a makeover!

**Tuesday, September 3, 1996**
Comic actor Damon Wayans (*Bulletproof*)

Singer Celine Dion performs from her CD *Falling Into You.*
Funnyman Anthony Clark (TV's *Boston Common*)

ROSIE: Can I tell ya somethin'? My dogs [two long-haired Chihuahuas named Buster and Valentine] have fleas. The fleas were so full on my dogs they couldn't even jump. They were, like, *lounging* on my dogs. Oh, and my son is at this stage that he puts everything in the toilet bowl.

## Wednesday, September 4, 1996
Actress Estelle Getty (*Golden Girls*)
Actress and model Isabella Rossellini
Actor Vincent Perez (*The Crow: City of Angels*)
Soap star Robin Mattson (*All My Children*)

ROSIE: Oh, my Lord, the problem I started in my building. I started a riot. For the record, my apartment building is flea-free.
ROSIE: Do I look different? I'll tell ya why. I'm wearing a Wonder Bra. I feel like I have superpowers. They didn't used to make Wonder Bras in my size. But now they do.
ROSIE TO ESTELLE GETTY: You've been married forty-nine years. How's your husband?
GETTY: How the hell should I know?

## Thursday, September 5, 1996
Actress Whoopi Goldberg (*The Associate*)
Singer Tramaine Hawkins performs.
Actress Mary Kay Place (*Manny & Lo*)

## Friday, September 6, 1996
Actress Kate Mulgrew (*Star Trek: Voyager*'s Captain Janeway)
A visit and a song from Kermit the Frog (and Gonzo)
Stage and screen star Patti Lupone (Broadway's *Master Class*) sings.

## Monday, September 9, 1996
Actress and new children's book author Jamie Lee Curtis
Actress Lee Meriwether (*All My Children*)

Actor John Turturro (*Grace of My Heart*)
Jazz saxophonist Dave Koz sits in with the band.

### Tuesday, September 10, 1996
Actress and talk-show host Ricki Lake
Talk-show pioneer Virgina Graham

On yesterday's show, Mayor Ed Rendell of Philadelphia was in the audience, part of an hourlong celebration of the show's upgrade to 11:00 A.M. on that city's WPVI-TV (where it had formerly been slotted at 2:00 A.M.).

As Rosie opened today's show, she was informed that she had a telephone caller: Mayor Rendell phoning in from Philadelphia, apparently with some subsequent good wishes. What happened next was heard only by affiliates with a live feed of the program; everyone else heard an edited version. The caller's comments were bleeped entirely, and a small box at the bottom covered up the original subtitle "On the Phone: ED RENDELL," with the words "CRANK CALL." Here's what was said:

ROSIE: Okay, who's on the phone, hello, phone person?
CALLER: [*In a smooth voice*]: Hellooo. Rosie, this is Mayor Rendell.
ROSIE: Mayor Rendell from Philadelphia?
CALLER: Yes. [*Drops suave voice*] Howard Stern says you're a fat pig, you know that?
ROSIE: Who did what?
CALLER: Howard Stern says you're a fat pig.
ROSIE: Oh. [*Adopts fake-bubbly manner*] Really interesting. Thanks for calling!
CALLER: You're welcome, you fat pig!

Rosie recovered fairly well, but it was obvious that she was stunned by the incident. She was also very upset with her staff for being fooled by the caller and allowing him on the air. She was especially disappointed in her producer, Daniel Kellison, and this mistake probably had something to do with his being fired only six weeks later. Turns out this was the same prank caller who had once gotten through to Larry King on his television show and asked why Larry couldn't stay married.

**Wednesday, September 11, 1996**

Actress, author, and comedian Brett Butler (*Grace Under Fire*)

Actress Halle Berry (*A Rich Man's Wife*)

Actor Jay Thomas (the upcoming film A *Smile Like Yours*)

Blues artist Keb'Mo sits in with the band.

Rosie starts a ten-day countdown until she finally gets to meet Tom Cruise at the American Cinemathèque Moving Picture Ball in Los Angeles. This included a flip-chart counting down the days and paper dolls to ask the audience to help her decide what to wear.

**Thursday, September 12, 1996**

Emmy Award–winning sitcom star Cybill Shephard (*Cybill*)

Actor Eric Stoltz (*Grace of My Heart; 2 Days in the Valley*)

From his long-running, one-man off-Broadway show *Defending the Caveman*, Rob Becker

**Friday, September 13, 1996**

Actress Tiffani Amber Thiessen (*Beverly Hills 90210*)

Former stuntperson and author Heidi Von Beltz (*My Soul Purpose*)

**Monday, September 16, 1996**

The multitalented Bette Midler (*The First Wives' Club*)

Pop singer Bryan Adams performs from his CD *18 Till I Die*.

Actor Sean Nelson (*American Buffalo*)

Rosie introducing Bette Midler: "As far as I'm concerned, our first guest is quite simply the Queen of All Things. Ladies and gentlemen, the one, the only, Emmy-winning, Grammy-winning, Tony-winning, Golden Globe–winning, Oscar-nominated, Her Highness, Royalty, Bette Midler." Rosie then got down on her knees and bowed to her idol in an "I'm not worthy" gesture.

**Tuesday, September 17, 1996**

Actor Hugh Grant (*Extreme Measures*)

Singer and now painter Tony Bennett shows off his new book of paintings.

Funnyman Jon Stewart
Legendary singer Rosemary Clooney performs one of her classics.

**Wednesday,
September 18, 1996**
Comic actor and drummer
  Dan Aykroyd
Actor Karyn Parsons
  (TV's *Lush Life*)

Dan and Rosie both show
off their skills on drums,
doing a very impressive
"battle of the drums"
segment.

**Thursday, September 19, 1996**
Actress Valerie Bertinelli (the upcoming TV movie *Two Mothers For
  Zachary*)
Country star Waylon Jennings performs

**Friday, September 20, 1996**
Actress Goldie Hawn (*The First Wives' Club*)
Actor Andrew Shue (*Melrose Place*)
Singer Natalie Merchant performs.
Soap couple Darnell Williams and Debbie Morgan (*The City*)

Tomorrow night Rosie meets Tom Cruise in Los Angeles as she emcees
an awards show for him.

**Monday, September 23, 1996**
Actor Tim Allen (*Home Improvement*)
Supermodel turned movie producer (*Extreme Measures*) Elizabeth
  Hurley
The director and star of the movie *Big Night*, Stanley Tucci
Singer Billy Porter performs his single from *The First Wives' Club*
  soundtrack.

**Tuesday, September 24, 1996**
Actor Michael J. Fox (*Spin City*)
Actress Teri Hatcher (*Lois & Clark*)
Country singer Vince Gill performs from his CD *High Lonesome Sound*

**Wednesday, September 25, 1996**
Comedian Ellen Degeneres (*Ellen*)
TV icon Shirley Jones (*The Partridge Family*)
Supermodel and recurring show feature Iman "Listen to Iman"
A performance from country singer Trisha Yearwood

Supermodel Iman, who worked with Rosie on the film *Exit to Eden*, presents offbeat advice in this first of several segments called "Listen to Iman." For example, Katie Couric asked, "I'm so sick of being called cute and perky. What should I do?" Iman's advice: "Katie, listen to Iman: Kill a drifter."

ROSIE: So, lots of rumors in the press about Ellen Morgan. Let's straighten the whole thing out. What's going to happen to Ellen Morgan?

ELLEN: We were really trying to build this up slowly and reveal it in a way that would change people's opinions. We do find out that the character is Lebanese.

ROSIE: Just out of the blue?

ELLEN: No, there have been clues. You've seen her eating hummus, and a big, big fan of Casey Kasem and Kathy Najimy.

ROSIE: Hey! I'm a big fan of Casey Kasem. Listen . . . (Rosie pushes a button on the DigiCard, and you hear Casey say, "You go, girl!")

ROSIE: Maybe *I'm* Lebanese!

ELLEN: You could be Lebanese.

ROSIE: I could be Lebanese myself. I didn't know that.

ELLEN: That's odd. Sometimes I pick up that you might be Lebanese.

ROSIE [*nods*]: Yeah. Well, I think that's great. A lot of networks wouldn't take the risk.

ELLEN: Half of Hollywood is Lebanese.

ROSIE: Really? People don't know.

(We all get the joke now that Ellen has outed herself.)

**Thursday, September 26, 1996**

Rosie welcomes two legends of television:

Carol Burnett and Mister (Fred) Rogers

Former *Who's the Boss?* star Alyssa Milano talks about her new movie
*Glory Days*

Singer Suzanne Vega performs from her new CD, *9 Objects of Desire.*

**Friday, September 27, 1996**

*World News Tonight* anchor Peter Jennings

*Beverly Hills 90210*'s Tori Spelling

Supermodel Cheryl Tiegs

Comedian and TV actor Tom Rhodes (*Mr. Rhodes*)

**Monday, September 30, 1996**

Rosie welcomes talk-show host Jerry Springer

*Beverly Hills 90210*'s Tiffani-Amber Thiessen

Dance diva Cece Peniston performs from her new CD.

Injured stuntwoman Heidi Von Beltz talks about her book *My Soul
Purpose.*

**Tuesday, October 1, 1996**

Oscar-winning actress and fitness maven Jane Fonda (*Cooking For
Healthy Living*)

Actress Nicolette Sheridan from the upcoming TV movie *The People
Next Door*

Award-winning playwright Neil Simon talks about his forthcoming
memoir, *Rewrites.*

The Goo Goo Dolls perform.

ROSIE: John F. Kennedy Jr. and his girlfriend were married. It was an
uneventful ceremony, except when the preacher asked if anyone
objected to their union, half the women in America yelled out, "I do!"

**Wednesday, October 2, 1996**

Former Rosie costar Tom Hanks (*Sleepless in Seattle*) talks about his
directing and screenwriting debut (*That Thing You Do*).

Actor Dom DeLuise

A performance from country legend Willie Nelson

For the first time since the show began, Rosie forgoes the prepared jokes and the taped-to-the-desk routine to simply ad-lib anecdotes about her previous evening. Although it would take another six months or so, this what-I-did-last-night dialogue with bandleader John McDaniel would eventually become the standard set piece for her opening monologues.

Also on this show Rosie borrowed Groucho Marx's "Magic Word" from *You Bet Your Life*. If one of her guests said the word, a little swing would come down from ceiling with an Elmo doll on the swing and the secret word on his lap. And each member of the studio audience would win an Elmo doll. She used this a couple of more times over the next few weeks, and then it was (thankfully) dropped.

Tom Hanks showed a clip from *A League of Their Own* in which Rosie tripped over a microphone cable on the baseball field.

**Thursday, October 3, 1996**
Actress Katey Sagal (*Married . . . With Children*)
Actor Tony Shaloub (*Big Night*, *TV's Wings*)
Singer Phoebe Snow performs.
We learn that Katey Sagal was also a Harlette.

**Friday, October 4, 1996**
Rosie talks to Murphy Brown herself,
    Candice Bergen.
Actor and activist Edward James Olmos
    (*Caught*)
Actress Clea Lewis (Audrey on TV's *Ellen*)
"Listen to Iman" segment

**Monday, October 7, 1996**
Comic actress Madeline Kahn (*Cosby*)
Actress Judith Light (from the upcoming TV movie
    *Murder At My Door*)
Singer Shawn Colvin performs a song from her new CD.
Actress Shannon Sturges (*Savannah*)

**Tuesday, October 8, 1996**
*NBC Nightly News* anchor Tom Brokaw
Chart-topping saxophonist Kenny G
Cajun chef and host of *Essence of Emeril*, Emeril Lagasse
Comedian Margaret Smith

ROSIE: I watch you every night.
BROKAW: I heard you say the exact same thing to Peter Jennings.
ROSIE [*almost flustered*]: I have picture-in-picture on my set.

**Wednesday, October 9, 1996**
Actress Demi Moore (Rosie's *Now and Then* costar; currently starring
   in HBO's *If These Walls Could Talk*)
Actress Gillian Anderson (*The X-Files*)
Actor Peter Strauss (*Maloney*)
A performance from the children of the East Harlem Violin Project

ROSIE: Kmart is opening its first store in New York City, on Thirty-
   fourth Street. You can get a blue-light special in the red-light district.

**Thursday, October 10, 1996**—repeat from September 3, 1996
(Originally scheduled guests: Chris O'Donnell, French Stewart, Los
   Lobos)

An electrical fire at 30 Rockefeller Plaza in New York City, the home of
*The Rosie O'Donnell Show*, resulted in replacement of this show with
a repeat and canceled the afternoon taping of Monday's show, featuring
Melissa Etheridge.

**Friday, October 11, 1996**—repeat from September 4, 1996. (Some stations aired a repeat of the July 4, 1996, show, which was actually taped
during the practice weeks.)
(Originally scheduled guests: Wynonna, Geena Davis, Lela Rochon)

Smoke damage from yesterday's fire resulted in replacement of this
show with a repeat.

**Monday, October 14, 1996**—live from the Ed Sullivan Theater
Actress Geena Davis
Actress Lela Rochon
Actor Steve Zahn
Actor and singer Mandy Patinkin
(Originally scheduled guests: Peter Gallagher, Melissa Etheridge, Jamie
    Luner)

This show was originally to have been taped Thursday afternoon, October 10. That's why the guests are different from the original schedule. David Letterman, whose show was on vacation this week, graciously allowed Rosie to use the Ed Sullivan Theater until she could return to her own studio. In another fire-related gesture, Geena Davis gave up leaving on a vacation and stayed in New York over the weekend so she could be on the show. That prompted Rosie to say: "Geena Davis, you rock." Davis: "Nothing's too big a sacrifice for you, Rosie."

ROSIE: "It's so much fun to be here. Why do I feel the urge to do this?"
    Rosie took a pencil and flung it over her shoulder, to the sound of
    breaking glass, à la Letterman.

**Tuesday, October 15, 1996**—
from the Ed Sullivan Theater
Actress turned clothing designer Delta Burke
Teen country sensation LeAnn Rimes performing
    from her breakout CD *Blue*
Comic actor Robert Klein
Actor Bill Pullman

ROSIE: We asked Urkel [of TV's *Family Matters*]
    to be on the show, and he said, "No."

Rosie was overwhelmed by Delta Burke, whom
she had never met. "I loved her. I just met her and felt a real connection."

**Wednesday, October 16, 1996**—from the Ed Sullivan Theater
Rosie says hello to television legend Mary Tyler Moore.
New York Yankee star pitcher Andy Petitte

*The Nanny*'s Charles Shaughnessy
The cast from *Smokey Joe's Café*

ROSIE: If I had a butt like Sharon's [Lawrence, of *NYPD*], I would do this show naked right now. (Then Rosie stood up and turned her back to audience and bent over!)

Rosie showed us a composition book filled with notes she compiled while watching the *Mary Tyler Moore Show*. "I used to watch every episode of the *Mary Tyler Moore Show* and take notes and copy it over into my Mary Tyler Moore book." She started with the first episode in 1970, through the closing episode on March 17, 1977.

**Thursday, October 17, 1996**—from the Ed Sullivan Theater
Actress Ann-Margret (from the upcoming TV movie *Blue Rodeo*)
A performance from singer Chris Isaak
Animal expert Vicky Croake
Actor David Charvet

The true facts are revealed that Jaleel "Urkel" White didn't diss Rosie, it was his agent! Jaleel loves the show, and Rosie apologized to him for thinking that he dissed her. Rosie: "Highly replaceable agent, I might add."

Vicky brought a cougar, a Siberian tiger, an African hedgehog, a marmoset, and a Canadian lynx. It's obvious that Rosie is not at all comfortable around strange animals.

ANN-MARGRET: You look like you're having a really good time.
ROSIE: Well, I am, when I meet people I really adore.
ANN-MARGRET: Do you really talk like that?

**Friday, October 18, 1996**—back home in her studio at 30 Rockefeller Plaza.
Rosie chats with supermodel Cindy Crawford.
Stage and screen actress Linda Lavin (currently in Broadway's *Cakewalk*)
Comedian and author Al Franken (*Rush Limbaugh Is a Big Fat Idiot*)
A performance from breakout musical group the Wallflowers

Opening takeoff from *The Wizard of Oz*: Rosie is in the Ed Sullivan Theater telling John McDaniel that she wants to go home. Rosie has her magic red sneakers on, and John tells her that she can go home; she just has to believe. In black and white, Rosie awakens in her own studio, surrounded by the band—John, Tracy, Mo, Ray, and Rodney—and the wizard? The wizard is Letterman regular Calvert DeForest. who says, "Hit it, John!"

ROSIE: Only seventeen days left until the election, or as I like to refer to it, Bob Dole's retirement party.

ROSIE: You know why Cindy Crawford looks the way she does? She never heard of Drake's cakes!

## Monday, October 21, 1996

Actor Mark Harmon (*Chicago Hope*)
Country singer turned talk-show host Naomi Judd
Singing sensation Luther Vandross tries to perform (sound problems).
The one-and-only Rip Taylor
Tennis legend Chris Everet

When Luther Vandross tried to perform, there was no sound coming from the band's keyboard, which was supposed to play the song's intro. After several people quickly tried to correct the problem, Rosie came over and said, "It's a live show. We are gonna go to commercial and fix it." After the break, we learned that the difficulty could not be found, so Luther would return to the show soon to perform. Interestingly, this sets up the incredible Luther Vandross/Roberta Flack reunion duet that occurred just four days later.

## Tuesday, October 22, 1996

Actor Liam Neeson (*Michael Collins*)
Chart buster Michael Bolton performs.
Photographer William Wegman (*William Wegman's Mother Goose*)
Comic actress Andrea Martin (soon to open in *Candide* on Broadway)

Rosie's entrance each day begins with little "dance" from the curtain to her mark. In rhythm with her theme song she takes small, bouncing steps while snapping her fingers or moving her hands back and forth a little at her waist. Well, it seems Rosie read a message last night on America Online from a man who wrote that he hated her show-opening dance. "A man wrote to say he hates that little dance I do when I walk out. He also said he hates that I tell jokes at the beginning of the show. What am I supposed to do? This man hated everything."

She didn't do anything different for this morning's opening, but she mentions the message several times during the show and eventually responds on the November 4, 1996, show.

### Wednesday, October 23, 1996

Actor Matt LeBlanc (*Friends*)

Actress Annie Potts (star of the TV version of the hit movie *Dangerous Minds*)

Seventies singing sensation Bobby Sherman (author of *Still Remembering You*)

Actress Cathy Moriarty cooks.

ROSIE: Scientists have determined that a low-fat diet may not be beneficial to your health. . . . Today there are thighs clapping everywhere.

Matt LeBlanc presented Rosie with a large bouquet of flowers "as a last-ditch effort," he said, "to take you away from your infatuation with Tom Cruise. And if you just want to be friends . . . well, that's *not* okay."

ROSIE: I'm trying to keep my options open in case things with Nicole don't work out for him.

LeBLANC: I understand. (*dejected look*)

Bobby Sherman is another of Rosie's teenage idols. "He has the Dick Clark gene; he never ages." Rosie asks Sherman to sing his 1970 hit "Easy Come, Easy Go," which he does, even going up into the audience to dazzle the ladies.

### Thursday, October 24, 1996

Actor Tim Daly (*The Associate;* TV's *Wings*)

Actor and Calvin Klein underwear model Antonio Sabato Jr. (*Melrose Place*)

Funnyman Jon Lovitz (*High School High*)

Actress Nancy Travis (TV's *Almost Perfect*)

We finally get to meet the members of the band. Rosie introduces them all.

### Friday, October 25, 1996

Actress Sissy Spacek (*The Grass Harp* and HBO's *If These Walls Could Talk*)

A special reunion performance from singers Luther Vandross and Roberta Flack

Actress Rosetta Lenoire (TV's *Family Matters*)

Author Jonathan Kozol (*Amazing Grace*)

This is the first time Luther and Roberta have sung a duet on television. Luther was a backup singer for Roberta until she fired him for no other reason than to force him to pursue a solo career.

### Monday, October 28, 1996

From the *Nanny*, actress Fran Drescher

Hip-hop sensation A Tribe Called Quest

Actress Lee Meriwether (*All My Children*)

Actress Nell Carter

This show was prerecorded to be shown on Wednesday. (There are several references to "tomorrow" being Halloween.) Rosie spent the prior weekend in Los Angeles shooting Kmart commercials, visiting Madonna and her new baby, and attending Paula Abdul's wedding, so this show was moved up so she could stay an extra day.

Joey Kola, the comic who "warms up" the audience each day, also selects each show's opening announcer. Rosie has him tell about a mother who offered him $1,000 in cash if he would choose her daughter to "do the announcing." Joey said he turned her down. "Wait a minute," said Rosie. "She put a thousand dollars cash in your hand and you said, 'No?'" "I can't," Joey said, claiming that he's not the person who decides who does the announcing. When Joey wasn't looking, Rosie mouthed that Joey alone chooses who does the announcing. Instead of the daughter, today he selected a grandmother from New Jersey.

**Tuesday, October 29, 1996**—repeat from July 26, 1996

**Wednesday, October 30, 1996**
Actress Kirstie Alley (*Veronica's Closet*)
The one and only RuPaul (singer; host of VH1's *The RuPaul Show*)
Actor Gavin MacLeod (*The Love Boat* and *Mary Tyler Moore*)
Comic actor Steve Harvey (from the Warner Bros. Network's *Steve Harvey Show*)

Kirstie gave Rosie a special gift—Tom Cruise's home phone and car-phone numbers. Rosie: "These numbers will be tattooed on my thigh by tomorrow morning."

**Thursday, October 31, 1996**
Actress Phylicia Rashad (*Cosby*)
Pop music legend Phil Collins performs from his new CD *Dance Into the Light*
Director Garry Marshall (*Dear God*)

Phil and Rosie both did voices for Disney's animated feature *Tarzan*, due summer of 1998.

**Friday, November 1, 1996**
TV legend Carol Burnett
Action hero, actor Kevin Sorbo (*Hercules: The Legendary Journeys*)
Rocker John Mellencamp performs from his latest CD *Mr. Happy Go Lucky.*

ROSIE: Barbra, if you're listening, dial 1-800-ROSIE.

Carol, of course, did her famous Tarzan yell for Rosie.

**Monday, November 4, 1996**
Legendary newsman Walter Cronkite
Chart topper Lionel Richie performs.
Chef extraordinaire Julia Child
Actor Kenny Blank (TV's *The Parent Hood*)

Because of a complaint Rosie got about her little opening dance (October 26, 1996), she demonstrates some other possibilities. She bunny-hops, does the hokey-pokey, makes like Zorba the Greek, does the Macarena, tries disco dancing to "Staying Alive," and finishes with the tango!

Walter celebrated his eightieth birthday. Rosie helped him blow out all the candles.

Julia admits to a fondness for McDonald's french fries.

**Tuesday, November 5, 1996**
Actor Mel Gibson (*Ransom*)
From TV's *I Dream of Jeannie*, actress Barbara Eden
Singer Paul Anka performs.

Paul, who wrote the song "Puppy Love" that Rosie forced Donny Osmond to sing, says that only *he* can properly sing that song to Rosie, with these new lyrics:

> Way off base that Donny Osmond,
> That canine costume should it fit,
> Got himself into the dog house,
> Acting like a little ShihTzu.

**Wednesday, November 6, 1996**
*Late Night* host Conan O'Brien
Jan Brady herself, actress Eve Plumb
Rapper turned actress Queen Latifah (*Set It Off*; TV's *Living Single*)

The highlight of today's program was hearing Maya Angelou recite her poignant poetry to the scat singing of R & B artists Ashford and Simpson.

**Thursday, November 7, 1996**
Actor David Hasselhoff (*Baywatch*)
Actress Susan Dey (*Partridge Family, LA Law*)
Actress Jackee Harry (TV's *Sister, Sister*)
Singer Huey Lewis performs.

**Friday, November 8, 1996**
The one-and-only Bill Cosby
R & B diva Chaka Khan performs.
Actor Gary Sinise (*Ransom*)

**Monday, November 11, 1996**
Actor John Lithgow (*3rd Rock from the Sun*)
Actor Matthew Fox (*Party of Five*)
From the miniseries *Pandora's Clock*, actress Daphne Zuniga
Children's TV favorites Shari Lewis and Lambchop

ROSIE: I went to the premiere of a new movie last night called *The Mirror Has Two Faces*, starring and directed by Barbra Streisand. (Rosie attended the reception afterward at Tavern on the Green. Near 11:00 P.M., as Rosie went to the cloak room to leave the party, Streisand arrived, walked over to Rosie, extended her hand, and said: "Thank you for being so kind to me on your program." Rosie told the audience: "My heart stopped.")

Chris Velarde is invited out of the audience to come onstage, where he proposes to his girlfriend, Lisa. Rosie presented the happy couple with special *Rosie O'Donnell Show* jackets that read: "I Got Engaged!" Rosie mentions that Daphne has been on the show before—for one of the practice shows that has never aired.

**Tuesday, November 12, 1996**—Rosie's 100th Show Celebration!
Actor Jeff Bridges (Streisand's costar in *The Mirror Has Two Faces*)

Country great Reba McEntire performs.
TV's *That Girl*, actress Marlo Thomas

### Wednesday, November 13, 1996
A performance from Barry Manilow
Actress Cheryl Ladd (*A Tangled Web*)
Actress Blair Underwood (TV's *High Incident*)
Actress Brenda Vaccaro (*The Mirror Has Two Faces*)
In honor of Rosie's 101st show, Ronald McDonald brings Rosie the *101 Dalmatians* Happy Meal toys.

### Thursday, November 14, 1996—Rosie's Look-alike Day!
Actor Burt Reynolds (*Mad Dog Time*)
Mrs. Brady herself, actress Florence Henderson
Singer Mary Chapin Carpenter performs.
Jazz saxophonist Joshua Redman sits in with the band.

The entire audience was dressed in black suits with white shirts and included a few men, a couple of children and at least one midget, all looking more or less like Rosie. The guest introductions were done by a few of the more convincing look-alikes.

### Friday, November 15, 1996
Pop superstar Elton John performs.
The Dutchess of York, Sarah Ferguson

Rosie told Elton how her father would come home drunk and listen for hours to Elton's recording of "Levon." Elton sang it for Rosie, and it brought tears to her eyes.

Rosie gets so many questions about Madonna and her new baby, she decided to call Madonna near the end of the show. (This was about 7:50 A.M. in California.):

ROSIE: Hi, Mo! How's the baby?
MADONNA: Why are you calling me so early?

ROSIE: So many people ask me about you and your baby. How's the baby?

MADONNA: She's great!

ROSIE: How are you?

MADONNA: Great, except I am suffering from sleep deprivation, so I ask, Why are you calling me?

ROSIE: I am sitting here with Sarah Ferguson.

MADONNA: Great, give her my love and tell her I want a free book!

ROSIE [*To Sarah*]: She wants a free book.

SARAH: Yeah, sure.

**Monday, November 18, 1996**
Soap superstar Susan Lucci (*All My Children*)
Actor Rob Schneider (*Men Behaving Badly*)
Gilligan's Mary Ann, actress Dawn Wells
Country star Alan Jackson performs.

**Tuesday, November 19, 1996**
Actress Heather Locklear (*Melrose Place*)
Singer Natalie Cole performs from her CD *Stardust*.
Actor Delroy Lindo (*Ransom*)
Octogenarian chef Marjorie Johnson
ROSIE: This is a really good job. How'd I get this? I'm really lucky.

**Wednesday, November 20, 1996**
Legendary actress Lauren Bacall (*The Mirror Has Two Faces*)
Country superstar Garth Brooks
Actor and director Emilio Estevez (*The War at Home*)
From *ER*, actor and director Eriq La Salle (director of HBO's movie *Rebound*)

**Thursday, November 21, 1996**
From *Friends*, actress Courteney Cox
Pop superstar Mariah Carey
Comic actor Phil Hartman (*Jingle All the Way*; TV's *Newsradio*)

### Friday, November 22, 1996

Superman himself, actor Dean Cain
   (*Lois & Clark*)
From *Melrose Place*, actor Thomas Calabro
Seventies icon David Cassidy

ROSIE TO AUDIENCE: Stop it! You are out of control.
   What do you think this is, *The Ricki Lake Show?*

Dean Cain said that often he says to himself: "I'm
a grown man. What am I doing in these tights?"
   Rosie got David to sing his signature song, "I
Think I Love You."

### Monday, November 25, 1996

Actress Glenn Close (*101 Dalmatians*; *Mars Attacks!*)
Actor Martin Sheen
Actor Malik Yoba (TV's *New York Undercover*)
Jazz violinist Vanessa-Mae performs.

ROSIE: A study has found that people who work at home are more flexible than people who work at the office. And people who work for
   Gumby are more flexible than anyone.

### Tuesday, November 26, 1996

The legendary actress Angela Lansbury
Actor Hector Elizondo (*Chicago Hope*)
Comedienne Julia Sweeney (*SNL* alum; currently on Broadway in *God
   Said Ha!*)
Chart-topping musical group Blackstreet performs.

ROSIE: I don't use the bathroom. I'm a talk-show host. I'm like Barbie
   and Ken: all smooth down there; genderless.

### Wednesday, November 27, 1996

Country superstar Dolly Parton performs from her new CD, *Treasures*.
Star of stage and screen, actress Tyne Daly
Actor Beau Bridges (the upcoming cable movie *Hidden in America*)

Early in her stand-up career, Rosie toured as Dolly's opening act. Dolly's show included a sad little song called "Me and Little Andy," about a small child and a dog who, left all alone in the cold, both die. The crew made fun of Rosie because that song always made her cry.

Dolly tells another story about that song. Seems she got a request to change the words from a man who complained, "It was one thing for the kid to die, but did you have to let the dog die, too?"

**Thursday, November 28**—repeat from September 27, 1996

**Friday, November 29, 1996**
*Dateline NBC* anchor Jane Pauley
Legendary singer and songwriter Joni Mitchell performs from her new
   *Hits* CD.
From *Gilligan's Island,* Ginger herself, actress Tina Louise
Actor Kyle Chandler (TV's *Early Edition*)

**Monday, December 2, 1996**
Action megastar Sylvester Stallone (*Daylight*)
Comic actor Jamie Foxx (TV's *The Jamie Foxx Show*)
Bebe Neuwirth, Lillith from TV's *Cheers* and *Frasier,* performs with
   the cast of the Broadway sensation *Chicago.*

**Tuesday, December 3, 1996**
From *20/20,* newswoman Barbara Walters
Fitness guru Richard Simmons
From TV's classic *Mary Tyler Moore Show,* actress Cloris Leachman
R & B hit makers Tony! Toni! Toné!

**Wednesday, December 4, 1996**
Actress Sarah Jessica Parker (*Mars Attacks!*; Broadway's *Once Upon a*
   *Mattress*)
Actress Stockard Channing (from the upcoming TV movie *Unexpected*
   *Family*)
The musical group Jackopierce performs.

**Thursday, December 5, 1996**
Funnyman Martin Short (*Mars Attacks!*)
Acress Shelley Long (from *Cheers* and the upcoming TV movie *A Different Kind of Christmas*)
Singer Amanda Marshall performs from her self-titled CD.
From *Baywatch*, actor David Chokachi

**Friday, December 6, 1996**
Director Penny Marshall (*The Preacher's Wife*)
International singing superstar Julio Iglesias
Actress Neve Campbell (*Scream* and TV's *Party of Five*)
Toy expert David Hoffman

**Monday, December 9, 1996**
Actor Denzel Washington (*The Preacher's Wife*)
Actress Swoosie Kurtz (*Citizen Ruth*)
Actress Sandy Duncan
Legendary soul performers The Isley Brothers

Rosie went Christmas shopping over the weekend at the Paramus Mall in New Jersey. "I spent the entire day there saying, 'No, I really am Rosie O'Donnell.' Because people would look at me and go, 'You look like Rosie O'Donnell.' 'Yeah, I know. I am her—' 'No, you're not. What the heck would she be doing at the Paramus Mall?'"

**Tuesday, December 10, 1996**—Rosie's big day. She finally welcomes . . .
Superstar Tom Cruise and his costars from *Jerry Maguire:*
Actor Cuba Gooding Jr.
Actress Renee Zellweger

ROSIE: I don't know if you've been watching the show . . . I've got a little crush on you. You don't mind it, do you?
CRUISE: No.
ROSIE: Does it scare you a little bit, like I'm an inch away from being a stalker? Because I fear that I may scare your entire family.
CRUISE: No, they love it.
ROSIE: Nicole's all right with it?

CRUISE: Oh yeah, absolutely.

ROSIE: I just want you to live in my house and mow my lawn . . . I want you to do yard work around my house.

Tom, as usual on talk shows, was not very talkative. Rosie didn't seem to mind, but at the end of the interview she had to resort to playing her DigiCard machine because she ran out of questions to ask.

**Wednesday, December 11, 1996**
Talk-show hostess Kathie Lee Gifford
Singer Neil Diamond performs one of his classics.
Actress Laura Dern (*Citizen Ruth*)

Still aglow from yesterday's Tom Cruise appearance, Rosie sings a song (the tune of "The Morning After"):

> Oh, how I love the morning after
> Visions of Tom dance in my head
> The next time that Tom comes on my show
> That could be the day we wed.

**Thursday, December 12, 1996**
Actress Nicole Kidman (*The Portrait of a Lady*)
Actor James Woods (*Ghosts of Mississippi*)
Comedian Richard Lewis
Kidman told Rosie that her husband, Tom Cruise, is still talking about his appearance on her show.

KIDMAN: That kiss. . . . He looked at you differently than he looks at me.

ROSIE: Really?

KIDMAN: I'm a little jealous.

ROSIE [*Beaming*]: A little threatened?

Rosie shows a clip of James Woods in a *Welcome Back Kotter* segment. James was told at the time that he should pause for the laughter each time he had a funny line. He told the director, "If you can tell me which lines are supposed to be funny, I'll know when to pause."

**Friday, December 13, 1996**
Singer and actress Whitney Houston (*The Preacher's Wife*)
Actor Henry Winkler
Singer Tracy Chapman performs from her chart-topping CD *New Beginning.*

ROSIE: Fifty-two percent of Americans say their favorite Stooge is Curly, 31 percent chose Moe, and 17 percent picked Kato.

Winkler, a Yale-trained actor, told the story of how he got his first role on TV, a small one on the *Mary Tyler Moore Show*, just weeks after he had arrived in Los Angeles.

ROSIE: And all your friends in New York were mad and jealous 'cause you went to L.A. and got something.

WINKLER: And a lot of them said, "We cannot do television. We were trained for the theater. It goes against our aesthetic grain" . . . and then they all came to visit me on the set and said, "Can you introduce me to somebody?"

**Monday, December 16, 1996**
Actress Debbie Reynolds (*Mother*)
Actor William Hurt (*Michael*)
The one-and-only Phyllis Diller

**Tuesday, December 17, 1996**
Actress Drew Barrymore (*Scream; Everyone Says I Love You*)
Country great Clint Black performs.
Actress Courtney B. Vance (*The Preacher's Wife*)

**Wednesday, December 18, 1996**
Actor, writer, and director Albert Brooks (*Mother*)
Actor and director Kenneth Branagh (*Hamlet*)
Singer Natalie Merchant performs.
Actress Kaye Ballard (*The Mothers-In-Law*, one of Rosie's favorite TV memories)

Rosie and Brooks discussed how, during their stand-up careers, they hated being on the road.

BROOKS: I hate hotel minibars.

ROSIE: Yeah, they're deadly.

BROOKS: At home in L.A., I can control what I eat. I put locks on the refrigerator.

ROSIE: Yeah! [*laughs*]

BROOKS: But minibars have every brand of candy, and the pieces are so small you can eat them all. When I was in Washington, the chocolate was on a spring, and I just open the door and boiing, it's in my mouth!

### Thursday, December 19, 1996

Actress Whoopi Goldberg (*Ghosts of Mississippi*)
Actress turned singer Crystal Bernard (TV's *Wings*) performs.
Supermodel turned actress Kathy Ireland
And special guest appearances by Elmo and Luther Vandross

Before singing "Rudolph the Red-Nosed Reindeer" with surprise guest Luther Vandross, Elmo and Rosie bickered briefly.

"You usually have to be about five to come on the show," Rosie reminded Elmo. "And you're only two and a half."

ELMO: What about Parker?

ROSIE: Oh, he's *privileged!*

Later, Elmo says he wants a Cadillac! Rosie says he might just get one. Whenever she mentions a product on the show, she always seems to get it.

This is the last live show of the year. At the end, we see a collection of clips of recent guests all singing "The Twelve Days of Christmas," some of them messing up. The singers include

Here's a bit of a little Rosie ditty to put you in the holiday spirit (Sung to the tune of "I'll Never Fall in Love Again"):

What do you get when the mailman comes?
You get a sticky loaf that's aggravating
With cherries and nuts, it's constipating
I'll never eat fruitcake again . . .

Garth Brooks, Penny Marshall, Neil Diamond, John McDaniel and the band, Elmo, Rosie, Mort and Sylvia Drescher, Tracy Chapman, and others.

**Friday, December 20, 1996**
Actress turned director Sally Field (the upcoming TV movie *The Christmas Tree*)
Actress Bonnie Hunt (*Jerry Maguire*)
Singer and actress Jennifer Lewis (*The Preacher's Wife*) performs.

John and Rosie have a CD—*Holiday Classics*. This is a collection of Christmas standards all sung to the tune of the show's "Who do you look like?" theme (i.e., the notes that are played when Rosie goes into the audience to see what famous people audience members look like).

**Monday, December 23, 1996**—repeat from July 19, 1996
**Tuesday, December 24, 1996**—repeat from September 16, 1996
**Wednesday, December 25, 1996**—repeat from July 22, 1996
**Thursday, December 26, 1996**—repeat from July 24, 1996
**Friday, December 27, 1996**—repeat from July 25, 1996
**Monday, December 30, 1996**—repeat from August 13, 1996
**Tuesday, December 31, 1996**—repeat from August 16, 1996
**Wednesday, January 1, 1997**—repeat from July 9, 1996
**Thursday, January 2, 1997**—repeat from September 20, 1996
**Friday, January 3, 1997**—repeat from September 24, 1996

**Monday, January 6, 1997**
In his first interview as cohost of *The Today Show:* Matt Lauer
Actor Alan Alda (*Everyone Says I Love You*)
Writer and director Nora Ephron (*Michael*)

**Tuesday, January 7, 1997**
Actor Alec Baldwin (*Ghosts of Mississippi*)
A performance from The Artist Formerly Known as Prince
Comedienne Joan Rivers

Rosie to the Artist Formerly Known as Prince: "You know, I've been referring to you as TAFKAP. Do you mind if I call you Taffy?" He responded with a glassy stare.

**Wednesday, January 8, 1997**
Comic actress Tracey Ullman (HBO's *Tracey Takes On . . .*)
From TV's classic *Dallas*, actor Larry Hagman (*Orleans*)
Author Mary Higgins Clark (*My Gal Sunday*)

**Thursday, January 9, 1997**
Pop superstar and actress Madonna (*Evita*)
Actress Lauren Holly (*Turbulence*)

Madonna surprises everyone by walking onstage with a baby in her arms, and the audience thinks it is her new baby girl. But it isn't hers; it belongs to a staff member; Madonna "borrowed" the baby from the show's day-care center.

**Friday, January 10, 1997**
Actress Jamie Lee Curtis (*Fierce Creatures*)
Actress Marlee Matlin (star of the HBO thriller *Dead Silence*)
Actress Barbara Hershey (*The Portrait of a Lady*)

"Jamie Lee Curtis was on two weeks after Christmas, saying she tells her kids that Santa Claus isn't real. I said, 'Yes he is, Jamie Lee. I know he's very real, and he was on the show last week.' I knew there were four-year-olds watching, so I got her off that subject."

**Monday, January 13, 1997**
Comedy superstar Eddie Murphy (*Metro*)
Actress Kim Delaney (*NYPD Blue*)
Comedian Rob Becker (Broadway's *Defending the Caveman*)

Rosie invites a little boy to the stage from the audience, eight-year-old Paul Iacono. He does singing impressions of Ethel Merman and Frank Sinatra. He says, "I love you Rosie; you're the best," and then he leans over and gives her a kiss.

**Tuesday, January 14, 1997**—repeat from June 21, 1996

**Wednesday, January 15, 1997**
Actor Matt Dillon (*Albino Alligator*)
Actor Rocky Carroll (*Chicago Hope*)
Singer Helen Reddy performs.

**Thursday, January 16, 1997**—repeat from October 2, 1996
**Friday, January 17, 1997**—repeat from September 23, 1996

**Monday, January 20, 1997**
Talk-show host Sally Jessy Raphael
From *The Drew Carey Show*, actress Kathy Kinney
Actress Vivica A. Fox (from the new Arsenio Hall show and *Independence Day*)
Singer Englebert Humperdinck

**Tuesday, January 21, 1997**
Actor Kevin Bacon performs with his band, The Bacon Brothers.
From TV's classic *Dynasty*, actress Linda Evans
Actor Frank Langella (currently on Broadway in *Present Laughter*)

**Wednesday, January 22, 1997**
Political activist and host of CNN's *Both Sides*, Jesse Jackson
Actor Michael Knight (*All My Children*)

**Thursday, January 23, 1997**
Actor Chris O'Donnell (*In Love And War* and *Batman & Robin*)
Singing sensation Celine Dion performs.
Actor Rob Estes (*Melrose Place*)

Rosie mentions that she got Magnavox's Web TV last night—and loves it! Within a week she would change her mind, saying she much prefers the more civil confines of America Online.

**Friday, January 24, 1997**
Actor Kevin Kline (*Fierce Creatures*)
Singer Tori Amos performs.
Actor Steve Guttenberg (*Zeus & Roxanne*)
Actor Ossie Davis (*I'm Not Rappaport*)

Where is Luther? Over the next few weeks Rosie will follow Luther Vandross on tour with a large map. This Sunday he will be singing at the Super Bowl, so Luther is in New Orleans.

Steve brings pizza from Long Island's Pappa Lardo's Pizza. Rosie: "I don't think any pizza place should have the word *lardo* in it."

**Monday, January 27, 1997**
Soap star Anthony Geary (*General Hospital*)
Actress Catherine Hicks (*Turbulence*; TV's *Seventh Heaven*)
From Broadway's *Grease*, actresses Tracey Nelson and Jasmine Guy
Author Frank McCourt (*Angela's Ashes*)

**Tuesday, January 28, 1997**
*Today Show* weatherman Al Roker
Actor turned director Vondie Curtis-Hall (*Chicago Hope; Gridlock'd*)
From TV's *Family Matters*, Reginald Vel Johnson
Actress Marcia Lewis performs a showstopper from Broadway's *Chicago*.

**Wednesday, January 29, 1997**
From *Friends*, actor David Schwimmer
Comic actor Damon Wayans (appearing in an HBO Comedy Hour: *Still Standing*)
Actress MacKenzie Astin (*In Love And War*)

**Thursday, January 30, 1997**
Actress Jane Leeves (*Frasier*)
Actor Jack Wagner (*Melrose Place*)
Comic actor Ray Romano (*Everybody Loves Raymond*)
Breakout musical group the Cardigans perform.

Julie Andrews is going to be on the show tomorrow, and Rosie is very excited to meet her childhood idol. Rosie: "I wanted Julie Andrews to marry my father. I wanted her to come and live with me and make me clothes out of curtains. I kid you not!"

### Friday, January 31, 1997
Legendary actress Julie Andrews (Broadway's *Victor/Victoria*)
Actor David James Elliot (*J.A.G.*)

ROSIE [*To Julie*]: It's so weird to meet you because I love you.

As the show ends, Rosie says, "Thank you, Lucie Arnaz." Her fans have wondered about this ever since. Did she mean to say Julie Andrews? Or was there some reason for her to really be thanking Lucie Arnaz?

### Monday, February 3, 1997
Hillary Rodham Clinton
Actor Michael J. Fox (*Spin City*)
From *Sesame Street*, Oscar the Grouch

ROSIE, TO JOHN MCDANIEL: "Ya know, I'm a big fan of the Clintons; I don't know if you've heard."

Hillary brought Oscar the Grouch some White House garbage for his collection.
    Rosie made television history by getting the first lady to sing *The Telephone Song* from *Bye Bye Birdie* with her.

### Tuesday, February 4, 1997
Actress Lindsay Wagner (from the upcoming TV movie *Their Second Chance*)
Bestselling author Jackie Collins (*Vendetta: Lucky's Revenge*)
*Good Morning America*'s Joan Lunden

ROSIE: Look at me crossing things off; I'm so anal retentive now. (Rosie has completely abandoned the daily magazine and newspaper and

instead keeps a list of things she wants and needs to talk about, crossing them off as she goes.)

ROSIE: I'm a big fan of yours! And I have your doll. [*holds up Bionic Woman action figure*]

WAGNER: I'm a big fan of yours. And I don't have your doll. Do you have a Betty here somewhere?

ROSIE: The thing about your doll, though, is it was sort of like a *Charlie's Angel* doll, and then they drilled a hole in your ear and painted it silver.

WAGNER: Do you know how much that hurt? They measured my face—my eyes, my ears, my nose—so carefully, and then they made the doll. And it was Farrah.

## Wednesday, February 5, 1997

Actor Grant Show (*Melrose Place*)
Actress Beverly D'Angelo (*Vegas Vacation*)
Writer, director, and star of the critically acclaimed film *Sling Blade*, Billy Bob Thornton

Rosie tells us that Elizabeth Taylor, who was scheduled to appear on the show later this month, will not be able to do *The Rosie O'Donnell Show* in California. (Liz would be recovering from surgery.)

## Thursday, February 6, 1997

Actress Fran Drescher (*The Beautician and the Beast*; TV's *The Nanny*)
Actress Ving Rhames (*Rosewood; Mission: Impossible*)
Actress Julia Ormond (*Smilla's Sense of Snow*)
Illusionist Joseph Gabriel

Rosie said to John, "I really didn't do anything last night, so I thought you could fill in the time for me."

Later, Rosie and John uncharacteristically bickered about Rosie's not liking coffee.

"Well, don't drink coffee, then," said John.

"I talk to you a little extra, and you get feisty!" retorted Rosie as John backpedaled and, amid nervous laughter, kept saying, "No!"

"All of a sudden you have an attitude," she continued. "You're gonna be forced to listen to Donny Osmond records."

Today is Zsa Zsa Gabor's birthday. "Zsa Zsa and I are friends from way back," Rosie revealed, "from before I was even on TV or anything." She has known her for fifteen years. Rosie would like to have Zsa Zsa on one of her California shows.

**Friday, February 7, 1997**—a special show: Rosie's Commack South High School Reunion
Jackie Ellard, Jeanne Davis, Bob Costas, Ruth Ann Swenson, Kevin Williams, Ciro Gentile, Craig Minervini, Craig Schulman, Laurie Zummo
(All guests attended Rosie's high school, although not necessarily the same years as Rosie.)

ROSIE: The teachers in America need to be applauded every day because they save the lives of kids! I know they saved mine.
COSTAS: My sister still lives on Long Island, and she'll say, "I saw this guy or that guy at the store, and boy, he says he was really your best friend and he loves you and he's so happy. He saw you on the Super Bowl, and he always knew you'd do well." And I'll say, "Oh, who was that?" And she'll say, "Oh, Tommy Desso . . . Charlie Kickler. . . ." And all I can remember is these guys beat the crap outta me.

**Monday, February 10, 1997**—from Universal Studios Hollywood
Legendary talk-show host Merv Griffin
Actor Ed Asner (appearing with Mary Tyler Moore in the TV movie *Payback*)
Ed and Rosie sing a song together to the tune of the *Mary Tyler Moore Show* theme. After they finish, Ed says, "That sucked."

Rosie announces that Warner Books, a division of Warner Bros., is going to make a book of the kid jokes (which will ultimately be called *Kids Are Funny*). All profits will go to charity, and it is expected to be available around Mother's Day.

**Tuesday, February 11, 1997**—from Universal Studios Hollywood
Comic actress Roseanne
From TV's *Frasier* Kelsey Grammer
Actor Randy Quaid (*Vegas Vacation*)

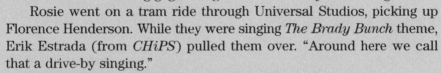

*Rosie on Roseanne:* "She's one of the women who paved the way for other women in television, including myself. Also, after her, every other female stand-up was offered a sitcom because she did it well and brilliantly for years."

Rosie "visits" Rockefeller Plaza. Rosie shows an empty studio except that all the *Sesame Street* characters are there, and they are pretending to be doing a Rosie show: *The Rosita O'Donnell Show* (starring Muppet Rosita). This is the start of a running gag throughout Rosie's stay in Los Angeles.

Rosie went on a tram ride through Universal Studios, picking up Florence Henderson. While they were singing *The Brady Bunch* theme, Erik Estrada (from *CHiPS*) pulled them over. "Around here we call that a drive-by singing."

Rosie and Roseanne have a fun time singing a duet (to the tune of *The Patty Duke Show*'s theme song):
> We're Rosies
> Identical Rosies all the way.
> One pair of chubby bookends
> It's easy both night and day . . .

**Wednesday, February 12, 1997**—from Universal Studios Hollywood
Actor David Hasselhoff (*Baywatch*)
Actress *Melanie Griffith* (Rosie's *Now and Then* costar)
From countless Disney classics, actor Dean Jones (now in the remake of *That Darn Cat*)

**Thursday, February 13, 1997**—from Universal Studios Hollywood
Actress Brooke Shields (*Suddenly Susan*)

Actress Bridget Fonda (*Touch*)
Singing sensation Chaka Khan performs
Roger the "peanut guy" from Dodger Stadium comes to the audience
   and throws peanuts.

Fonda is starring in a new movie *Touch* with Christopher Walken.
Fonda likes Walken; Rosie thinks he's creepy. The actress also mentioned that she has a seminude scene in the film.

ROSIE: Was Christopher Walken in the scene where you were naked?
FONDA: No.
ROSIE: Because I don't know if I could see it if—
FONDA [*Whispering*]: I wish.
ROSIE [*Exploding*]: You wish! She said, "I wish!"
FONDA: It's just something to dream about.
ROSIE [*Nodding knowingly*]: Are you familiar with Tom Cruise?

**Friday, February 14, 1997**—from Universal Studios Hollywood
Comedy legend Carol Burnett
From *Ink*, costars Ted Danson and Mary Steenburgen
Comic actor Jeff Foxworthy (*The Jeff Foxworthy Show*)

Rosie was a little sad because *USA Today* reported that Scope mouth-
wash did a survey of one thousand of its customers, who voted Rosie
the celebrity they'd least like to kiss. To get revenge, she pulled out a
bottle of Listerine and did a quick endorsement. "We just want to say:
'Scope—you stink!' "

**Monday, February 17, 1997**—from Universal Studios Hollywood
Comic actor and frequent Academy Awards master of ceremonies Billy
   Crystal
Funnyman Drew Carey (*The Drew Carey Show*)
Musical group The Presidents of the United States of America

Billy Crystal and Rosie reveal that at the beginning of their stand-up
careers, they both performed at Dickson's White House Inn on Long
Island.

Elmo is there. Rosie asks Elmo about the fact that she gave him the key to her dressing room in New York and that the Muppets have been messing around on the set!

**Tuesday, February 18, 1997**—from Universal Studios Hollywood
Actor Paul Reiser (*Mad About You*)
From *Friends*, actress Lisa Kudrow
Actress Patricia Richardson (*Home Improvement*)

ROSIE: Thank you for doing the show.
REISER: Oh, it's my pleasure. This is so fun. I watch you, I gotta say, like these people, I watch you regularly. And I've known you for many years, so I'm watching you work very hard, and you're singing, and big stars are coming and talking with you, and this is as close to not really having a job as you could come.
ROSIE: You're not kidding, man.
REISER: You're a step away from being in your pajamas and having people come right to your house. And how did you get away with that?

**Wednesday, February 19, 1997**—from Universal Studios Hollywood
It's Superman! Actor Dean Cain (*Lois & Clark*)
Actor Jason Priestley (*Beverly Hills 90210*)
Actress Valerie Bertinelli (from the upcoming TV movie *Night Sins*)

ROSIE: Say nope to Scope. I will teach them to mess with me!
ROSIE: Hey, y'know what? Yesterday was John Travolta's birthday; did ya know that? For forty-three years he's been [*singing*] Stayin' alive, stayin' alive . . . [*speaking*] anybody know the words to that? I don't.

Rosie visits Waterworld because some guys stole her Elmo. Rosie is on a jet ski with a water gun and her Koosh ball shooter. She takes out the bad guys and rescues Elmo!

**Thursday, February 20, 1997**—from Universal Studios Hollywood
Director and Kmart pitchwoman Penny Marshall

A performance from singer Bonnie Raitt
Princess Leia herself, actress and author Carrie Fisher

Carrie, Penny, and Rosie sing "Together Forever" (to the tune of "Wherever We Go"):
> Wherever we go, it's Car, Pen, and Ro
> We'll always get through it together.

**Friday, February 21, 1997**—from Universal Studios Hollywood
Editor in Chief of *George*, John F. Kennedy Jr.
From *3rd Rock from the Sun*, comic actress Jane Curtin
Actor Scott Wolf (*Party of Five*)
Actress Estelle Getty (*Golden Girls*)

Estelle says that she is Rosie's biggest fan. She says she was out the other day and realized she might miss *The Rosie O'Donnell Show*. So she went to the mall, found a store, found the TV section, and had the salesman turn to the right channel so she could watch the show.

**Monday, February 24, 1997**—from Universal Studios Hollywood
Talk-show host turned sitcom star Arsenio Hall
Country sensation Wynonna performs.
Actor Johnny Depp (*Donnie Brasco*)

Rosie played a video clip of her with Elmo in which his December wish for a new Cadillac came true. When the two prepared to drive away, Elmo cracked, "Let's hear some tunes, Rosie. And no Streisand this time." They peeled out singing "Sesame Street" as she and Elmo drove off into the "Sunset" (Boulevard).
    The Cadillac folks came through! The car will be auctioned off in a benefit Rosie is doing in April.

HALL: Now I just hang out, stuff you never get to do. . . . Stevie Wonder took me to watch Prince work, and then Stevie went up onstage with him. And I'm, like [*look of utter contentment*], "I'm unemployed!"
ROSIE [*Laughing*]: Got nowhere to be!
HALL: Did you know Stevie Wonder wears a watch?
ROSIE: A Braille watch?

HALL: I don't know what it is, and you don't wanna ask. But Stevie wears a watch. And I could swear at one point I saw him do this [*looks at his wrist*]. We know he's a genius, and I think he can see, too.

ROSIE [*Cracking up*]: The scandal of the decade!

**Tuesday, February 25, 1997**—from Universal Studios Hollywood
Award-winning actor Jack Lemmon
From *ER*, actor Noah Wyle
The one-and-only Zsa Zsa Gabor
Actress Lea Thompson (*Caroline in the City*)

ROSIE: So Zsaz, you saw my son?

GABOR: Oh, I love your son. But you made a big boo boo with your son.

ROSIE: Should we tell them? You tell them, go ahead.

GABOR: She said, "You know Zsa Zsa, maybe you should be the grandmother of my son." *Well*, I nearly had a heart attack. How could I ever be a grandmother? That ages me. [Gabor is eighty—amazing but true.]

ROSIE: Exactly! When he was a newborn, I talked to Zsa Zsa on the phone and said, "He's so beautiful, and I don't have a mom. Maybe you could be his grandmother?" [*Imitates a shrieking Gabor*] "Don't you ever say grandmother to me!" Click!

Rosie tells Noah that she wants to be on *ER*. She says she wants to play a corpse in the emergency room, with blood all over her.

**Wednesday, February 26, 1997**—from Universal Studios Hollywood
Actor Matthew Perry (*Friends; Fools Rush In*)
Comic actor Jason Alexander (*Seinfeld*)
A performance from chart-topper Babyface

This is the show's last day in Hollywood: "I can hardly believe we're done. We had fun."

Everyone sings "Happy Birthday" to John McDaniel, who is thirty-six today.

JASON ALEXANDER: Did you go to school in Boston?

ROSIE: Yes, I went to B.U.

ALEXANDER: So did I.

ROSIE: But you didn't finish, either, right?

ALEXANDER: No, I got kicked out.

ROSIE: I got kicked out, too. It's this program for acting and they kick you out if they think you're not good enough. But you have to know this: [*Very bitterly*] You were on Broadway at the time, and they kept saying to us students, "Jason *Al-ex-an-der* graduated from here. Jason *Al-ex-an-der* is on Broadway. You're not as good as Jason *Al-ex-an-der*." They rubbed our face in you.

ALEXANDER: Well, you know when I was there they used to say, "Faye *Dun-a-way*". . . . They kicked her out, too.

ROSIE: And do they ever send you letters saying they wanna like give you an honorary something?

ALEXANDER: Uh, I'm a doctor now.

ROSIE: Oh.

As the show ends, we get to see highlights of the last two weeks. Next week, back in New York again.

Rosie and Florence Henderson put a cap on L.A. month with a song "Goodbye L.A." (sung to the tune of "Leaving on a Jet Plane"):

Oh, my bags are packed,
I'm done with the show,
I've got my desk, chair, and Elmo.
I hate to leave L.A., its fun and sun . . .

**Thursday, February 27, 1997**—repeat from November 20, 1996
**Friday, February 28, 1997**—repeat, from November 15, 1996

**Monday, March 3, 1997**
Rock legend David Bowie performs from his new CD *Earthling*.
Actor Dylan McDermott (*The Practice*)
Actress Marg Helgenberger

Rosie says she has big news. She received flowers from Barbra Streisand! Rosie holds up to the camera the note that Barbra sent with them:

Dear Rosie—

It's so nice to see someone win with kindness. I truly appreciate your compliments and sincerity.

Congratulations on your enormous success. And who knows, Rosie, maybe someday. . . .

somehow . .

somewhere . . .

With gratitude,

Barbra          2/97

### Tuesday, March 4, 1997

Musician, actor, and activist Sting (*Gentlemen Don't Eat Poets*)
Actor Adam Arkin (*Chicago Hope*)
Actress Debi Mazar (*Temporarily Yours*)
Young actress Joanna Proccini

Rosie says she will be taking a long weekend this week to attend the Cystic Fibrosis Charity Auction and to ski with Parker and other members of her family.

Rosie asks Sting about a film that he was in, saying: "I loved you in that film *Buster*." Except that it was Phil Collins, not Sting, who was in that movie.

ROSIE: "This is the worst interview I have ever done." (Rosie would poke fun at her faux pas with her song parody "Torn Between Two Rockers.")

Joanna won a contest to play the lead in a revival of *Annie*, but she was fired just before the show opened.

Debi was scheduled for the show that was canceled the day of the fire at Rockefeller Plaza.

### Wednesday, March 5, 1997

Actress Whoopi Goldberg (Broadway's *Funny Thing Happened on the Way to the Forum*)
Actor Chad Allen (TV's *Dr. Quinn Medicine Woman*)
Actress Blair Brown (*Feds*)

**Thursday, March 6, 1997**

Oscar-nominated actress Brenda Blethyn (*Secrets & Lies*)

Actress Laura San Giacomo (TV's *Just Shoot Me*)

Oscar-nominated composer and musician Marc Shaiman (*The First Wives' Club*)

Laura talks about how she steals props and costumes from some of the films she's been in. Rosie complains that they wouldn't even let her keep her baseball mitt from *A League of Their Own*.

**Friday, March 7, 1997**—repeat from November 27, 1996

**Monday, March 10, 1997**—repeat from December 13, 1996

**Tuesday, March 11, 1997**

Actor George Segal (*Just Shoot Me*)

Actress Salma Hayek (TNT's *The Hunchback; Fools Rush In*)

Singer and songwriter Duncan Sheik performs.

Rosie participated in the Cystic Fibrosis Charity Auction. Over the three-day weekend, they raised more than $3 million! Rosie says that Elmo's Cadillac was auctioned off for $90,000. And who bought it? Rosie!

The president of Listerine called last week and said that the company will donate $1,000 for each guest Rosie kisses between now and sometime in May. The donations will be made to Rosie's For All Kids Foundation, and there is *no* limit! She's off to a good start with $13,000 on today's show.

**Wednesday, March 12, 1997**

Comic actress Janeane Garofalo (currently guest-starring on *Law and Order*)

MTV VJ and comic actor Bill Bellamy (*Love Jones*)

Actress Kaye Ballard

Seems that the Listerine folks are surprised! They didn't expect *every* guest to kiss Rosie and really didn't expect some guests to kiss her twice. But they will stand by their $1,000-per-kiss offer.

ROSIE TO KAYE: "Keno is for people who can't handle the excitement of Bingo."

**Thursday, March 13, 1997**
Funnyman Martin Short (*Jungle 2 Jungle*)
Actress Lolita Davidovich (*Jungle 2 Jungle*)
Olympic diver turned author Greg Louganis
A performance from musical group 88 Butterfly

**Friday, March 14, 1997**
R & B legend Roberta Flack performs.
Oscar nominee for *The Crucible*, actress Joan Allen
Actress Mary Louise Parker

Roberta presented Rosie with a thong, underpants that are little more than a G-string. Flack explained that because thongs only come in one size, big gals like Rosie didn't have to feel embarrassed hanging them up to dry in the bathroom. She also said they were great because they didn't leave a panty line. This gift would eventually lead to Rosie's doing an entire week of shows (April 7–11, 1997) dedicated to the thong.

ROSIE: It doesn't feel like dental floss? 'Cause I'd imagine I'd be sitting there like, "Whoo, boy!"
ROBERTA: As a matter of fact. . . . Uh, let me stop!
ROSIE: You're a little feisty today, Roberta.

**Monday, March 17, 1997**—St. Patrick's Day Show
Actress and fitness maven Suzanne Somers
Irish choreographer and dancer Michael Flatley (*Lord of the Dance*)
Broadway actress Helen Gallagher

**Tuesday, March 18, 1997**
Actor Mark Hamill (*Return of the Jedi*)
From the Broadway smash *Chicago*, actor Joel Grey
Comic actor Anthony Clark (*Boston Common*)
Actress Kellie Martin (*Crisis Center*)

**Wednesday, March 19, 1997**

From *Melrose Place*, actress Laura Leighton

Formerly from *Empty Nest*, actress Park Overall (on Broadway in *Psychopathia Sexualis*)

A performance from cast members of Broadway's *Les Miserables*

**Thursday, March 20, 1997**

Actress Halle Berry (*BAPs*)

Oscar nominee for *Secrets & Lies*, Marianne Jean-Baptiste

Actress Jennifer Lopez (*Selena*)

**Friday, March 21, 1997**—Rosie's birthday

Legendary actor Christopher Plummer (on Broadway in *Barrymore*)

Actor Brendan Fraser (*The Twilight of the Golds; George of the Jungle*)

Actress Lucie Arnaz

Rosie found the letters that Lucie Arnaz wrote to her when Rosie was a kid. She couldn't find them the last time Lucie was on the show (August 11, 1996).

Rosie sings this funny song parody about herself (the tune of "Stayin' Alive"):

> Well you can tell by the way I walk onstage
> That I'm no kid—I look my age.
> I still feel great, don't be alarmed
> I've got style and sausage arms . . .

**Monday, March 24, 1997**

Actress Olympia Dukakis (from the upcoming TV movie *A Match Made in Heaven*)

Singer and actress Bernadette Peters performs.

Former Brat Pack actor Andrew McCarthy (currently on Broadway in *Psychopathia Sexualis*)

**Tuesday, March 25, 1997**

Actor Rip Torn (*The Larry Sanders Show*; Broadway's *The Young Man From Atlanta*)

Actor Ralph Macchio (currently touring in the play *How To Succeed in Business . . .*)
Actor Kadeem Hardison (*The Sixth Man*)

Rosie tells us that, starting next week, they will begin taping each show the previous afternoon. This will allow her and Parker to sleep several hours later each day. That way, she can go out more at night, to Broadway shows, charity events, film premieres, and such. She promised that the taped shows will not be edited in any way.

## Wednesday, March 26, 1997
Big-screen superstar Harrison Ford (*The Devil's Own*; the *Star Wars* trilogy)
Singer Robert Palmer performs.
Comic actress Anne Meara (*All My Children; The Daytrippers*)

## Thursday, March 27, 1997
Actor Willem Dafoe (*The English Patient*; on Broadway in *The Hairy Ape*)
Actor Lesley Anne Warren (on Broadway in *Dream*)
TV's John Boy, actor Richard Thomas (*A Walton Easter*)

## Friday, March 28, 1997
Comic actress Christine Baranski (*Cybill*)
Rapper MC Lyte performs.
Funnyman Eddie Griffin (TV's *Malcolm & Eddie*)

## Monday, March 31, 1997
Actress Mia Farrow talks about her memoir *What Falls Away*.
Country great Randy Travis performs from his latest CD *Full Circle*.
Actress Peta Wilson (TV's *La Femme Nikita*)

## Tuesday, April 1, 1997
Teenage World Figure Skating champion Tara Lipinski
Soap star Linda Dano (*Another World*)
Actor Stephen Collins (*7th Heaven*)
A visit from performers from Ringling Bros. Barnum & Bailey Circus

ROSIE, TO JOHN MCDANIEL: What's new? How's life?

JOHN: It's good. I had an incredible night last night.

ROSIE: What'd you do?

JOHN: I had dinner with Barbra Streisand.

ROSIE: Excuse—

JOHN: April Fool!

ROSIE: *Arrrrrggghh!* You piece of turd.

JOHN: I'm sorry . . . I'm sorry.

ROSIE: You are a piece of turd for doing that.

**Wednesday, April 2, 1997**

Producer and director Ron Howard (*Inventing the Abbotts*)

Country legend Tanya Tucker performs and talks about her autobiography.

Actress Jennifer Connelly (*Inventing the Abbotts*)

Author James McBride (*The Color of Water*)

**Thursday, April 3, 1997**

Action star Jean-Claude Van Damme (*Double Team*)

Comedy legend and director Carl Reiner (*That Old Feeling*)

Singer Nanci Griffith performs.

TV's *The Pretender*, actor Michael T. Weiss

**Friday, April 4, 1997**

Actress Bette Midler (*That Old Feeling*)

Actress Meredith Baxter-Birney (the upcoming TV movie *The Inheritance*)

Actress Kathy Baker (*Inventing the Abbotts*)

**Monday, April 7, 1997**—Thong Week (see March 14th show)

Actress Cicely Tyson (the upcoming Showtime movie *Riot*)

Actress Liv Tyler (*Inventing the Abbotts*)

Actor Dennis Farina (*That Old Feeling*)

ROSIE TO LIV TYLER: First of all you're strikingly beautiful. I guess that gets annoying to hear, doesn't it?

TYLER: No.

**Tuesday, April 8, 1997**
From *Good Morning, America*, Joan Lunden
Actor Jon Voight (*Anaconda*)
From TV's classic *Eight is Enough*, actor Dick Van Patten

**Wednesday, April 9, 1997**
Actor Daniel Stern (*Gun*)
Actress Dixie Carter
Actor Rob Lowe
A performance from the cast of Broadway's new *Annie*

**Thursday, April 10, 1997**
Actress Glenn Close (*Paradise Road*; HBO's *In The Gloaming*)
Actress Minnie Driver (*Grosse Pointe Blank*)
Singer Paula Cole performs.
Minnie Driver (*talking about Thong Week*): "It feels like me bum ate me underwear."

**Friday, April 11, 1997**
Actor John Cusack (*Grosse Pointe Blank, Con Air*)
Actress Toni Collette (*Cosi, Muriel's Wedding*)
Musical group Veruca Salt performs.
Actor Doug E. Doug

**Monday, April 14, 1997**
Fitness guru Richard Simmons
Musical group Mint Condition performs.
Actress Diane Lane (*Murder At 1600*)

SIMMONS: If we were married I would get up every morning and I
would be your little aerobic personal trainer!
ROSIE: I don't know if you've realized, but I'm not generally into the
workout routine right now.
SIMMONS: I'll just clean!
ROSIE: Clean is good.

**Tuesday, April 15, 1997**
Actor Jimmy Smits (*NYPD Blue*)
Actress Peri Gilpin (*Frasier*)
Singer Amanda Marshall performs.

**Wednesday, April 16, 1997**
Actor Joe Pesci (*8 Heads in a Duffle Bag*)
Actress Melissa Joan Hart (*Sabrina the Teenage Witch*)
Singer Maureen McGovern performs

**Thursday, April 17, 1997**
Actress Shannen Doherty (the upcoming TV movie *Sleeping with the Devil*)
Musical group INXS performs.
Comedian Howie Mandel

**Friday, April 18, 1997**
Actor Dudley Moore
Actress Justine Bateman (*Men Behaving Badly*)
Actress Jennifer Ehle (*Paradise Road*)
Surprise guest Barry Manilow

ROSIE: You never know when you might need to be in the bush! (After Mutual of Omaha's Jim Fowler presented Rosie with a bush jacket. Mutual of Omaha is donating $10,000 to Rosie's For All Children Foundation. They are also providing Rosie with $10,000 limb insurance on her lips, so that if she can't kiss someone for some reason, she's covered.)

While telling a story about the filming of *10*, Dudley Moore used the word plinth.

ROSIE: What's a plinth? Is that a word?

MOORE: A plinth means a thing on which awards go.

ROSIE: Oh, a plinth. I've never heard of a plinth. I thought it was some kind of Jewish delicacy.

MOORE: Well, I don't know if you can eat it.

**Monday, April 21, 1997**
Actor Bill Paxton (*Traveler*)
Actress Anne Heche (*Volcano*)
Actor David Charvet (*Melrose Place*)

**Tuesday, April 22, 1997**
Actress Christine Lahti (*Chicago Hope*)
Actress Gloria Reuben (*ER*)
Actress Kate Nelligan (Broadway's *An American Daughter*)

**Wednesday, April 23, 1997**
*Friends* star Lisa Kudrow (*Romy & Michelle's High School Reunion*)
Broadway actress Linda Eder performs.
Actress Leila Kenzle (*Mad About You*)

Rosie shows us the beeper that will only give the Dow Jones report. She leaves the beeper near the microphone to prove that the Dow Jones report comes up automatically.

Rosie's Emmy-nominated hairstylist David Evangelista came out to give his first in a series of hair tips—and the beeper goes off!

Although Rosie convinced her to sing a few bars of "The Piña Colada Song," Kudrow sweetly undermined Rosie's very reason for living:

ROSIE: You never did any musical theater? Not even in high school or college?
KUDROW: No.
ROSIE: Never?
KUDROW: No, I'm sorry.
ROSIE: That's okay.
KUDROW: I just don't enjoy musicals. I just don't.
ROSIE: At all?
KUDROW: Uh-uh.
ROSIE: *The Sound of Music?!* Can I just say—
KUDROW: Well, the movie—I liked that a lot.

**Thursday, April 24, 1997**—Barbra Streisand's birthday
Action star Steven Seagal
Actress Sharon Lawrence (*Fired Up*; *NYPD Blue*)
Actress Roma Downey (TV's *Touched by an Angel*)

ROSIE [*To Sharon Lawrence*]: Let's just say, if my butt looked like yours, I'd be naked right now!

**Friday, April 25, 1997**
Actor Anthony Edwards (*ER*)
Actress Rosie Perez (*A Brother's Kiss*)
Singer Boz Scaggs

**Monday, April 28, 1997**
From *ER*, actress Julianna Margulies (*Traveller*, *Paradise Road*)
Actor Steven Weber (star of the ABC miniseries *Stephen King's The Shining*)
Comedienne Paula Poundstone
Sixteen-year-old blues musician Jonny Lang sits in with the band.

**Tuesday, April 29, 1997**
Actor Kurt Russell (*Breakdown*)
Twin actresses Mary Kate and Ashley Olsen (TV's *Full House*)
Musical group Brandy and Ray-J perform.
Rosie announces that *Kids Are Punny* is currently number two on the *New York Times* Best Seller List.

**Wednesday, April 30, 1997**
Comic actor Mike Myers (*Austin Powers: International Man of Mystery*)
Actress Elizabeth Hurley (*Austin Powers: International Man of Mystery*)
Actor Robert Wagner (*Austin Powers: International Man of Mystery*)
A performance by singer Jon Secada

**Thursday, May 1, 1997**

Actress Joan Collins (*Pacific Palisades*)

Actress Joely Fisher (*Ellen*)

Singer Deana Carter

Actor Patrick Dempsey

Listerine presents Rosie with a check for $500,000 to end the $1,000-a-kiss marathon that began last Valentine's Day, when Scope declared Rosie "least kissable." John McDaniel gave Rosie the last kiss.

Rosie and Patrick juggle Koosh balls. So, Rosie has another talent: She can also juggle.

**Friday, May 2, 1997**

Actor Luke Perry (from the miniseries *Robin Cook's Invasion*)

Actor Alec Baldwin

Musical group Indigo Girls performs.

Rosie taught Parker his first complete sentence: "Show me the money."

Alec pulls a lady from the audience, a Swedish girl named Ingelina, to teach her the ways of New York. Alec and Ingelina start to grill pancakes with M & M's while Rosie squirts their mouths full of canned whipped cream.

**Monday, May 5, 1997**

Funnyman Garry Shandling (*The Larry Sanders Show*)

Comic actor Robert Townsend (*The Parent Hood*)

From TV's classic *Knots Landing*, actor Ted Shackelford

Musical group Hanson performs.

Brian Hefferman, a thirteen-year-old Broadway fan, sent Rosie a letter asking to be her escort to the Tony Awards, and Rosie accepts!

**Tuesday, May 6, 1997**

A special show: Rosie's studio audience picks their favorite moments from the show's past season.

**Wednesday, May 7, 1997**

The one-and-only Mary Tyler Moore is reunited with Valerie Harper!
Child actress Emily Mae Young (*Step By Step*)
From *All My Children*, actor Maxwell Caulfield (bumped because of time)

Seven-year-old Emily Mae Young was blown away by Rosie's kindness. Knowing that the young girl's pet hamster had recently died, Rosie presented Emily with a new one. Emily was so excited that she was at a loss for words.

**Thursday, May 8, 1997**

Actor John Goodman (*Roseanne*)
Actor Judd Nelson (*Suddenly Susan*)
Actor Danny Aiello (from the miniseries *Mario Puzo's The Last Don*)
Disco sensation K.C. and the Sunshine Band perform.

Judd was thrilled to see his friend Tracy (Wormworth, the bass player) in Rosie's band.

**Friday, May 9, 1997**

Talk-show host and new mom Ricki Lake
Singer Rosemary Clooney performs.
From TV's classic *One Day at a Time*, Bonnie Franklin

**Monday, May 12, 1997**

Funnyman Martin Short
Actress Kelly McGillis
A performance from the cast of Broadway's *Titanic*

After six weeks of taping each show the previous afternoon, *The Rosie O'Donnell Show* is airing live again. Even though Rosie had promised otherwise, they had been editing and retaping things more and more often, simply because they could. Returning to a live broadcast keeps things "more spontaneous, more exciting."

This is Martin's fourth visit to the show, a record. Rosie presents him with a plaque to commemorate the occasion: "You are the king of all guests."

Kelly lived with an Amish family as preparation for filming *Witness*. One of the boys in the home said to her: "Did you know that women go into heat once a month?"

Kelly gave Rosie a hat worn by Tom Cruise, saying, "You have to smell it."

ROSIE: I was going to wait until commercial. Otherwise, I'd get letters.
   Do you think I'm crazy?

### Tuesday, May 13, 1997
Comic actress Roseanne and Jessica Gruvay from *The Wizard of Oz*
Mary Hart (cohost of *Entertainment Tonight*)
Actor Peter Reckell (*Days of Our Lives*)

### Wednesday, May 14, 1997
Actor Andy Garcia (*Night Falls on Manhattan*)
Actress Tisha Campbell (*Martin*)
Actor Malcolm Gets (*Caroline in the City*)
Actor Robert Cuccioli from Broadway's *Jekyll and Hyde*

Tisha starts singing a song from *Little Shop of Horrors*, then suddenly stops: "I need to dance with David [Evangelista]." Rosie calls David out, and Tisha and David dance while Tisha sings.

### Thursday, May 15, 1997
Rapper and actress Queen Latifah (*Living Single*)
Country-music artist Travis Tritt performs.
Actor Dana Delaney (*True Women*)

### Friday, May 16, 1997
Rosie celebrates her first anniversary by welcoming her first show's
   guests:

Actor George Clooney (*ER; Batman and Robin*)
Soap superstar Susan Lucci (*All My Children*)
Grammy-winning chart topper Toni Braxton performs.

Rosie facts: number of times Rosie has mentioned Tom Cruise: 2,017
Rosie facts: number of songs or song fragments Rosie has sung with
and without guests: 574

**Monday, May 19, 1997**
Superstar Julia Roberts and her costars (from *My Best Friend's Wed-*
    *ding*):
Actress Cameron Diaz
Actor Dermot Mulroney
Actor Rupert Everett

**Tuesday, May 20, 1997**
Actor David Hyde-Pierce (*Frasier*)
Music group En Vogue
Actress Kristen Johnston (*3rd Rock From the Sun*)

**Wednesday, May 21, 1997**
Actress Meg Ryan (*Addicted to Love*)
Actor James Brolin
Musical group Savage Garden performs.

Rosie has Meg's high school yearbook and shows some pictures of her.
At the end of the interview, Rosie gives the book to Meg. It later turns
out that the book had been borrowed from a rental service that makes
celebrities' school yearbooks available to shows like Rosie's. This was
their only copy of this yearbook, and Rosie ends up paying the service
several hundred dollars' compensation.

**Thursday, May 22, 1997**
Actor Jeff Goldblum from the blockbuster *The Lost World*
Singer James Taylor performs.
Soap star Peter Bergman (*The Young and the Restless*)

**Friday, May 23, 1997**
Actress Julianne Moore (*The Lost World*)
The cast of the Broadway musical *Chicago* performs.
Actress Kelly Preston (*Addicted to Love*)

**Monday, May 26, 1997**
In anticipation of Rosie's hosting of the Tony Awards, she presents a *Best of Broadway* show featuring some of the best Broadway performances from her show's past season. Plus Rosie introduces her date to the awards—thirteen-year-old Ryan Heffernan.

**Tuesday, May 27, 1997**
Director Penny Marshall
The cast of Broadway's Tony-nominated *Titanic* performs.
Comedian Bill Engvall

This is Penny's fourth appearance on the show, and she asks Rosie where her plaque is, referring to the one Rosie presented Martin Short when he made his fourth visit.

**Wednesday, May 28, 1997**
Former *CHiPs* star turned author Erik Estrada
Comedian George Wallace

A performance from Sam Harris from Broadway's *The Life*
Rosie's brother Eddie and his wife, Trish, had a baby this morning, naming him Ryan. He is Rosie's first nephew.

**Thursday, May 29, 1997**
From *Seinfeld*, comic actor Michael Richards (*Trial and Error*)
Actor-turned-director Griffin Dunne (*Addicted to Love*)
A performance from the cast of Broadway's Tony-nominated *Steel Pier*

**Friday, May 30, 1997**
Actor Matthew Broderick (*Addicted to Love*)
Eight-year-old singer Paul Iacono
Award-winning author Alice Walker (*Anything We Love Can Be Saved*)

A performance from Lillias White of Broadway's Tony-nominated *The Life*

Tyco sent Rosie a Rosie O'Donnell Doll for her birthday. She is thinking of marketing the dolls at Christmas, with a portion of the money going to charity. Rosie says: "I have a feeling people might enjoy those dolls."

**Monday, June 2, 1997**
Actor Patrick Duffy (*Step By Step*)
Former *ET* anchor turned musician John Tesh performs.
Actor James Mitchell (*All My Children*)

**Tuesday, June 3, 1997**
Actress Patricia Richardson (*Home Improvement; Ulee's Gold*)
Master chef Julia Child (*Baking With Julia*)
Direct from Broadway—a performance from *Chicago*'s Marcia Lewis
Guitar great Dick Dale sits in with the McDLTs.

**Wednesday, June 4, 1997**
Actor and author Charlton Heston (*To Be a Man*)
A performance from David Bowie
Actor Vince Vaughn (*The Lost World*)

**Thursday, June 5, 1997**
Actress Kathleen Turner (*A Simple Wish*)
Singer k.d. lang performs.
Author Kay Willis (*Are We Having Fun Yet? 16 Secrets of Happy Parenting*)

**Friday, June 6, 1997**
Actress Rene Russo (*Buddy*)
Musical group Luscious Jackson performs.
Actress Vanessa Lee Chester (*The Lost World*)—bumped because of time
Author Bill Adler Jr. (*Outwitting Squirrels*)

As Adler, the squirrel man, was explaining ways to keep them off bird feeders by applying Vaseline to the pole, Rene started talking about KY jelly. Rosie, who has been on the floor pretending to be a squirrel, goes over the Rene and says "Ix-nay on the Y-Kay elly-jay!"

All this talk of defending her home against squirrel attack had prompted Rosie on an earlier show to sing "All the Squirrels" (to the tune of "To All the Girls I Loved Before"):

> To all the squirrels I've terrified,
> I made you feel electrified.
> I know you had your needs,
> But try acorns not my seeds.
> Ask any squirrel I've shocked before.

## Monday, June 9, 1997
Soap star Robert S. Woods (*One Life to Live*)
Former *Welcome Back Kotter* star turned children's book author Ron Paolillo
Chef Marcel Desaulniers (*Death by Chocolate*)

ROSIE: "I don't like playing solitaire on the computer because you can't cheat. They should make the game with a cheat button!"

## Tuesday, June 10, 1997
Actress Farrah Fawcett
Singer Steve Winwood performs.
Comic actor Andy Dick (*NewsRadio*)

ROSIE TO FARRAH: "If I looked like you, I would be naked every day. I would do my show naked. I would go shopping totally nude." This bit is from Rosie's stand-up act, and she uses it occasionally with beautiful guests, especially those who have done nude scenes or appeared in *Playboy* magazine.

**Wednesday, June 11, 1997**—repeat from January 31, 1997
**Thursday, June 12, 1997**—repeat from December 12, 1996

**Friday, June 13, 1997**
Actor Jason Patric (*Speed 2: Cruise Control*)
Actress Gail O'Grady (*Two Voices*)
Musical group Erasure performs.
The voice of Disney's *Hercules*, actor Tate Donovan

This is the last live show for the first season. All of the new shows between June 13, 1997, and August 15, 1997, were taped during May and early June.

There's a surprise appearance from Carol Channing, singing a song she wrote about Rosie's squirrel problems, *Rosie Is a Squirrel's Best Friend*.

**Monday, June 16, 1997**
The legendary Lena Horne
Twelve-year-old Vanessa Lee Chester (*Harriet the Spy; Jurassic Park: The Lost World*)
Actor Jonathan Taylor Thomas (*Wild America;* TV's *Home Improvement*)
Rapper Coolio performs.
A performance from *Bring in 'Da Noise Bring in 'Da Funk*

Rosie tells Savion Glover that he looks like Jesus.

The interview with Vanessa was supposed to happen on a show which aired *after* this one (June 25, 1997), but there wasn't enough time.

**Tuesday, June 17, 1997**—repeat from December 17, 1996
**Wednesday, June 18, 1997**—repeat from May 20, 1997

**Thursday, June 19, 1997**
Actress and author Isabella Rossellini talks about her autobiography, *Some of Me*.
Comic actress Kathy Griffin (*Suddenly Susan*)
Actor Richard Kind (*Spin City*)
Singer Laurie Beechman performs.

Laurie's performance is rerun on March 11, 1998, three days after her death from ovarian cancer.

**Friday, June 20, 1997**
Broadway legend Liza Minnelli
From *Melrose Place*, actor Jack Wagner
A performance from singer k.d. lang
Tony Award–winning actress Julie Harris (*The Gin Game*)

This was a special show commemorating the Day of Compassion, one day every year on which the television industry unites to show compassion for those who have AIDS, people who are HIV positive, and to honor those who have already died of AIDS.

**Monday, June 23, 1997**—repeat from May 19, 1997
**Tuesday, June 24, 1997**—repeat from February 3, 1997

**Wednesday, June 25, 1997**
Superstar John Travolta (*Face/Off*)
R & B sensation Mary J. Blige performs.
Actress Josie Bissett (*Melrose Place*)

**Thursday, June 26, 1997**—repeat from January 10, 1997
**Friday, June 27, 1997**—repeat from January 29, 1997

**Monday, June 30, 1997**
Actress Delta Burke
A performance from pop sensation Spice Girls
From *Melrose Place*, actress Courtney Thorne-Smith

Delta Burke shellacs everything. She gives Rosie a necklace of shellacked potato chips.
    The Spice Girls name Rosie "Tough Sassy Spice."

**Tuesday, July 1, 1997**—repeat from January 21, 1997
**Wednesday, July 2, 1997**—repeat from April 14, 1997

**Thursday, July 3, 1997**—repeat from April 11, 1997, and the last day of Thong Week!

**Friday, July 4, 1997**—repeat from January 23, 1997

**Monday, July 7, 1997**
Actor Tim Robbins (*Nothing To Lose*)
Musical group The Brand New Heavies perform.
From *Melrose Place*, actor Rob Estes
Kid cartoonist Andy Holmes

A fan sent Rosie a toilet-lid cover with pictures of Tom Cruise, top and bottom.

Tim is the first guest to hit the drop box with a Koosh ball. The drop box is a wooden box filled with goodies that is mounted on a track over the audience. There's a target on front that, when hit, triggers the opening of the bottom of the box.

**Tuesday, July 8, 1997**—repeat from January 9, 1997

**Wednesday, July 9, 1997**
Comic actor Martin Lawrence (*Nothing to Lose*)
Actress Mara Wilson (*A Simple Wish*)
Author Thomas Kelly (*Payback*)

ROSIE TO THE AUDIENCE: It's weird, but you all look familiar. (Apparently this show was taped using the same audience that saw another show. They tried to bring in a different audience for every taping, even when they taped two shows in one day, but this must have been an exception.)

**Thursday, July 10, 1997**
Actress Jodie Foster (*Contact*)
Actor Robert Pastorelli (*A Simple Wish*)
Actress Laura Innes (*ER*)

**Friday, July 11, 1997**—repeat from May 12, 1997

**Monday, July 14, 1997**—repeat from February 10, 1997, from Universal Studios Hollywood

**Tuesday, July 15, 1997**—repeat from February 11, 1997, from Universal Studios Hollywood

**Wednesday, July 16, 1997**—repeat from February 12, from Universal Studios Hollywood

**Thursday, July 17, 1997**—repeat from February 13, 1997, from Universal Studios Hollywood

**Friday, July 18, 1997**—repeat from February 14, 1997, from Universal Studios Hollywood

**Monday, July 21, 1997**—repeat from February 17, 1997, from Universal Studios Hollywood

**Tuesday, July 22, 1997**—repeat from February 25, 1997, from Universal Studios Hollywood

**Wednesday, July 23, 1997**—repeat from February 18, 1997, from Universal Studios Hollywood

**Thursday, July 24, 1997**—repeat from February 24, 1997, from Universal Studios Hollywood

**Friday, July 25, 1997**—repeat from February 19, 1997, from Universal Studios Hollywood

**Monday, July 28, 1997**—repeat from February 20, 1997, from Universal Studios Hollywood

**Tuesday, July 29, 1997**—repeat from February 21, 1997, from Universal Studios Hollywood

**Wednesday, July 30, 1997**—repeat from February 26, 1997, from Universal Studios Hollywood

**Thursday, July 31, 1997**
Actress Jennifer Aniston (*Picture Perfect*, TV's *Friends*)
Comic actress Kim Coles (*Living Single*)
Actress Erin Murphy (Tabitha from the TV series *Bewitched*, now grown up)

Erin stumps Rosie with a *Partridge Family* trivia question. Under her breath Rosie says, "You'll never be back."

**Friday, August 1, 1997**
Superstar Sylvester Stallone and his costars from the new film *Cop Land*
Actress Annabella Sciorra
Actors Ray Liotta and Peter Berg

Todays opening announcements are done by Bette Midler's aunt, Ethel Midler.

Rosie mentions that Parker is now two and that she is experiencing an itch to adopt another little one.

**Monday, August 4, 1997**—repeat from December 10, 1996
**Tuesday, August 5, 1997**—repeat from March 4, 1997
**Wednesday, August 6, 1997**—repeat from May 2, 1997
**Thursday, August 7, 1997**—repeat from April 28, 1997
**Friday, August 8, 1997**—repeat from April 9, 1997
**Monday, August 11, 1997**—repeat from May 7, 1997
**Tuesday, August 12, 1997**—repeat from April 2, 1997

**Wednesday, August 13, 1997**
Emmy nominee, actor Dennis Franz (*NYPD Blue*)
Hollywood heavy, actor Christopher Walken (*Excess Baggage*)
Actress Lisa Vidal (*High Incident*)
Comedian and Rosie's warm-up guy Joey Kola

When Rosie introduced "the always entertaining but mildly frightening" Christopher Walken, she acted somewhat frightened of him. Christopher acted hurt, saying no one he knew thought him scary. Still, he played up the scary role by carrying a case with a skull and crossbones stenciled on it. After a while, he opened the case and pulled out a bouquet of flowers and a heart-shaped box of chocolates.

WALKEN: I hear you collect children's jokes.
ROSIE: Yes, I do. I have a book called *Kids Are Punny*.
WALKEN: I have one. Okay, a duck walks into a drugstore. And he says to the druggist, "Do you have any Chapstick?" And the druggist says, "Certainly, sir, will this be cash or charge?" And the duck says, "Put it on my bill."

ROSIE: That's a good one! Christopher Walken with a kid joke!

Dennis cooks his tuna casserole with Rosie.

**Thursday, August 14, 1997**
Actress Demi Moore (*G.I. Jane*)
Actor Patrick Swayze
Actress Robin Wright-Penn (*She's So Lovely*)

**Friday, August 15, 1997**
Actress Alicia Silverstone (*Excess Baggage*)
Director Rob Reiner
Broadway legend Chita Rivera
Comic actor Chris Tucker (*Money Talks*)

Rob tells a story of being fourteen years old and on the set of the *Dick Van Dyke Show*, which his father, Carl Reiner, directed: "I grabbed Mary Tyler Moore's tush! I got a long lecture from my father."

**Monday, August 18, 1997**—repeat from May 22, 1997
**Tuesday, August 19, 1997**—repeat from May 30, 1997
**Wednesday, August 20, 1997**—repeat from May 29, 1997
**Thursday, August 21, 1997**—repeat from April 23, 1997
**Friday, August 22, 1997**—repeat from April 30, 1997
Leading Ladies' Week (where each repeat features a different major film actress):
**Monday, August 25, 1997**—repeat from April 4, 1997
**Tuesday, August 26, 1997**—repeat from March 6, 1997
**Wednesday, August 27, 1997**—repeat from March 31, 1997
**Thursday, August 28, 1997**—repeat from May 21, 1997
**Friday, August 29, 1997**—repeat from April 10, 1997
**Monday, September 1, 1997**—repeat from April 15, 1997
**Tuesday, September 2, 1997**—repeat from May 14, 1997
**Wednesday, September 3, 1997**—repeat from April 25, 1997
**Thursday, September 4, 1997**—repeat from March 26, 1997
**Friday, September 5, 1997**—repeat from April 29, 1997

**Monday, September 8, 1997**
Singer Billy Joel performs.
Actor Joe Lando (*Dr. Quinn: Medicine Woman*)
Comedienne and special correspondent for *The Rosie O'Donnell Show*
  Paula Poundstone

Rosie suggested that in memory of Princess Diana folks should quit buying tabloid magazines for a year. She understands the curiosity of people regarding celebrities, so go ahead and *read* them while you're shopping. Just don't buy them.

**Tuesday, September 9, 1997**
TV news personality Bryant Gumbel *Private Eye;* host of Emmys)
Basketball superstar Michael Jordan
Superstar musical trio The Bee Gees perform.

A surprise visit by future *Today Show* anchor Matt Laurer
Rosie relegates several of last year's "comedy bits" to a time capsule: her obsession with Tom Cruise, hair tips from David Evangelista, Listerine, and Ring Dings.

**Wednesday, September 10, 1997**
Actor Noah Wyle (*ER*)
Singer Jon Bon Jovi performs.
Comic David Alan Grier (Broadway's *A Funny Thing Happened on the Way to the Forum*)

**Thursday, September 11, 1997**
Actress Michelle Pfeiffer (*A Thousand Acres*)
Lucy Lawless performs (TV's *Xena: Warrior Princess;* Broadway's *Grease*).
Legendary newsman Mike Wallace

Rosie tells us that sometimes she laughs so hard that she, well, needs to wear Depends.

**Friday, September 12, 1997**
Barbara Walters
From Broadway's *Last Night at Ballyhoo*, actress Kimberly Williams
WNBA star Cynthia Cooper
Joey Green, author of *Wash Your Hair With Whipped Cream*

Green's segment inspires Rosie to start a food fight with her stage-hands.

**Monday, September 15, 1997**
Actor and author Kirk Douglas
Actor Scott Wolf (*Party of Five*)

**Rosie List: FAVORITE ACTORS**
Pierce Brosnan
Tom Cruise
Emilio Estevez
John Travolta
Robin Williams

**Tuesday, September 16, 1997**
Actor Tom Selleck (*In and Out*)
Actress Yasmine Bleeth (*Baywatch* and TV movie *Crowned & Dangerous*)
Marilu Henner performs from her role in Broadway's *Chicago*
A performance by country singers Brooks & Dunn

**Wednesday, September 17, 1997**
Academy Award–winning actress Jessica Lange (*A Thousand Acres*)
Penny Marshall
Singer Belinda Carlisle performs.

**Thursday, September 18, 1997**
Actress Kim Basinger (*LA Confidential*)

Actor and Calvin Klein model Antonio Sabato Jr.
Comic actor Andy Dick (*NewsRadio*)
Young accordionist Hunter Hayes

Rosie describes a new candy product, Nestle's Magic. This is "like a Happy Meal toy in a ball covered with chocolate."

Andy Dick strips to his briefs and wildly dances and sings, "I'm the new guy in Calvin Kleins. I look good like you knew I would in sexy briefs."

### Friday, September 19, 1997
Actress Brooke Shields (*Suddenly Susan*)
Country-music superstar Trisha Yearwood performs from her album *Song Book*.
Tennis legend Martina Navratilova talks about her book *Killer Instinct*.

### Monday, September 22, 1997
Stars from the movie *The Peacemaker:*
Actor George Clooney
Actress Nicole Kidman
Actor Michael Boatman

### Tuesday, September 23, 1997
Actress Janeane Garafolo (*The Matchmaker*)
A performance from singing group sensation Boyz II Men
Comic actor Jaleel White (Urkel from *Family Matters*)

Janeane and Rosie complain about Joan Rivers and her satirical humor. This fuels rumors of a minispat between Joan and Rosie.

Rosie retells the situation with Jaleel from her October 17, 1996, show.

### Wednesday, September 24, 1997
Actor and dancer Gregory Hines (*The Gregory Hines Show*)
Actress Christina Ricci (*Ice Storm*)
Singer and songwriter Sarah McLachlan
British TV chefs Two Fat Ladies promote their new cookbook.

**Thursday, September 25, 1997**
Actor Alec Baldwin (*The Edge*)
Actor Russell Crowe (*LA Confidential*)
Actress Jennifer Lopez (*U-Turn*)
Animator Chuck Jones

Alec Baldwin shows his sense of humor—and his hometown rivalry with Rosie—by singing a duet with her (to the tune of "Oklahoma"):
    ALEC: Massepequa, exit 30 off the Southern State.
    Where kids wall-to-wall hit the Sunrise Mall,
    It's the cheapest place to bring a date.
    ROSIE: I'm from Commack
    Where the high school Spartans always win.
    And the action's hot in the parking lot
    Of the lovely Commack Motor Inn . . .

**Friday, September 26, 1997**
Actress Candice Bergen (*Murphy Brown*)
Pint-sized actor Jonathan Lipnicki (TV's Meego)
Dancer June Taylor (June Taylor Dancers)
*Saturday Night Live*'s Molley Shannon

Rosie chats about when she went to a nutritionist, whom she would later call a wacko quacko. Rosie, who knows a good running gag when she finds one, will continue to talk about her wacko nutritionist over the next few months.

**Monday, September 29, 1997**
Actress Whoopi Goldberg
A performance from singer Gladys Knight
Actress Laura San Giacomo (*Just Shoot Me*)

Rosie buys a German shepherd guard dog named Donna, which turns out to be kissy-face loving instead of scary-protective. And Parker loves it too much to return it to its trainer. We won't learn about it for several more weeks, but Rosie also adopted Chelsea Belle over this weekend. That may have something to do with buying the guard dog.

Parker also has a *Building a Skyscraper* video which he just loves, but Rosie can't bear to watch it because it's so boring.

Whoopi says she will not eat eggs; she'll eat things with eggs in them, like cakes, but not eggs.

Laura brings Rosie the mitt Rosie used in *A League of Their Own!* See March 6, 1997.

Rosie and Whoopi don tuxes and sing backup with Gladys Knight.

### Tuesday, September 30, 1997
Actress Fran Drescher (*The Nanny*)
Actor Kevin Anderson (*Nothing Sacred; A Thousand Acres*)
Actress Lee Grant (*Save It, Fight It, Cure It*)
Singer Pat Benatar performs.

Rosie is doing the voice for a couple of cartoon commercials for the California Prune Board, in exchange for a $350,000 donation to the National Breast Cancer Coalition. Rosie shows one of the commercials, in which she is Cleopatra.

Rosie didn't sleep last night because she watched a commercial for Ashley Judd's new film, *Kiss The Girls*, which gave her stomach cramps. Rosie: "It took me three years in therapy to get over *Silence of the Lambs*. No, you won't get me in the theater for that film. I'll be at home watching *Chitty Chitty Bang Bang.*"

### Wednesday, October 1, 1997
Musical superstar and Rosie's idol Elton John performs.
Joost Elfers, food artist and author of *Play With Your Food*
Ten-year-old stand-up comic Josh Peck

Rosie's brother Danny does today's show's opening announcements.

Rosie's book *Kids are Punny* is back on the bestseller lists. And as a result, Rosie wins a bet with her publisher.

### Thursday, October 2, 1997
Talk-show host Regis Philbin
Singers Hall & Oates perform.
Actor Cary Elwes (*Kiss The Girls; The Princess Bride*)

Parker pulled a television set off a shelf, bruising his head. This leads to Rosie's talking about Mallomars, because she ate three boxes of them after Parker's accident.

Rosie has to stall during the opening because Regis is hurrying over from *Live With Regis and Kathy Lee*. Regis teased Rosie, who filled in for Kathy Lee a few times, about her wanting Kathy Lee's job.

Rosie said: "She wouldn't quit, so I had to get my own show."

**Friday, October 3, 1997**
Actress Jane Fonda
A perfomance from *Riverdance*
Actress Kate Capshaw (*The Locusts*)
Actress Emily Mae Young (*Step By Step*)

Jane was on the show in response to Rosie's excitement over the fact that Jane's husband, Ted Turner, is donating $1 billion to UN charities. (Maybe Jane had heard Rosie sing her parody, "One Singular Donation," which she sang to the tune of "One" from the musical *A Chorus Line*.)

Emily still has the hamster (named Jelly Bean) that Rosie gave her the last time Emily was on the show.

**Monday, October 6, 1997**
Actress and singer Vanessa Williams performs.
Actress Jennifer Jason Leigh talks about her two new films, *A Thou-sand Acres* and *Washington Square*.
Actor Thomas Gibson from the TV show *Dharma and Greg*

Rosie sadly tells us that Nestlé's has discontinued their "Magic Ball" chocolate candy with a toy inside (i.e., Nestlé's Magic).

Jennifer's personal trainer, Bob Harper, wants to be Rosie's trainer.

ROSIE: Oh, really? Is he in New York?
JENNIFER: No, he's in L.A.
ROSIE: Thank God!

**Tuesday, October 7, 1997**
Actor Dan Aykroyd talks about his new show, *Soul Man*.

A performance by the singing sisters The Wilsons
Actor Dan Cortese from NBC-TV's *Veronica's Closet*

Rosie plays a call that came in on the Comment Line. The caller says the show was much better when David Evangelista was on it. The caller sounds suspiciously like David Evangelista.

The Wilsons used to be two-thirds of the group Wilson Phillips. Their father is Beach Boy Brian Wilson.

### Wednesday, October 8, 1997
Actor, author, and comedian Paul Reiser (*Mad About You; Babyhood*)
Funnyman Mel Brooks (new book, *The 2,000 Year Old Man in the Year 2000*)
Actor and director Carl Reiner (coauthored *The 2,000 Year Old Man in the Year 2000*)
Singer Billy Porter performs.

Rosie plays another call from the Comment Line that sounds like David Evangelista.

Tyco will be making a "Rosie O'Doll" for Christmas this year, with ten dollars from each sale going to charity.

Rosie sings the mammogram song, which became a classic. (Sung to the tune of "Put on a Happy Face"):

Your boobs are gonna cheer up
Go get a mammogram
No need to pout and tear up
Put them in expert hands . . .

BILLY PORTER: You really know when you've hit the big time when you make the DigiCard.

Rosie wins a bet with Paul Reiser over the fact that Carol Burnett's name was misspelled on the credits of *Mad About You* when she appeared recently.

### Thursday, October 9, 1997
Actor John Lithgow (*3rd Rock From The Sun*)
Actress Parker Posey (*House of Yes*)

Broadway diva Betty Buckley

Rosie plays yet another call from the Comment Line that sounds like David Evangelista.

Rosie's wacko-quacko nutritionist has her eating nothing but red snapper.

## Friday, October 10, 1997
TV's odd couple, Tony Randall and Jack Klugman
Actor Jim Belushi talks about his new TV show, *Total Security* and his new movie, *Gang Related*.
Actress and singer Eartha Kitt
Today we see David Evangelista, caught on a hidden camera, calling the Comment Line.

## Monday, October 13, 1997—the All Kids Show
Superstar twins Mary Kate and Ashley Olsen
Teen heartthrob Jonathan Taylor Thomas (*Home Improvement*)
Actor Matthew Lawrence (*Boy Meets World*)
Singer Alliyah performs.

## Tuesday, October 14, 1997
Actor David Duchovny (*X-Files* and *Playing God*)
A performance by Duran Duran
Olympic superstar Jackie Joyner Kersee

A Hershey candy factory in Connecticut will be introducing a new candy product in November, and Rosie wants to know what it is. Rosie invites any of the Hershey employees to contact the show and assures them that they will not be sorry.

## Wednesday, October 15, 1997
Actor Keanu Reeves (*The Devil's Advocate*)
Actress Victoria Principal (*Love in Another Town*)
Singer Deborah Gibson (Broadway's *Beauty and the Beast*)
Actress Charlize Theron (*The Devil's Advocate*)

Rosie was filling in for Kathie Lee today on *Live with Regis and Kathie Lee*, which made her a few minutes late for her own show.

## Thursday, October 16, 1997
Vice President Al Gore's wife, Tipper Gore
Actor, author, and rapper L L Cool J performs.
Cancer survivor and activist Carol M. Baldwin and son, actor Billy Baldwin

## Friday, October 17, 1997
Singer and songwriter Carly Simon performs.
Actor and rapper Ice-T (*Players*)
Actress Jennifer Love Hewitt (*Party of Five*)

Rosie replays her mammogram song for those who missed it the first time.
Jennifer Love Hewitt agrees to sing, but first she needs a dance partner and requests David Evangelista. The show ends with Jennifer, David, and Rosie singing and dancing to the McDLTs.

## Monday, October 20, 1997
Academy award–winning actor Kevin Kline (*In & Out*)
Pop singer Amy Grant
Roving reporter Paula Poundstone

This is the first Interactive Monday; Rosie has her computer on her desk and chats on America Online during the commercial breaks.

## Tuesday, October 21, 1997
Actor Dennis Franz (*NYPD Blue*)
A performance by Neil Patrick Harris (*Rent; Starship Troopers*)
Film star Joan Allen (*Ice Storm*)

## Wednesday, October 22, 1997
Emmy-winning actress Kim Delaney (*NYPD Blue*)
Scottish TV and film actor Billy Connolly (*Mrs. Brown*)

A performance by rap star Missy "Misdemeanor" Elliot

Rosie has the new Hershey candy, and she was quite disappointed. The candy is a small, hard candy called the Classic Caramel, which also comes in a version with a chocolate center.

Davenia McFadden, who calls herself the "black Rosie O'Donnell," sends Rosie a home video challenging Rosie to a Mary Tyler Moore trivia contest. The video ends with Davenia saying, "Bring it on! Bring it on!" Mary Tyler Moore is scheduled to be on the show November 6, and Rosie accepts the challenge, saying, "You too, Davenia! Get your sorry butt here!"

### Thursday, October 23, 1997
A performance by Salt 'n Pepa
Actor Ethan Hawke (*Gattaca*)
Actress Annie Potts (*Over the Top*)

Rosie asked Annie about potty training her youngest boy. Annie says friends have told her that her older boys will teach him. Rosie: "Just leave it in their hands. So to speak."

### Friday, October 24, 1997
A performance by Wynonna
TV Star Jenny McCarthy
Bestselling author Anne Rice (*Violin*)

WYNONNA: Rosie, you're the only person who can imitate me singing.
ROSIE: It's because I know the secret. You squeeze your butt cheeks.

### Monday, October 27, 1997
Actor Patrick Stewart (*Othello; Star Trek: Next Generation*)
Actor Matthew Fox (*Party of Five*)
Actress Jamie Luner (*Melrose Place*)
Singer Gary Barlow

Jamie is another guest who was supposed to appear on the show on the day of the fire at Rockefeller Plaza.

**Tuesday, October 28, 1997**
Actor Kevin Bacon and his band The Bacon Brothers
Actor Fred Savage (*Working*)
Actress Carol Leifer (*Alright Already*)
Actor Marcus Paulk (*Moesha*)

MARCUS: I don't like chocolate. It makes me thirsty.
ROSIE: Water, Marcus. You eat a little chocolate and you drink water.

Rosie gets Fred Savage, who recently saw Wayne Newton in Vegas, to sing "Danke Shoen." Except that John McDaniel doesn't know how to play the song.

ROSIE: I can't believe it. This is the first time John has been stumped.

**Wednesday, October 29, 1997**
Actress Angela Lansbury (*Murder She Wrote: South by Southwest*)
Actor Patrick Muldoon (*Starship Troopers*)
Actor and comedian David Spade (*Just Shoot Me*)
Olympic gymnast Kerri Strug

**Thursday, October 30, 1997**—the Cinderella Show; all of today's guests appear in ABC-TV's *Cinderella*, which airs on Sunday, November 2, 1997.
Actress and singer Whitney Houston (did not appear)
Actress and singer Brandy
Actress Bernadette Peters
Actor Paolo Montalban (appeared in place of Whitney Houston)

Whitney Houston, giving only forty-five minutes' notice, canceled her appearance, claiming stomach flu. Rosie was visibly upset ("I hope she's *very* ill"), and several times during this and subsequent shows made a point to mention what Whitney had done.

**Friday, October 31, 1997**
The "Queen of All Things," the exquisite Bette Midler
A performance by The Village People
Actor Mark Wahlberg from *Boogie Nights*

For Halloween, today's theme is *The Wizard of Oz*, and the stage looks like the Emerald Forest. Rosie is Dorothy, holding a fake Toto, and even the McDLTs and the stagehands are dressed appropriately. John McDaniel is the scarecrow, Tracy Wormworth is the wicked witch, Mo Goldberg is the tin man, Rodney Jones is the cowardly lion, and Ray Marchica is in drag as the good witch, with a cigar hanging from his mouth. The camera crew is dressed like flying monkeys.

**Monday, November 3, 1997**
Actor John Travolta (*Mad City*)
Singer Bobby Brown performs.
Actress Jane Seymour (*Dr. Quinn, Medicine Woman*)

Rosie dances with John Travolta and eats Gummy Bears with Bobby Brown, trying to see who can stuff the most into their mouth.

   Neither Rosie nor Bobby bring up the recent incident involving Mrs. Bobby Brown, i.e., Whitney Houston.

**Tuesday, November 4, 1997**
Actor David Hyde Pierce (*Frasier*)
Singer Beth Nielsen Chapman performs with superstar Bonnie Raitt.
Actor Jason Gedrick (*The Third Twin*)

**Wednesday, November 5, 1997**
Actress Cybill Shepherd (*Cybill*)
A performance by Steve Lawrence and Eydie Gorme

Last year Rosie appealed to Drake's to bring back the Swiss Roll. On today's show, Rosie shows us Drake's Swiss Rolls. They are back, and a portion of the sales will go to the Cystic Fibrosis Foundation.

**Thursday, November 6, 1997**
Actor Anthony Edwards (*ER*)
Teen country singer LeAnn Rimes sings.
Actor Mandy Patinkin and his mother, Dora Lee (*Grandma Dora Lee's
   Jewish Family Cookbook*)

### Friday, November 7, 1997

Television icon Mary Tyler Moore (*The Dick Van Dyke Show; The Mary Tyler Moore Show*)
Trivia diva Davenia McFadden brings it on!
The cast of Broadway's *The Lion King* performs.

The trivia contest with Davenia and its follow-up on *The People's Court* were choreographed stunts to attract ratings during the November sweeps. McFadden is an actress with small parts in ten films to her credit, having most recently worked with Whoopi Goldberg in *Eddie*, Julia Roberts in *My Best Friend's Wedding*, and Howard Stern in *Private Parts*.

   She was good on the show, but she was no Donny Osmond. Rosie's song parody kind of sums up the Davenia "rivalry" (sung to the tune of "How Do You Solve a Problem Like Maria" from *The Sound of Music*):

   How do you solve a problem like Davenia?
   How do you win a Mary Tyler war?
   How do you find a way to tell Davenia
   That when it comes to MTM she's empty and won't score?

### Monday, November 10, 1997

Movie actor Wesley Snipes (*One Night Stand*)
TV's Gilligan, actor Bob Denver
A performance by singing sensation Harry Connick Jr.!

### Tuesday, November 11, 1997

Academy award–winning actress Susan Sarandon
Singer Naomi Judd
Pop singer Michael Bolton performs.

Rosie starts to tell us an anecdote about last night, being in bed totally nude, when suddenly Al Roker breaks in with a special news report. When we come back to the show, Rosie is laughing hysterically.

   Rosie talked with Hershey's master chocolate chef about the kind of candy bar she would like to see made, and he's coming on the show soon to let her demonstrate.

### Wednesday, November 12, 1997
Hollywood heartthrob Richard Gere (*Red Corner*)
Legendary singer Carole King and The Sugar Beats perform.

Rosie announces that she has adopted a baby girl, Chelsea Belle, born on September 20.

A caller on the Comment Line is upset that Rosie was preempted yesterday as she was telling the story about being nude in bed. Rosie begins telling it again and again gets preempted by Al Roker.

Rosie mentions that she might reverse her desk and the guest chairs so that the guests sit on Rosie's left. Rosie gives several reasons for the change, but many fans realize this is our first clue that Barbra Streisand will be a guest soon. Streisand is probably the only guest for whom Rosie might rearrange the set to favor Barbra's demands. Sure enough, two days before the Streisand show is taped, the furniture is changed, only to be changed back a couple of weeks later.

We see *The Adventures of Hair Man*, starring David Evangelista.

The Sugar Beats is a pop band starring Carole King's daughter Cheri that brings the songs of the sixties to today's kids. Their latest album *Back to the Beat*, includes songs like "Locomotion," "Mockingbird," and "Mony, Mony."

### Thursday, November 13, 1997
A performance by the queen of soul, Aretha Franklin
TV and film actress Claire Danes (*The Rainmaker*)

When Aretha mentioned that she'd been sick the night before with a 103 degrree fever, Rosie took the opportunity to again diss Whitney Houston.

Rosie was flabbergasted to learn that Claire Danes was only eighteen years old and planning to attend Yale next fall.

### Friday, November 14, 1997
The one-and-only Bill Cosby (*Cosby*)
Actress Ally Walker (*The Profiler*)
Singer Lisa Stansfield performs.

Rosie announces that Barbra Streisand will be her guest in one week.

Bill Cosby does a few minutes of monologue, the first comic to do that on *The Rosie O'Donnell Show* in over a year.

### Monday, November 17, 1997
Comic genius Robin Williams (*Flubber*)
Actress Marcia Gay Harden (*Flubber*)
A performance by Jamiroquai

Rosie has rearranged her desk and the guest chairs so that the guests sit on Rosie's left. Friday's show with Barbra Streisand will be taped on Wednesday evening.

### Tuesday, November 18, 1997
Grammy Award–winning superstar Celine Dion
Fitness guru Richard Simmons
The cast of Broadway's *Cats*

Rosie announces that she will be suing Davenia on *The People's Court*.

During a cooking segment, Rosie turns her nose up after tasting Richard's low-fat s'mores.

RICHARD: If Tom Cruise were here making this kaka stuff, you'd *love* it.

Richard then offers Rosie a chocolate mousse cake. When Rosie says she isn't fond of mousse, Richard casually tosses the cake onto the floor behind him.

### Wednesday, November 19, 1997
Former president Jimmy Carter
Emmy Award–winning comedian Chris Rock
Performance by Roberta Flack

On this show, Rosie and Roberta Flack sang a silly song parody in response to the Rosie show's recent Thong Week, instigated by Roberta (sung to the tune of Roberta's hit "Killing Me Softly"):

Roberta, when you stopped by,
You said this thong I'd dig.

At home I tried it on,
And God my butt looked big . . .

**Thursday, November 20, 1997**
Movie actor Danny DeVito
Octogenarian chef Julia Child
A performance by Sheryl Crow

**Friday, November 21, 1997**
The one-and-only Barbra Streisand!
Rosie's sister, Maureen, does the opening announcements.

ROSIE: So, why are you here today?
MAUREEN: I'm here to help keep you calm. And if you faint, it's *my* show!

After a year and a half of begging and pleading—Barbra Suck-up Day was way back on August 7, 1996!—Rosie finally got her hour with Barbra. The stage was awash in roses. Rosie apparently brought with her everything she owns of Barbra memorabilia: albums, CDs, eight-track tapes, a coffee mug, a notepad. Each commercial break begins and ends with Barbra film clips and montages.

    Rosie started to cry as she announced Barbra. Seeing Barbra enter from behind the curtains and walk to her chair must have reminded Rosie of her mother, who was a big Streisand fan. "I will get better . . . it feels like my mom walking through the curtain." Barbra brushed a tear from Rosie's cheek and tried to get her to quit crying.

ROSIE: You were a constant source of light in an often dark childhood. I am profoundly grateful to you. [*Now even Barbra is crying. Rosie continues*]: I don't remember my life without you in it.
BARBRA [*admitting that she is nervous*]: How do I fulfill your fantasy?
ROSIE: No, my feelings about you are reality based.
BARBRA: There is nothing that is perfection.
ROSIE: I gotta tell you, you come pretty close!
BARBRA: How can I live up to what people write about me?

Rosie ends the show with a champagne toast to Barbra Streisand and James Brolin: "To you two, for years of happiness and for all the joy you have brought to me and others."

Rosie was noticeably ill at ease throughout the hourlong interview. That may explain some of the lapses she had in her interviewing. We didn't need to hear again about her diarrhea, and even Barbra was alarmed when Rosie belted out the opening words to "People." On top of that, asking questions about Ring Dings and playing the DigiCard should be reserved for her less interesting guests, when she runs out of things to talk about.

Still, this show has to be considered one of the high points to date of *The Rosie O'Donnell Show.*

## Monday, November 24, 1997

Comic Tim Allen (*For Richer or Poorer; Home Improvement*)
Actress Kirstie Alley (*For Richer or Poorer; Veronica's Closet*)

Rosie and Davenia McFadden meet again, this time in Edward Koch's courtroom—*The People's Court.* Rosie wins the chance to meet Davenia in a rematch of their Mary Tyler Moore trivia challenge.

## Tuesday, November 25, 1997

Actress Whoopi Goldberg
Singer Mariah Carey performs.
A performance by Jason Raize from the new Broadway musical *The Lion King*

The Hershey doctor, Dr. Charles Duncan, makes the candy bar that Rosie would like to see sold. Wafers, peanut butter, chopped peanuts, caramel, crisped rice, all coated in chocolate. Dr. Duncan called this the "Rosie Bar." He even presented Rosie with an Honorary Ph.D. in chocolate!

## Wednesday, November 26, 1997

Actress Sigourney Weaver (*Alien Resurrection*)
Rap artists Puff Daddy & Mase perform.
Rosie's sister, Maureen O'Donnell
A performance from the cast of the Broadway musical *Titanic*

Rosie gets a Christmas CD from Donny Osmond. Donny's note: "I was thinking about who I want to wish a Merry Christmas to. Of all the people I have rolled around on the floor with, you are it."

Rosie shows us what she does behind the curtain just before the show starts: jumping rope, making balloon animals, dancing with David Evangelista, playing Twister, getting her nails manicured, and making burgers on a barbecue grill. Rosie says, "That's what happens!"

**Thursday, November 27, 1997**—repeat from October 1, 1997
**Friday, November 28, 1997**—repeat from September 9, 1997
**Monday, December 1, 1997**—repeat from September 18, 1997
**Tuesday, December 2, 1997**—repeat from October 8, 1997
**Wednesday, December 3, 1997**—repeat from September 16, 1997
**Thursday, December 4, 1997**—repeat from September 10, 1997
**Friday, December 5, 1997**—repeat from September 25, 1997

**Monday, December 8, 1997**
Actress Courteney Cox (*Scream 2; Friends*)
Actor Kyle Chandler (*Early Edition*)
Actor Anthony LaPaglia (from Broadway's *A View From the Bridge*)
Actress Kelly Ripa and actor Mark Consuelos (*All My Children*)

**Tuesday, December 9, 1997**
Actor Sir Anthony Hopkins (*Amistad*)
Actress Bridget Fonda (*Jackie Brown*)
Actor Danny Aiello (*Dellaventura*)
A performance by the Trans-Siberian Orchestra

**Wednesday, December 10, 1997**
Actor Ralph Fiennes (*Oscar & Lucinda*)
Former teen idol Frankie Avalon performs.
Sheryl Swoopes of the WNBA cooks with Rosie.
Rosie's friend singer Sam Harris performs.

Country singer Mary Chapin Carpenter did the opening announcements today.

### Thursday, December 11, 1997
Actor Matt Damon (*The Rainmaker; Good Will Hunting*)
Actor Alex D. Linz (*Home Alone 3*)
Actress Shemar Moore (*The Young & The Restless*).
A performance from the Broadway musical *A Street Corner Symphony*

Rosie is the first person to call the new toll-free Broadway Line. During the conversation, Rosie begins singing songs from *Funny Girl*. The Broadway Line operator tells Rosie, "I'd really like to hear you sing all day, but I have to take other calls, too."

Rosie and Alex Linz both provided voices for Disney's upcoming animated feature film *Tarzan*, scheduled for a summer release. Alex is Tarzan as a child, while Rosie voices his friend Terk.

### Friday, December 12, 1997
Actor Nathan Lane (*Mouse Hunt*)
Actress Shelley Duvall (Horton Foote's *Alone*)
The music of Enya

Along with Nathan was his mouse costar, which proceeded to make a little stain on Nathan's Armani suit.

### Monday, December 15, 1997
The cast of *The Postman*, including:
Actor and director Kevin Costner
Actress Olivia Williams
Actor Larenz Tate

### Tuesday, December 16, 1997
Actress Emma Thompson and
Her mother Phyllida Law (*The Winter Guest*)
Singer Luther Vandross performs.
Morgan the vacuum boy

Luther, to people who chide him about his weight: "I can lose this weight; you are *stuck* with that face."

Staffer Debbie Casper sings and dances in a Rudolph the Red-Nosed Reindeer outfit.

Rosie sings this funny song parody (to the tune of "Winter Wonderland"):

> Got a cold—nose and my throat's clogged,
> Can't see straight and my head's fogged,
> I do a live show, I cough and I blow [my nose],
> Living in a winter virus land . . .

**Wednesday, December 17, 1997**

Actor Tim Curry (*Doom Runners; Beauty and the Beast: Enchanted Christmas*)
Actor Greg Kinnear (*As Good as it Gets*)
Actor Ingo Rademacher (*General Hospital*)
Actress Patty Duke (*A Christmas Memory*)

Dave Thomas, founder of Wendy's restaurants, opened today's show. Dave brought Rosie a new chicken sandwich. (Dave was adopted as a child, and he's working to make it easier for people to adopt.)

**Thursday, December 18, 1997**

The cast of *Tomorrow Never Dies*, including:
Actor Pierce Brosnan
Actor Jonathan Pryce
Actress Michelle Yeoh

John McDaniel went to the jazz club Birdland last night to see his friend Billy Stritch (see January 13, 1998 show).

Michelle Yeoh appeared on Rosie show last July 24th, using the pseudonym Michelle Khan.

JONATHAN: I did my own stunts, but I had a double for the acting.

> **Rosie List: FAVORITE CHRISTMAS SPECIALS (her rankings)**
>
> 1. How the Grinch Stole Christmas
> 2. It's a Charlie Brown Christmas
> 3. Rudolph the Red-Nosed Reindeer
> 4. Miracle on 34th Street
> 5. It's a Wonderful Life
> 6. White Christmas
> 7. Scrooge (British 1970 version)
> 8. Mrs. Santa Claus
> 9. The Santa Clause
> 10. Frosty The Snowman

**Friday, December 19, 1997**
Comic actor Leslie Nielsen (*Mr. Magoo*)
Actor Tom Everett Scott (*An American Werewolf in Paris*)
Singer Bryan Adams performs.
Actor Jim Davidson (*Pacific Blue*)

Leslie Nielsen gave Rosie a device to make vulgar noises, but it was Jim Davidson who stole the show, singing a beautiful "Edelweiss" (from *The Sound of Music*) with Rosie.

Staff writer Alan Katz, wearing gloves with cat faces on them, performs a catty version of "Silent Night."

**Monday, December 22, 1997**—repeat from November 24, 1997

**Tuesday, December 23, 1997**
Actress Helen Hunt (*As Good as It Gets; Mad About You*)
Country singer Shania Twain performs.
*The Rosie O'Donnell Show*'s roving reporter Paula Poundstone

Rosie says Shania is the best Koosh shooting guest she's ever had on the show.

**Wednesday, December 24, 1997**—a Very Rosie Christmas (all pre-taped segments)
Hillary Clinton performs a spoken-word Christmas classic accompanied by The Boys Choir of Harlem.
Billy Porter performs.
Luther Vandross performs.
Roberta Flack performs.
Tony Bennett performs.
Donny Osmond performs.
Indianapolis's Caroling Cops perform.
. . . and Elmo!

The first lady showered Rosie with gifts: a platter of cookies, two gifts for Parker, one gift for Chelsea, and a White House Christmas ornament.

**Thursday, December 25, 1997**—repeat from October 2, 1997
**Friday, December 26, 1997**—repeat from October 24, 1997
**Monday, December 19, 1997**—repeat from October 14, 1997
**Tuesday, December 30, 1997**—repeat from November 3, 1997
**Wednesday, December 31, 1997**—repeat from November 13, 1997
**Thursday, January 1, 1998**—repeat from October 22, 1997
**Friday, January 2, 1998**—repeat from November 17, 1997

**Monday, January 5, 1998**
Soap diva Susan Lucci (*All My Children*)
Actor Joan Cusack (*In and Out*)
Game-show host and actor Alan Thicke (*Pictionary*)

Joan talks about Hostess Bakery's HoHo's, and Rosie reminds Joan that she once slammed Drake's Yodels. Rosie has a plate of HoHo's and Yodels for a test taste. Joan easily recognizes the HoHo's, while Rosie, much to her surprise, discovers she, too, prefers the HoHo's. Rosie says that Joan may have jeopardized Rosie's role as spokesperson for Drake's cakes.

**Tuesday, January 6, 1998**
Actor Peter Fonda
Actress Kathy Najimy (*Veronica's Closet*)
Olympic skater Oksana Baiul with her new book *Secrets of Skating!*
Junior paleontologist Justin Hoffmann
Barney the purple dinosaur makes a surprise visit (his first) to *The Rosie O'Donnell Show*.

**Wednesday, January 7, 1998**
Actor Samuel L. Jackson (*Jackie Brown*)
Fashion designer Michael Kors
Singer Jai performs.

**Thursday, January 8, 1998**
Talk-show host Matt Lauer (*Today Show*)

Actress Pam Grier (*Jackie Brown*)
A performance by She Moves

Pam, who loves Bob Vila as much as Rosie loves Barbra Streisand: "When I get married, I'm going to be registered at ACE Hardware."

**Friday, January 9, 1998**
Actress Minnie Driver (*Good Will Hunting*)
Stage and screen star Natalie Portman (*Beautiful Girls*; Broadway's *Diary of Anne Frank*)
Nine-year-old singer Paul Iacono performs with Minnie and Rosie.

A young girl named Ashley opened the show today. Carrie was chosen to be the announcer, but she let her friend Ashley do the opening announcement. Ashley and Carrie had just met waiting in line to see the show.

**Monday, January 12, 1998**
Comic actress Tracey Ullman (*Tracey Takes On*)
Actor John Dye (*Touched by An Angel*)
Actor Kris Kristofferson (TNT's *Two for Texas*)
Fashion designer Tommy Hilfiger

Tracey shows a gimmicky hair-care product, Tap Teaser, that she ordered from an infomercial. It is nothing more than a pair of rattail combs for teasing the hair. She gets them entangled in both hers and Rosie's hair, saying: "Tap, tap, tap is crap, crap, crap!"

**Tuesday, January 13, 1998**
Actress Kate Winslet (*Titanic*)
Actor John Leguizamo (one-man Broadway show *Freak*)
Actress Wendy Jo Sperber (*Murphy Brown*)
A performance by singer Uncle Sam

For the first time ever, John McDaniel has called in sick. His more-than-able replacement is Billy Stritch. Billy tells us that he got a 6:00 A.M. call from John, who said, "I'm so glad you're there." Rosie tells John that Billy even knows how to play "Danke Shoen."

A younger, yet envious Kate tells Rosie that although Rosie is thirty-five, she has no wrinkles. Rosie shares her beauty tip for avoiding them: "Keep an extra forty ponds on. Chubby people don't get wrinkles."

John Leguizamo, whose family is Latino: "There are no Latinos on *Star Trek*. We have no future."

**Wednesday, January 14, 1998**
Actress Linda Lavin (*The Diary Of Anne Frank*) performs.
Anchorman Tom Brokaw
Actor Michael Beach (*ER; Ruby Bridges*)
Actress Chaz Monet (*Ruby Bridges*)

**Thursday, January 15, 1998**
Actor Peter O'Toole
Hockey legend Wayne Gretzky
Fashion designer Cynthia Rowley

**Friday, January 16, 1998**
Actor and director Kenneth Branagh (Robert Altman's *Gingerbread Man*)
Singer Patti LaBelle performs.
Comedian Colin Quinn (*Saturday Night Live*)
A performance from Marc Salem's *Mind Games*

**Monday, January 19, 1998**
Actress Gloria Reuben (*ER*)
Actor Michael Bergin (*Baywatch*)
Actor Michael Rapaport (*Illtown*)
Another performance from the cast of Broadway's *Ragtime*

**Tuesday, January 20, 1998**
Actor Charles Grodin (CNBC's *Charles Grodin; Beethoven*)
Actor Richard Kind (*Spin City*)
Singer Marie Osmond performs a song from Broadway's *The King And I*.

**Wednesday, January 21, 1998**
Actor/comedian Adam Sandler (*The Wedding Singer*)

Actress Victoria Rowell (*Diagnosis Murder*)
A performance by Darlene Love

**Thursday, January 22, 1998**
Actor Michael J. Fox (*Spin City*)
Actor Michael Badalucco (*The Practice*)
Actress Tina Louise (*Gilligan's Island*; and book *Sunday: A Memoir*)

**Friday, January 23, 1998**
Actor Michael Keaton (*Desperate Measures*)
A performance by singer Martina McBride
Actress Lili Taylor (*Illtown*)

**Monday, January 26, 1998**
Actor Bill Pullman (*The Zero Effect*)
Actor James Van Der Beek (*Dawson's Creek*)
A performance by The Kinleys
Actor Michael T. Weiss (*The Pretender*)

**Tuesday, January 27, 1998**
Actress Patti LuPone (*The Old Neighborhood*)
Cast of Broadway's revival of *The Sound of Music*
Actress Madeline Kahn (*Cosby*)

**Wednesday, January 28, 1998**
Actors Dan Aykroyd and John Goodman (*Blues Brothers 2000*)
Actor Harry Hamlin (*The Hunted*)
Designer Nicholas Graham of Joe Boxer

**Thursday, January 29, 1998**—mostly a repeat from November 7, 1997
Clips from previous shows featuring:
Television icon Mary Tyler Moore (*The Dick Van Dyke Show; The Mary Tyler Moore Show*)
Trivia diva Davenia brings it on!
The cast of *The Lion King* performs.

**Friday, January 30, 1998**

More clips from previous shows featuring:

Comic and talk-show host Chris Rock (*The Chris Rock Show*; author of *Rock This*)

Actor Nathan Lane and friend (*Mouse Hunt*)

Actor and flatulist Leslie Nielsen

A cooking demonstration by the Two Fat Ladies

**Monday, February 2, 1998**—from Warner Bros. Studios, Burbank

Actor Matt LeBlanc (*Friends*; the upcoming film *Lost in Space*)

A performance by Jewel

Rosie learned from Matt's mother that he played the Cowardly Lion in a sixth-grade production of *The Wizard of Oz*. She coerces him into singing a little of "If I Were King of the Forest." And he does so quite well, too. Rosie will have several more members of the cast of *Friends* on her show this month and will ask each of them to show off their hidden talents.

**Tuesday, February 3, 1998**—from Warner Bros. Studios, Burbank

Actor Andy Garcia (*Desperate Measures*)

Actress Peri Gilpin (*Frasier*)

Rock 'n' roll legend Little Richard performs.

Actress Journee Smollett (*Eve's Bayou; NYPD Blue*)

Severe weather knocked out a satellite, causing most stations that carry the show live to lose their feed. New York City and others saw a repeat of the August 14, 1997, show with Demi Moore instead.

Eleven-year-old Journee sang an incredible rendition of "Yesterday, When I Was Young" with the band.

ROSIE: Janet Jackson has nothing on you!

**Wednesday, February 4, 1998**—from Warner Bros. Studios, Burbank

Actress Drew Barrymore (*The Wedding Singer*)

Actor Wallace Langham (*Veronica's Closet*)

Rockers Sugar Ray perform.

Rosie tells us she spent the morning doing the cartoon voice for Terk, Tarzan's pal in the upcoming Disney animated feature. As a result of many takes of her screaming while being chased by cartoon elephants, her voice is very hoarse. For this and the next two shows, she sounds like a twelve-year-old boy whose voice is changing.

**Thursday, February 5, 1998**—from Warner Bros. Studios, Burbank
The entire cast of *ER*, including George Clooney, Anthony Edwards, Julianna Margulies, Noah Wyle, Eriq LaSalle, Laura Innes, Gloria Reuben, Alex Kingston, and Maria Bello

For the first time ever, Rosie skipped her opening dialogue with John McDaniel so that the full hour could be dedicated to the cast of *ER*. At this announcement, the audience groaned in disapproval.

At the end of the show, four audience members get to ask questions of the cast. The first, a very pregnant young lady, asks Clooney if he's ever kissed a lady who was eight months' pregnant. He jumps out of his chair and runs up the aisle to give her a kiss. As he sits back down, he protests, "I never touched her!"

**Friday, February 6, 1998**—from Warner Bros. Studios, Burbank
Actress Gwyneth Paltrow (*Sliding Doors; Great Expectations*)
Actor Marlan Wayans
Chef Madam Wu
A performance by R & B legends Earth, Wind and Fire

For the very first time, Rosie, standing in the front row of the audience, did her own opening announcements today so that she could introduce Earth, Wind and Fire at the top of the show.

Rosie tells us that her weekend stand-up shows at Caesars Palace in Las Vegas are being filmed for a future HBO special.

Rosie welcomed three of the twelve winners of a Kraft Macaroni and Cheese contest. Eleven-year-old Anjuli won.

ROSIE: You're a very talented young lady.
ANJULI: Of course.

Madam Wu, a famous L.A. chef, prepared her Cary Grant Chinese
Chicken Salad with Rosie.

**Monday, February 9, 1998**—from Warner Bros. Studios, Burbank
Actor Matthew Perry (*Friends*)
Talk-show host Keenan Ivory Wayans
A performance by Boyz II Men

Rosie tells Matthew that fellow *Friends* cast member Matt LeBlanc
sang on the show last week and invites Matthew to sing something.
Matthew says he is a musician, not a singer, and brings out a cello case.
Inside is a triangle for himself and a kazoo for Rosie. The McDLTs play
"Wipe Out" while Matthew and Rosie trade solos during the drum
interludes.

**Tuesday, February 10, 1998** —from Warner Bros. Studios, Burbank
Actor David Schwimmer (*Friends*)
Rap star turned actress Queen Latifah (*Sphere*)
Actor Judd Nelson (*Suddenly Susan*)
Comedian Andy Dick (*NewsRadio*)

While in Los Angeles, Rosie is doing her stand-up act on weekends at
Caesars Palace in Las Vegas. She will be there again in May and finally
in December. At Saturday's show, she was sick. Forty minutes into her
act, she had to leave the stage and "threw up all over Luther Vandross's
dressing room." Judy Gold, a stand-up comic and a segment producer
on *The Rosie O'Donnell Show*, was in the audience, and she finished
for Rosie.

**Wednesday, February 11, 1998**—from Warner Bros. Studios, Burbank
Singer, actress, and onetime absentee guest Whitney Houston
Actress Kate Mulgrew (*Star Trek: Voyager*)
Four-year-old country singer Austin Burke performs.

Yesterday Rosie taped a week of shows for the celebrity game show
*Pictionary*, with Sally Struthers as her partner. She was told not to
give away the results, but Rosie says, "We kicked butt."

Whitney brings a note from her mother, which asks that she be excused from the October 30 show because "she had a virus and was throwing up."

Kate Mulgrew has hired a personal trainer. "Today I ran two miles!"

ROSIE: Are you striving to run a Marathon?

KATE: No, in that period of time I could have three glasses of wine and a dinner party.

**Thursday, February 12, 1998**—
from Warner Bros. Studios, Burbank
Actress Courteney Cox (*Friends*)
Oscar nominee Ben Affleck
    (*Good Will Hunting*)
Motown legend Smokey Robinson performs.

Rosie has a pimple just below her lower lip. Although her makeup person, Mariella Smith Masters, spent a great deal of time trying to hide it, Rosie takes a sharpie pen and colors it, creating a "beauty mark."

Like the other guests from *Friends*, Courteney has a hidden talent. She burns a bit of cork and shows Rosie how to use it to create dramatic eye shadow. Rosie than corks a mustache on Courteney, along with a few warpaint-like additions.

**Friday, February 13, 1998**—from Warner Bros. Studios, Burbank
Child actress Emily Mae Young (*Step By Step*)
Superstar Sharon Stone (*Sphere*)
Cast of TV's daytime drama *General Hospital*, led by diva Vanessa Marcil

SHARON: Ya know, we were once up for the same part.

ROSIE: No, you're being kind. We were not up for the same part, you were offered a role, you turned it down—wisely.

SHARON: Rosie took it.

ROSIE: I took it. It was a fabulous film called *Exit to Eden*. [*audience laughs*] But honestly, Sharon, and I've said this before in interviews, the only reason I took the role was because I wanted to tell people, "I took the role Sharon Stone turned down." Because I couldn't believe that at some big Hollywood meeting they went, "Hmmm, can't get Sharon Stone? LET'S GET ROSIE O'DONNELL!"

**Monday, February 16, 1998**—from Warner Bros. Studios, Burbank
Country star Reba McEntire cohosts with Rosie.
Actress Heather Locklear
*Sesame Street*'s Elmo!

**Tuesday, February 17, 1998**—from Warner Bros. Studios, Burbank
Actor Jimmy Smits (*NYPD Blue*)
Actress Sarah Michelle Gellar (*Buffy the Vampire Slayer*)
The cast of *The Young and the Restless*
A performance by Patti LaBelle

**Wednesday, February 18, 1998**—from Warner Bros. Studios, Burbank
Surprise guest Tom Cruise!
Actress Neve Campbell (*Party of Five; Scream 2*)
Actress Elisabeth Shue
A performance by Backstreet Boys

Tom surprises Rosie with a kiss and details on his top-secret upcoming film, costarring wife Nicole Kidman. He even seems more relaxed than during his previous appearances.

**Thursday, February 19, 1998**—from Warner Bros. Studios, Burbank
The cast of the upcoming *Lethal Weapon 4*:
Mel Gibson, Rene Russo, Danny Glover, Joe Pesci, and Chris Rock

**Friday, February 20, 1998**—from Warner Bros. Studios, Burbank
Actor Dylan McDermott (*The Practice*)
Actress Brooke Shields (*Suddenly Susan*)

# Cast and Crew
## THE ROSIE O'DONNELL SHOW CREDITS

| | |
|---|---|
| **Host** | Rosie O'Donnell |
| **Roving correspondent** | Paula Poundstone (from 9/97) |
| **Executive producers** | Daniel Kellison (6/10/96–12/6/96) Hillary Estey-McLaughlin (from 12/7/96) Rosie O'Donnell |
| **Director** | Arthur Forrest |
| **Supervising producer** | Andy Lasoner |
| **Comedy producer** | Janette Barber |
| **Writers** | Judy Gold Eric Kornfeld Rosie O'Donnell Beth Sherman Caissie St. Onge |
| **Segment producers** | Deidre Dod Deb Drucker Judy Gold David Perler Mimi Pizzi Lisa Mazie Rechsteiner |
| **The McDLTs** | John McDaniel, leader/piano Morris Goldberg, saxophone Rodney Jones, guitar Ray Marchica, drums Tracy Wormworth, bass |

| | |
|---|---|
| **Associate directors** | Yvonne De Mare |
| | Susan Quinn |
| **Stage managers** | Rose Riggins |
| | Smith W. Sumroy |
| **Production designer** | Kathleen Ankers |
| **Lighting designer** | Bob Dickenson |
| **Lighting director** | Alan Blacher |
| **Publicity** | Renee Koblentz |
| | Marc Liepis |
| **Assistants to Rosie** | Jennifer Kriegel |
| | Merrie Raker |
| **Talent executive** | Jeffry Culbreth |
| **Talent coordinator** | Corin Nelson |
| **Music/comedy talent coordinator** | Deirdre Dod |
| **Head talent researcher** | Amie Baker |
| **Researcher** | Perry Moore |
| **Researcher** | Lisa Mazia Rechsteiner |
| **Associate director** | John Dincecco |
| **Production coordinator** | Beth Boreanaz |
| **Production accountants** | John Cooke |
| | Santana Westbrook |
| **Script supervisor** | Susan Quinn |
| **Clearance coordinator** | Sandra Chin |
| **Stage managers** | Patty Sheehan |
| | Paul Pennolino |
| **Art direction** | Joe Aiello |
| **Titles/graphic designer** | Robin McCormick |

| | |
|---|---|
| **Director of creative services (East Coast)** | Denise Rolfe |
| **Promotion producer** | Jane Snyderman |
| **Associate promotion producer** | Debbie D'Amato |
| **Publicity relations** | Renee Koblentz<br>Marc Liepis |
| **Talent assistants** | Susan Claxton<br>Joanna Philbin<br>Bella Seikel |
| **Writers' assistant** | Mae Martin Conroy |
| **Production assistants** | Jennifer Essenfeld<br>Brendan Higgins<br>James H Petrozelli Jr. |
| **Correspondence coordinator** | Michael Summers |
| **Receptionist** | Jessica Landy |
| **Technical director** | Dick Sansevere |
| **Audio** | Al Centrella<br>Keith Carroll<br>Mike Ferrara<br>Kevin Hartman<br>Ed McQuewen<br>Jay Vicari<br>Allyson Vogel<br>Bob Batsche |
| **Camera** | Ken Decker<br>Manny Guitterez<br>Michael Inglesh<br>Manny Torres<br>Len Wechsler |
| **Videotape operators** | Jose Alvarez-Ugarte<br>Mike Cain |

| | |
|---|---|
| **Electronic graphics** | Debra J. Morrishow |
| **Cue cards** | Melanie Windenbaum |
| **Utility** | Frank Puma |
| | Neil Winikoff |
| **Technical manager** | Mike Matthews |
| **Studio manager** | Tom Popple |
| **Operations manager** | Mary Gallagher |
| **Outside props** | Doug Bleier |
| **Scenic artist** | Carol Suchy |
| **Stagehands** | Bobby Friend |
| | Janie Saizan |
| | Ray Kirchmer |
| **Wardrobe designer** | Rhea Landig-Giaimo |
| **Wardrobe (Rosie O'Donnell)** | Salon Z at Saks Fifth Avenue |
| **Wardrobe (John McDaniel)** | Men's Store at Saks Fifth Avenue |
| **Wardrobe** | Donna Richards ("The Dresser From Hell") |
| **Makeup (Rosie O'Donnell)** | Mariella Smith Masters |
| **Hair (Rosie O'Donnell)** | David Evangelista |
| **Makeup** | Cindy Gardner |
| **Hairstylist** | Jeffrey Swander |
| **Production facilities provider** | NBC (New York) |
| **Executive in charge of production** | Laurie J. Rich |
| **Development vice president** | Hilary Estey-McLaughlin |
| **Production vice president** | Kevin Fortsn |
| **President of Telepictures Productions** | Jim Paratore |

# Rosie Online

**AMERICA ONLINE— WARNER BROS.' ROSIE SITE**

In October 1996, just four months after *The Rosie O'Donnell Show* first aired, Warner Bros. unveiled the official Rosie site on America Online. Why did they put it there and not on the World Wide Web, where it would find a much larger audience? Simple: money. Warner Bros. gets paid for each minute that an AOL member spends in the Rosie site. With the site attracting half a million people a month, it adds up quickly.

Warner Bros. was also able to recruit unpaid volunteers to do most of the work of organizing and updating the vast amounts of information available on the site. All of these volunteers use assigned screen names that start with "TheR0," with the fifth character being the numeric zero, not the letter "o." Only Warner Bros. can assign screen names that begin with "TheR0" so that subscribers can tell when they come across someone officially associated with the Rosie site. Some of the older hands at the Rosie ranch include TheR0Monkey, TheR0Joe, TheR0Deb, and TheR0Elmo.

"I've been online for about eight years. I'm one of those people who is on there surfing every night," Rosie says. Even though she has her own high-speed T-1 connection to the Internet, Rosie mostly stays within the cozy confines of AOL, only occasionally venturing out into the real world of the World Wide Web. "I go into the Rosie site on AOL all the time. You can usually find me in the AOL chat rooms. I try to answer mail via the message boards." After trying out Web-TV (which can only access the Web, not AOL) for a few days, she admitted that she did not like it very much. So if you want to chat with Rosie, you have to subscribe to America Online. If you want to read her occasional replies to fans' comments and questions on the message boards, you have to subscribe to America Online.

Speaking of chatting with Rosie, it is a chaotic experience like no other. Dozens of people are typing questions to her all at once. Add to that the fact that Rosie's responses are very concise and sometimes cryptic, it is almost impossible to understand what is going on. What follows is a transcript of the beginning of a chat that took place on September 23, 1997, which shows the excitement and pandemonium Rosie creates when she appears in a chat room.

| | |
|---|---|
| Elvis Here: | ((((((((ROSIE)))))))))))))) |
| TangTang33: | Gumb {S jammy |
| PLIVY: | Seneca. . . . . . . . .I can do that |
| Shorti oh: | Tons |
| TheR0Marni: | People  ROSIE is on-line  but NOT in the chat rooms |
| Seneca4260: | ROISE********* |

| | |
|---|---|
| TheR0Marni: | Hi Tatm, TheR0SIE! I'm TheR0Marni your host |
| Mimipapa86: | Rosie********* |
| TheR0Marni: | this hour! |
| MOOKOLA: | LIN where are you? |
| Chazmoo2: | Rosie********** Helloooooooo |
| BillMu: | Rosie!!!!! |
| Gaddfan: | Hi Rosie |
| Gumbster: | R0sie****** |
| UItraWmn1: | Lnda do you have wavs? |
| Shorti oh: | Hi Rosie |
| Lailalyn: | Rosie I love you!!!!!!!!!!! |
| TheR0Marni: | keep your fingers crossed |
| TheR0SIE: | HELLO ALL |
| PLIVY: | HIYA ROSIE************** |
| T0NSofFUN: | Rosie*********** |
| Seneca4260: | Kewl PLIVY :D |
| THLCCL: | BBME>. . YOU MUST send an IM to her!! it will say not taking IM right now. . that means she is |
| TangTang33: | Rosie !!!!! |
| THLCCL: | ONLINE |
| LINENSLADY: | =ABosie |
| BillMu: | Rosie! How be ye? |
| Gumbster: | Hi Rosie*** it's me GUMBSTER |
| OlallaDi: | hi Rosie |
| LndaB: | ultra - what is wavs |
| Shorti oh: | i'm going to really get nervous |
| LViator102: | )((((((((((((((((((((((((((((((ROSIE))))))))))))))))))))))LOVE ya baby |
| BLTLSOH: | Hi Rosie! |
| Elvis Here: | ROSIE>. . . . . . . . . . . . .How are You. .BTW I made someone pee in there pants <g> |
| PBelliv683: | Hi Rosie |
| Mimipapa86: | THL, she is here |
| WinCanasta: | ROSIE hiya |
| LINENSLADY: | is she here? |
| Njhosea: | rOSIE,HI. |

| Chazmoo2: | ROSIE********** We love you!! How's the PUPPY? |
| | JPChevy 57: HI ROSIE!!! I AM A HUGE FAN OF YOURS!!! |
| Tom 8 Cat: | {{{{{{{{{{{{{{{{{{{{{{{{{{{{{{{{{{{{{ROSIE}}}}}}}}}}}}}}}}}}}}}}}}}}}}}}}}} HIYA |
| ThirtySixE: | Hiya ROSIE.....how are you cupcake? |
| TheR0SIE: | GOD I NEED A SUIT OF ARMOR WHEN ENTERING THE MESSAGE BOARDS |

Here's a list of all the other features available at Rosie's AOL site, along with a comparison showing how little of that information is available to World Wide Web users who don't pay to subscribe to AOL:

| Features Available to America Online Subscribers | Description | Available on the World Wide Web? |
| --- | --- | --- |
| Games and puzzles | Rosie Concentration, New York Jigsaw, Sliding With Rosie, Rosieoke, Dress Rosie. Most of these can also be downloaded in Mac and Windows versions. | no |
| Hey! Write to Rosie | Send messages to Rosie. | yes |
| Interactive Mondays | Rosie chats online with her fans during the first Monday show in each month. | no |
| Rosie's Fan Club | How to join the Official Rosie O'Donnell Fan Club | no |
| *Kids Are Punny* Online | Kids can post their jokes, and grown-ups can order the book. | no |

| | | |
|---|---|---|
| TV station listings | This list of stations where you can see *The Rosie O'Donnell Show* does not give the channel numbers and does not include any Canadian stations. | yes |
| Notes from the show | Information about contests and talent searches | some |
| Official Rosie staff | Forty-three volunteers who support and maintain AOL's Rosie site. They are the official staff for the Rosie online area. These friendly folks are hosts in Rosie's chat room and monitor the message boards. They all "work" for Warner Bros., but they are not affiliated with Rosie or the show. | no |
| Ro show overviews | Summaries of each day's show, written by AOL staff members | no |
| Rosie fan sites | Links to Web sites dedicated to Rosie. These have to be approved by Warner Bros., which can take months. Many sites are gone by the time they are approved and posted. | no |
| Rosie in the news | News items related to Rosie and the show | no |
| Rosie online FAQ | Information about the site and about Rosie | no |

| Media clips | sounds, pictures, and videos that can be downloaded | a few |
|---|---|---|
| Rosie's charities | information about a few of the charities Rosie supports; like other lists, it is months out of date. | no |
| Rosie's online newsletter | Promotion for Rosie's AOL site | no |
| Rosie's promotions | Videos of the Rosie announcing the next show's guests | no |
| Rosie's place | Chat room | no |
| Rosie's web links | Links to Web sites of interest to Rosie, such as Tom Cruise, Broadway, Streisand, Bette Midler, the Brady Bunch, etc. | no |
| Show talk | The message boards | no |
| Ticket information | How to order tickets for *The Rosie O'Donnell Show* | yes |
| Kooshball Club | Another set of message boards | no |
| Transcripts of Rosie live | Rosie's interview appearances on AOL | no |
| You oughta be in pictures | Photos of the AOL Rosie staff and anyone else who wants to send in a photo | no |

# Highlights of Rosie's Chat on Warner Bros. Online APRIL 10, 1997

**Rosie:** Hello everyone.

**Rosie:** How goes it?

**OnlineHost:** Nickelodeon Online is proud to present this year's Tenth Annual Kids' Choice Awards host Rosie O'Donnell. Not only is she the host of the show, but she's also a nominee for a Best Actress Award for her role in Nickelodeon's *Harriet the Spy*.

**Rosie:** I hope I win.

**Rosie:** Hello, kids.

**Question:** If you could be in any movie ever made, with any other actor/actress what movie would it be and who would it be with?

**Rosie:** I would love to be in the *Sound of Music* with Julie Andrews. It is my favorite movie ever!

**Question:** Rosie, do you intend on doing any TV cameos anytime soon? When can we expect to see you? I loved you on the *Nanny*.

**Rosie:** I don't think I will be on any other shows soon. I will be hosting the Nick Awards and the Tony Awards on June 1st aside from that I will be on my own show!

**Question:** Rosie, Do you like kissing all the guests on your show???

**Rosie:** I love kissing the guests especially for money. . . . . . . . . .all the money goes to charity which makes it even more fun.

**Question:** Which guest has been the nicest so far?

**Rosie:** Hmmmmm, well I think Florence Henderson, Delta Burke, Julie Andrews, Elton John and of course my Tommy!

**Question:** What is your favorite kind of food?

**Rosie:** Junk food. . . . . . candy cookies chocolate potato chips ect. . . !

**Question:** Do you really have a crush on Tom [Cruise]?

**Rosie:** Yes I really have a crush on Tom he makes my palms sweaty!

**Question:** Rosie, did you cry when Tommy didn't get the Emmy for best actor?

**Rosie:** Well I didn't cry but I was hoping he would win he was a good sport about losing the Oscar. . . . . . . . . . . . . . He is well kinda. . . . . . . . . . . . . . . . . . . . . . perfect !

**Question:** Do you ever watch your show?

**Rosie:** Not really I am usually at work when my show is on if I do watch it I am very critical which is bad!

**Question:** Congratulations on the work you've done for charity. I was reading a post regarding an idea for another book for charity, i.e. cook book or another joke book. Any plans to do a second book?

**Rosie:** Yes we plan on doing a *Kids are Punny 2* and maybe a cook book after that. I am thrilled to be able to generate money for so many worthy causes.

**Question:** Do you think that you will host Kids Choice again in the future???

**Rosie:** I will host it every year if they want me for.

**Question:** How does it feel to have major movie, a totally famous TV show and to host Kid's Choice Awards?

**Rosie:** Having a hit show feels pretty good. Being a mom feels great!

**Question:** Do you ever get tired?

**Rosie:** I am tired right now, good night :) Actually I am happy to host the awards and even if I am tired it is worth it!

**Question:** Rosie, is there a brother or sister in Parker's future?

**Rosie:** I hope so, but not till Parker is 3 or 4!

**Question:** Do you like Jell-O?

**Rosie:** Yes I do like Jell-O. Lime flavored!

**Question:** How many movies have you made and which was your favorite?

**Rosie:** I have made 12 movies some only tiny parts my favorite was *League of Their Own*!

**Question:** How much fan mail do you receive in a day?

**Rosie:** Well, we get a lot of letters. We have a staff of 5 to deal with just the mail!

**Question:** What is it like to live in Helen Hayes' house and to occupy the same space that many famous movie stars must have been in?

**Rosie:** I was at the kitchen sink last week looking at the window and I thought Helen Hayes looked out this window it was pretty inspiring. I adored her!

**Question:** I would like to know if Rosie wears an Irish claddagh ring.

**Rosie:** I used to wear my Moms claddaugh but it was stolen in 1989 while I was on a ski trip :( I think the maid took it!

**Question:** What is the best reward in donating to charities?

**Rosie:** The best part about doing charity work is being able to share the tremendous amount of blessings I have received in my life to use fame to benefit many then I can understand its purpose.!

**Question:** How is Parker doing after his episode with the croup? Do you hate zucchini too

**Rosie:** I am not a fan of zucchini and the croup was way way way way icky but Parker is much better now, thanks.!

**Question:** Do you think you will ever have Barney on your show?

**Rosie:** Barney is tough to have as a guest cause unlike Big Bird and Elmo, he doesn't speak. Someone speaks for him off stage!

**Question:** Do you feel like your show reflects your true personality?

**Rosie:** Yes, I do think it does.

**Question:** How has Parker influenced your life?

**Rosie:** Parker is the best thing that has ever happened to me. He has taught me to love in a way I never knew. To appreciate each day. I thank the universe for him every day.

**Question:** Do you know how many guests have given you kisses or gifts?

**Rosie:** Well kisses is easy to tell at least 400 cause Listerine has to pay that much. Gifts, wellll a lot.

**Question:** Rosie, what would you consider the hardest part of you're life is?

**Rosie:** The hardest part of my life is finding time to relax.

**Question:** Rosie, How do you plan on celebrating Parker's birthday on May 25th?

**Rosie:** I am having a party with his cousins and all a little family thing.

**Question:** Rosie, who is your favorite Disney character? Your favorite Disney movie?

**Rosie:** Disney movie. . . . . . . . . . . . . . *Beauty and the Beast.* Character? Mary Poppins.!

**Question:** Do you ever get nervous before a show?

**Rosie:** I don't get nervous before a show I do get excited!

**Question:** Where did she get the M&M gift box that was on her show once?

**Rosie:** The M&M people sent it over!

**Question:** How can you be so down to earth and not afraid to share personal things?

**Rosie:** Well I don't share everything.

**Question:** If you could have any name what would it be?

**Rosie:** Any name............... Hmmmmmm'............ Lucy Manning don't know, why?

**Question:** When do you have time for you?

**Rosie:** Well I don't have enough time for me lately, but I do have the summer off so I will then!

**Question:** Rosie, do you like *Star Trek*? BTW, I LOVE your show. :)

**Rosie:** I love *Star Trek* and all the spin offs!

**Question:** What are your hobbies?

**Rosie:** Tennis, painting, ready, AOL!

**Question:** Rosie, I like basketball, just like you. Will you ever have Michael Jordan on your show?

**Rosie:** I hope we can have Michael Jordan on he rocks!

**Question:** Do you like to dress up?

**Rosie:** I hate to dress up!

**Question:** I have seen some of your old comedy acts. While they were very funny, they were very adult. How was the transition for you to change your image for public TV?

**Rosie:** I knew doing a TV show I had to be TV appropriate, so it wasn't too tough when I do another HBO special it will be adult themed!

**Question:** OBubier sends a proposal, literally:) Dear Ms. O'Donnell, I am 17 going on 18, will you marry me next year?

**Rosie:** Ummmmm. . . . . . . . . . . . . . . . . . . . . I have to check with Tommy first, but thanks.")

**Question:** What do you pray Parker will grow up to be?

**Rosie:** I pray he will grow up to be happy.

**Question:** I luv chocolate and do you?

**Rosie:** I love chocolate too.

**Question:** Are u bored since u have done everything

**Rosie:** LOL, I never bungee jumped") I am not too bored don't worry:0).

**Question:** Do you like those little fluffie marshmallows? (you know peeps?)

**Rosie:** Ummm welll ummmmmmm . . . . . . . . . . . . . . . . . . . . . . yep.

**Question:** I heard something about a biography of you becoming available. Any truth to it?

**Rosie:** It is available but I didn't write it. . . . . . . . . . . . and didn't read it so I don't know if it is accurate or not.

**Question:** I love your show!!!!!!! Did you ever have any guests that you didn't like?

**Rosie:** Yes I have had guests I didn't like but I can't say who cause it would be mean.

**Question:** Hey Rosie, I just wanted to say that you are so very talented, does it run in the family?

**Rosie:** No Kristen no one else in my family is in entertainment.

**Question:** Love your show! I was wondering. . . . How do you choose who will be a guest on your show?

**Rosie:** We have a talent broker she asks me I say no or yes.

**Question:** Has Elmo ever been to your house?

**Rosie:** Yes Elmo sleeps over often.

**Question:** Was it hard to cry when you were leaving Harriet in the movie?

**Rosie:** No it wasn't hard to cry I just pretended I was Golly and I cried.

**Question:** Rosie, What is your favorite game to play with your son?

**Rosie:** My favorite game to play with my son is hide and seek. He loves it!

**Question:** Did you do any plays in high school?

**Rosie:** Yes I did *Dames at Sea, The King and I* and a variety show!

**Question:** What was the doll's name on the TV show, *Family Affair?*

**Rosie:** Mrs. Beasley!

**Question:** Do you remember Dawn and Angie dolls—there were 2 others—did you have them??

**Rosie:** I have 3 of em!

**Question:** I'm a catcher on my baseball team—any hints 4 me?

**Rosie:** Always wear a mask!

**Question:** What do you think of the Jaguars?

**Rosie:** I love natron means. I think they will win this year!

**NickEmcee:** All good things come to an end we must go. Last question:

**Question:** How much money have you spent in the Baby Gap?

**Rosie:** JAYNUE way way way way way way too much!

**AOLiveMCO:** Do you own stock in it by now?

**Rosie:** I have no stock in it but I should!

# World Wide Web: Official and Unofficial Pages

**ACME Rosie O'Donnell Page**
http://www.bestware.net/spreng/rosie/index.html
This is my Rosie web site. It is the oldest of all the Rosie pages.

**And Now, Here's Rosie**
http://www.cardnet.net/~alexdiaz/rosie/
Attractive, well organized. Typical of many of the Rosie sites.

**And Now . . . Here's Rosie**
http://www.geocities.com/Broadway/Stage/8623/

**Angel's Page**
http://users.interlinks.net/angel/rosie.htm

**BillMu's Page**
http://members.aol.com/HWNews/index.html

**Bobby's Rockin' Rosie Page**
http://members.aol.com/newyork2/index.htm

**Bro1414's Rosie Homepage**
http://members.aol.com/Bro1414/rosie.html

**CelebSite: Rosie O'Donnell**
http://www.celebsite.com/people/rosieodonnell/index.html
Mr. Showbiz's commercial page about Rosie. Useful for getting the latest Rosie news.

**Checkatnite's Home Page**
http://www.geocities.com/TelevisionCity/4823

**Eeyore's Place**
http://members.aol.com/eeyore8643/index.html

**Everything's Comin Up Rosie**
http://www.geocities.com/TimesSquare/5511/rosiemain.html
Rosie's entry at the Internet movie database

**KidRosie's Rosie WebSite**
http://members.aol.com/kidrosie/index.html

**Lilypad's Page**
http://members.aol.com/Lilypad341/

**MaineFlame's Home Page**
http://members.aol.com/MaineFlame/maine.index.html

**Pet2's Home Page**
http://members.aol.com/thepet2/

**RO Joe's Rosie Site**
http://members.aol.com/TheR0Joe/index.html
One of the best Rosie sites on the web. Very well done.

**ROFire' Page**
http://members.aol.com/TheR0Fire/index.html

**ROGuard's Home Page**
http://members.aol.com/ther0guard/

**ROMonky's Page**
ttp://members.aol.com/ther0monky/index.html
This is the web's number-one Rosie site. the FAQ section is terrific,
and the designer's personality shines though in this page.

**RH's ROSIE-ish PAGE**
http://members.aol.com/RHarrin505/rosie.html

**Rosie O . . . By: Billybobbo**
http://members.aol.com/billybobbo/rosiemain.html

**Rosie O'Donnell Show (Official)**
http://www.rosieo.com/

Warner Bros. spent all their efforts on the America Online site, so this web page is a real disappointment. But it does tell you how to subscribe to AOL.

### Rosie Oh! Photo Album
http://www.geocities.com/TelevisionCity/Set/6261/

### RosieLand!
http://www.geocities.com/TelevisionCity/5253/

### Sesame Street Parents
http://www.ctw.org/parents/weekly/199717/rosie.htm

### Soph's Rockin Planet Rosie
http://members.aol.com/SophieTckr/index.html

### The Queen of all Things!
http://www.mindspring.com/~moomoo/rosie.html

### The Rosie Page
http://members.aol.com/egggirl2/rosie.html

### Tiny Little Space of Rosie
http://members.aol.com/Stuff36/Rosie.html

These were the correct addresses at the time of this writing. Anyone who's web savvy knows that the Internet is in a constant state of flux. URLs constantly change, and pages are added constantly, while others drop off. I recommend doing a Rosie O'Donnell name search, using one of the major search engines. Happy surfing!

### MAILING LIST—OFFICIAL AND UNOFFICIAL
Long before there was the official Rosie Newsletter—a one-way mailing list of promotional items for Warner Bros. America Online Rosie Site—or even the USENET newsgroup, there was the Rosie List. Started in August 1996 by Californian Kamal Larsuel, the list usually has about 150 members, all diehard fans who have come together to discuss Rosie and to get to know each other better.

To subscribe (for free) to the unofficial Rosie mailing list, send E-mail to majordomo@nwlink.com, with any subject, and in the body of your message, type:

subscribe rosie-list myemail@whatever.com (your E-mail address)

Be prepared to receive fifty to a hundred messages a day from your new Rosie friends!

### USENET—ALT.FAN.ROSIEODONNELL

This news group got off to a terrible start; it was bombarded by hordes of anti-Rosie hooligans. But things have since settled down to become a very useful forum for the discussion of everything related to Rosie. You will see a lot of people asking for Rosie's E-mail address or how to get show tickets or how to get video copies of prior shows. But there's usually some interesting discussions going on, too. Check with your internet provider if you need help with USENET.

# Media

## BOOKS BY AND ABOUT ROSIE

### Rosie O'Donnell, Entertainer, Comedienne

*Rosie O'Donnell, Entertainer, Comedienne* (Women of Achievement Series), by Matina S. Horner, due to be published in 1998. Hardcover—Young Adult. List: $19.95; published by Chelsea House (Library); ISBN: 0791047105.

### Kids Are Punny: Jokes Sent by Kids to The Rosie O'Donnell Show

*Kids Are Punny: Jokes Sent by Kids to The Rosie O'Donnell Show*, by Rosie O'Donnell, a collection of jokes Rosie has read on the air along with many more. All profits go to the For All Kids Foundation for children's charities. This is a must-have book for every Rosie fan. Hardcover, 89 pages. List: $10.00; published by Warner Books; ISBN: 0446523232.

### Rosie: Rosie O'Donnell's Biography

The first biography of America's favorite comic turned TV host was *Rosie: Rosie O'Donnell's Biography* by James Robert Parish. Hardcover, 288 pages. List: $23.00; published by Carroll & Graf, April 1997; ISBN: 0786704101.

*Rosie* is the first full-length biography to present the complete, captivating story of how a girl from Commack, Long Island, became the first-class jokester she is today. Demonstrating a remarkable talent for researching his subject, Parish follows Rosie's path from the childhood loss of her mother to her successful career in TV and films. This biography uncovers information about Rosie that every fan will want to know. 20 photos.

### Rosie O'Donnell: Her True Story

*Rosie O'Donnell: Her True Story* by George Mair and Anna Green. Hardcover, 266 pages. List: $22.50; published by Birch Lane Press, July 1997. ISBN: 1559724161

*Rosie O'Donnell* offers an intimate look at the woman who has invigorated daytime television. From her unusual childhood to her stint on the eighties comedy circuit through her film career to her successful talk show and the adoption of her son, bestselling biographers George Mair and Anna Green tell Rosie's fascinating story with warmth and considerable insight. 44 photos.

### Rosie's Autobiography

Rosie signed a $2 million deal with Warner Books to write her own story, but she has decided not to start on it yet. "I had a deal to write one, but I will put it off for a while 'cause the prospect is a bit daunting for now," she explains.

## THE EMMYS

➤ Rosie: Emmy Winner for Outstanding Talk Show Host (Daytime), *The Rosie O'Donnell Show*, 1997

➤ Nominated for Outstanding Talk Show (Daytime), Rosie O'Donnell, Hilary Estey Mcloughlin, Daniel Kellison, executive producers; Andy Lassner, supervising producer; Bernie Young, coordinating producer; Deirdre Dod, Mimi Pizzi, Lisa Rechsteiner, Janette Barber, Judy Gold, Jeanne Willis, Peter Johansen, Tara Elia, producers; 1997 (lost to *Oprah*)

➤ Nominated for Outstanding Guest Actress in a Comedy Series, *The Larry Sanders Show* episode "Eight" (HBO), 1996

➤ Nominated for Outstanding Individual Performance in a Variety or Music Program, Rosie O'Donnell HBO Comedy Special from Faneuil Hall's Comedy Connection, Boston (HBO), 1995

## EMMYS—THE ROSIE O'DONNELL SHOW

➤ Emmy Winner for Outstanding Technical Direction/Electronic Camera/Video Control (Daytime), Gregory Aull, technical director; Robert Batsche, senior video; Leonard Wechsler, Michael C.

Inglesh, Ken Decker, Damien Tuffereau, Manny Gutierrez, electronic cameras; 1997 (Tied with *The Price is Right*)

➤ Nominated for Outstanding Talk Show Directing (Daytime), Paul Nichols, Bob Mckinnon, 1997 (lost to *Oprah*)

➤ Nominated for Outstanding Makeup (Daytime), Cindy Gardner, Mariella Smith-Masters, makeup artists, 1997 (Lost to *Leeza*)

➤ Nominated for Outstanding Hairstyling (Daytime), Jeffrey Swander, David Evangelista, hairstylists, 1997 (Lost to *Oprah*)

➤ Nominated for Outstanding Lighting Direction (Daytime), Alan Blacher, Bob Dickinson, lighting designers, 1997 (lost to *Secrets of the Cryptkeeper's Haunted House*)

## OTHER AWARDS AND HONORS

➤ *Entertainment Weekly:* "101 Most Powerful Players in Hollywood," October 1996. (Rosie was ranked eighty-fourth.)

➤ *Glamour:* 1996 Top 10 Women of the Year, November 10, 1996; included Rosie along with eight other women and the U.S. Olympic women's basketball team.
"We won!" shouted Rosie O'Donnell, honored "for giving us talk without trash" on her new syndicated talk show. "It's a great honor to be selected with this group of women who have succeeded," she added. "I try to be an inspiration to women and to kids, and well, it's been a phenomenal year."

➤ Blistex World's Most Beautiful Lips Awards, December 5, 1996: "Most Talkative" lips.

➤ People Online: 1996 Icon Award.

➤ *TV Guide:* 1996 Performer of the Year; Rosie finished behind Oprah Winfrey and John Lithgow.

➤ New York Women in Film & Television: Muse Award, December 17, 1996.

- *People* magazine: 25 Most Intriguing People of 1996.

- *Entertainment Weekly:* 1996 Entertainer of the Year.

- Mr. Showbiz: 1996 Person of the Year; Rosie finished second behind Mel Gibson.

- 11th Annual American Comedy Awards: February 1997; Funniest Female Leading Performer in a Television Series.

- Nickelodeon's 10th Annual Kids' Choice Awards; favorite movie actress, for her role in *Harriet the Spy.*

- *Entertainment Weekly* picked Rosie number eight of the 50 Funniest People, April 18, 1997.

- *Time* named Rosie one of the 25 Most Influential People for 1997.

- *TV Guide:* 1997 Performer of the Year (finished eighth).

Rosie's Charities

Recognizing that her success has given her a platform, Rosie supports many worthy causes. Here's how you can help, too.

**BEARABLE TIMES**
The Kids' Hospital Network
P.O. Box 533
Harwich, MA 02645
www.bearabletimes.org
Kids Helping Kids Through Love, Support, and Understanding!

The Kids' Hospital Network (TKHN) is an organization created for children that are ill or have challenges. We are believers in providing children and their families with support and resources to help them manage their lives and also strengthen ties in schools, hospitals, and friendships. TKHN is a caring group with an interest in networking with others to fulfill common goals. We have a positive outlook on change to help better a child's future. TKHN is an advocate for children and their families trying to open doors of communication and build bridges to connect them through education, health, and technology resources. Our goal is to break down barriers and typical stereotypes—to work with each other as individuals. Through love, support, and understanding, together we can make a difference!

## BIG BROTHERS AND BIG SISTERS OF AMERICA
230 N. 13th St.
Philadelphia, PA 19107
www.bbbsa.org

## CHILDREN WITH AIDS PROJECT OF AMERICA (CWPOA)
4141 West Bethany Home Rd., Suite 5
Phoenix, AZ 85019
1-800-866-AIDS
www.aidskids.org

CWA offers a variety of services for children infected/affected by AIDS or drug-exposed infants who will require foster or adoptive families. CWA works to create adoptive, foster, family-centered care programs that are both effective and compassionate.

## CHILDREN'S DEFENSE FUND
25 E Street NW
Washington, DC 20001
202-628-8787
www.childrensdefense.org

The Children's Defense Fund exists to provide a strong and effective voice for all the children of America, who cannot vote, lobby, or speak for themselves. We pay particular attention to the needs of poor and minority children and those with disabilities. Our goal is to educate the nation about the needs of children and encourage preventive investment in children before they get sick, drop out of school, suffer family breakdown, or get into trouble.

## COMPUTER RE-USE NETWORK
P.O. Box 1078
Hollywood, SC 29449
www.awod.com/gallery/probono/corn/

CoRN is a nonprofit organization which specializes in recycling computers and donating them to nonprofit organizations.

## CONCEPT: CURE

1-888-GMC-CURE

www.gm.com/about/community/cure/about.html

As part of the General Motors Cancer Foundation, the Concept: Cure program is an ongoing collaboration between General Motors and the Council of Fashion Designers of America (CFDA) to help find a cure for breast cancer.

## CYSTIC FIBROSIS FOUNDATION

6931 Arlington Rd.
Bethesda, MD 20814

## FOR ALL KIDS FOUNDATION

P.O. Box 225
Allendale, NJ 07401

## GILDA'S CLUB

195 West Houston Street
New York, NY 10014
647-9700
www.jocularity.com/gilda1.html

The mission of Gilda's Club is to provide a place where people with cancer and their families can join with others to actively involve themselves in building social and emotional support as a supplement to regular medical care. Free of charge and nonprofit, the facility offers groups, lectures, workshops, and social events in a conveniently located, nonresidential, homelike setting in the city of New York. Funding is solicited from private individuals, corporations, and foundations. Gilda's Club is named in honor of the late comedian Gilda Radner, who, in describing the psychological and social support she received in her own life, called for such places of participation, education, hope, and friendship to be made available to people with cancer and family members everywhere.

**HALE HOUSE**
152 West 122nd St.
New York, NY 10027
Dr. Larraine Hale, executive director
212-663-0700

Mother Hale began her work with children in 1942, becoming a foster parent to newborn infants whose parents could not afford them. In 1969, Mother Hale and her daughter, Dr. Larraine Hale, founded Hale House in Harlem and have since raised over eight hundred babies. Today the new challenge is the AIDS virus. The Hale House has met this challenge and continues to provide care for terminally ill children

**MAKE-A-WISH FOUNDATION OF AMERICA**
100 West Clarendon, Suite 2200
Phoenix, AZ 85013
722-9474
www.wish.org/

To grant the wishes of children with terminal or life-threatening illnesses.

**NATIONAL BREAST CANCER COALITION**
1707 L Street, NW, Suite 1060
Washington, D.C. 20036
(202) 296-7477
www.natlbcc.org/

The National Breast Cancer Coalition is a grass-roots advocacy effort in the fight against breast cancer. In 1991 the Coalition was formed with one mission, to eradicate breast cancer through action and advocacy.

**NATIONAL EDUCATION TECHNOLOGY INITIATIVE**
P.O. Box 55303
Sherman Oaks, CA 91413
780-3344

The National Educational Technology Initiative is raising money to supply schools with computers. "As we work together to promote computer literacy for all of America's students, I am grateful for your involvement." President Bill Clinton

## RONALD McDONALD HOUSE
Check your phone book for the Ronald McDonald House nearest you. Providing a warm, friendly, and low-cost housing alternative to parents and siblings already overwhelmed by the stress of illness and the financial challenge of receiving lifesaving treatment.

## ST. JUDE CHILDREN'S RESEARCH HOSPITAL
332 North Lauderdale St.
Memphis, TN 38105
1-800-822-6344
www.stjude.org/

St. Jude Children's Research Hospital, located in Memphis, Tennessee, is one of the world's premier centers for research and treatment of catastrophic diseases in children, primarily pediatric cancers.

## STAND FOR CHILDREN
1834 Connecticut Ave., NW
Washington, DC 20009
1-800-663-4032
www.stand.org/

Stand For Children is a national organization that encourages individuals to improve children's lives. Our mission is to identify, train, and connect local children's activists engaging in advocacy, awareness raising, and service initiatives on an ongoing basis as part of Children's Action Teams (CATs).

A nonprofit, nonpartisan organization in its structure, Stand For Children is a movement in its mission—a movement to Leave No Child Behind and to give every child a Healthy Start, Head Start, Safe Start, Fair Start, and Moral Start in life.

## STARLIGHT CHILDREN'S FOUNDATION
12424 Wilshire Boulevard, Suite 1050
Los Angeles, CA 90025
(310) 207-5558
www.starlight.org/

The Starlight Children's Foundation is dedicated to brightening the lives of seriously ill children through wish granting and state-of-the-art, in-hospital entertainment. Starlight's worldwide presence in hospitals is substantial and growing exponentially. Today over forty-six thousand children benefit from the Foundation's services each month.

## TOYS FOR TOTS
Marine Toys for Tots Foundation
Marine Corps Base
715 Broadway Street
P.O. Box 1947
Quantico, VA 22134
(703) 640-9433
www.toysfortots.org/

To support the U.S. Marine Corps Reserve Toys for Tots Program by raising funds that enable it to provide toys to supplement the collections of reserve units; provide promotional and support materials to reserve units to help them conduct more effective local campaigns; provide administrative, advisory, financial, logistic, and promotional support to reserve units; provide other support to the program that the Marine Corps, as a federal agency, cannot provide; and conduct public education and information programs about the benefits of Toys For Tots that calls the general public to action in support of this patriotic community-action program and its sponsor—the U.S. Marine Corps.

# About the Author

**Patrick Spreng** is a corporate senior computer analyst by day and a successful Webmaster by night. He has turned his passion for online research and Rosie O'Donnell into his own Acme Rosie Page web site (http://www.bestware.net/spreng/rosie/index.html), which led to this, his first book. Spreng has also produced web pages on the Los Angeles Dodgers, Dolly Parton, Joe Bob Briggs, Karen Allen, and Whoopi Goldberg. He lives in Tulsa, Oklahoma. You can E-mail him at spreng@kosher.com.